Seabrook (NH) Library

3 4604 00032195 9

W9-BXT-813

The
Joy of
Pickling

**Also by
Linda Ziedrich**

Cold Soups

The
Joy of
Pickling

200 Flavor-Packed Recipes

for All Kinds of Produce

from Garden or Market

Linda Ziedrich

Foreword by
Christopher Kimball

The Harvard Common Press • Boston, Massachusetts

SEABROOK LIBRARY
101 CENTENNIAL STREET
SEABROOK, NH 03874-4508

The Harvard Common Press
535 Albany Street
Boston, Massachusetts 02118

Copyright © 1998 by Linda Ziedrich
Illustrations copyright © 1998 by Rodica Prato

All rights reserved. No part of this publication may be reproduced
or transmitted in any form or by any means, electronic or mechanical,
including photocopying, recording, or any information storage or retrieval
system, without permission in writing from the publisher.

Printed in the United States of America
Printed on acid-free paper

Library of Congress Cataloging-in-Publication Data

Ziedrich, Linda.
    The joy of pickling : 200 flavor-packed recipes for all kinds of
produce from garden or market / by Linda Ziedrich.
        p.   cm.
    Includes index.
    ISBN 1-55832-132-2 (hardcover : alk. paper). — ISBN 1-55832-133-0
(pbk. : alk. paper)
    1. Canning and preserving. I. Title.
TX601.Z52 1998
641.4'2dc21

Special bulk-order discounts are available on this and other Harvard
Common Press books. Companies and organizations may purchase books for
premiums or resale, or may arrange a custom edition, by contacting the
Marketing Director at the address above.

Cover photograph by Craig Lovell
Interior illustrations by Rodica Prato
Cover design by Suzanne Noli
Text design by Barbara M. Bachman

10 9 8 7 6 5 4 3 2 1

CONTENTS

FOREWORD

I GREW UP on a small farm in the Green Mountains of Vermont and I remember stories of the old days when the pace of life was quite different. Everything moved by horsepower, up and down the main road. Mail was delivered by horse and buggy, and, in a tradition that continued through the 1960s, the mailman on his morning rounds was known to help out with chores, like checking the wood stove at Harry Skidmore's place when nobody was home.

When you needed to find a good spot to dig a well you hired a dowser. He would cut off a forked branch from an apple tree and hold it in front of him with arms crossed. The branch would pull downwards when water was near. Frasier Mears, who did the dowsing in our town, talked to his rod as if it were alive. "Tell me, Mr. Stick," he would say, "how far is it?" Or "Tell me, Mr. Stick, is it deep?"

Some of our neighbors still remember when they saw their first car. Russell Baines didn't see one until he was eleven years old, but they weren't good for much in those days. "If you could drive ten miles and back without a flat," he told me, "you bragged about it." One farmer figured he could solve the problem by putting rope in the tires so they would have something to run on. It worked fine until the rope heated up from friction and burst into flames. A horse, by contrast, has always been a more reliable means to get around. As Junior Bentley once said to me, concerning the difference between tractors and horses, "On a cold morning, I always know that a horse is going to start up."

In the 1950s, folks in our town were still picking dandelion, milkweed, and mustard, still turning milk into cheese and butter. For meat, there was wild game and a hog or steer raised out back—behind the chained beagle, who in the winter would be let loose just a half dozen times or so for hunting rabbits.

Since the growing season was so short, most everything was preserved. Beef tongue was pickled, fruits were made into jams and fruit butters, and corn was turned into succotash. Root vegetables were packed into crates and carried down to the cellar.

It is therefore with a great deal of admiration and enthusiasm that I first read *The Joy of Pickling*. By working a special magic on an abundance of garden produce, Linda Ziedrich has transformed what might have become a lost art into something both necessary and delightful. Who wouldn't head for the kitchen to make Spicy Crock Pickles, or Indian-Style Pickled Cauliflower, or Limed Green Tomato Pickle? This is a book not just about saving money or rescuing a surfeit of cucumbers and cherry tomatoes from the pitfalls of superabundance. It is about applying simple methods to simple ingredients to produce tastes and textures that are both unexpected and extraordinary. Even in an age marked by home kitchens used for reheating instead of cooking, pickling is a thoroughly modern notion, one that requires little time and expense and pays great dividends.

It is my great hope that as we taste our first batch of half-sours or Italian pickled raw eggplant, we will stand by the stove and recall the May planting; the young sprouts shooting up from the cool soil; the long, slow maturing of the fruit through the hot days of July and the cool nights of August; and, finally, the act of pickling itself—great crocks filled with their sharp, briny liquid, just-picked vegetables submerged and ready to change into something crisp and wonderful.

For too many of us, our crop of memories is hardly worth preserving, like a small, scarred fruit without a gardener and cook to see it through from simple beginnings to ripe fruition. I often think that in cooking one can find all things: recollection, experience, hope, nourishment, and a simple faith in providence. Pickling serves up crisp memories, summer fruits and vegetables alive with the scent and taste of life's possibilities.

—Christopher Kimball
PUBLISHER AND EDITOR OF COOK'S ILLUSTRATED, AND AUTHOR OF
THE COOK'S BIBLE: THE BEST OF AMERICAN HOME COOKING.

"My chutneys and kasaundies are, after all, connected to my nocturnal scribblings—by day amongst the pickle-vats, by night within these sheets, I spend my time at the great work of preserving. Memory, as well as fruit, is being saved from the corruption of the clocks."

—*Salman Rushdie*, Midnight's Children

PREFACE

NEVER A BIG pickle eater myself, I became inspired to write this book after my son Ben, then about seven years old, developed a taste for cucumber pickles. I hesitated to buy the ones in the grocery store, which were dyed and preserved with scary-sounding chemicals as well as the usual salt and vinegar. I'd occasionally made pickles from farm-grown cucumbers, but truly fresh ones were very hard to find. Although I kept a large vegetable garden, I had never grown my own cucumbers. So I planted some. Soon I was pickling homegrown cukes, and our abundant pears, plums, peppers, and beans as well.

I didn't get really interested in pickles, though, until I started making the fermented kind. My husband and I are both endlessly intrigued by the way invisible little creatures transform raw plant materials into wonderfully nourishing and tasty foods; this must be part of the reason he makes beer and wine and I make about ten pounds of bread each week. We relished the complex flavors of my home-brined pickles, each batch a little different from the one before. I was amazed, too, to discover that cucumbers aren't the only foods suitable for brine-pickling; many other vegetables, and even some fruits, are enhanced by this magical metamorphosis.

Not all of my experiments were entirely successful, though, for I had little guidance in learning the art of pickling. General preserving books gave scant attention to pickles of any sort, and the one book then in print that was wholly devoted to pickles concentrated on cucumbers. I wanted a more comprehensive book, on pickling all sorts of produce and in all sorts of ways—through brining, with vinegar, and through unusual methods such as Japanese miso and rice-bran pickling. My dream book started taking shape in my head, co-incidentally, about the time my first cookbook was published; I knew I'd soon have time for another project. If I needed a good pickling book, I figured, other people would probably find one helpful, too. I decided to write it for us.

I began to study pickling by searching through old, out-of-print books and, especially, ethnic cookbooks. In many parts of the world pickling is still a commonplace household art, and travelers and nostalgic emigrants have taken pains to record what they know of it. By comparing their accounts and trying their techniques, I began to piece together the puzzles of pickling methods used halfway around the world. Some of the recipes here are my renditions of traditional pickles; others are unique inventions, but even these are based on methods that have stood the test of time.

In Chapter 1 and in the text that introduces each chapter, I explain how each pickling method works. Throughout the book, also, I try to provide a sense of the range of possible variations for each traditional pickle. This approach, I hope, will allow you to vary the recipes to suit your tastes without worrying that your pickle may turn out bad-tasting or even unsafe to eat. (Before you get too creative, however, be sure to read Chapter 1.)

Friends and relatives helped me along the way. Ann Kaiser, Eleanor Thompson, Michael Kim, Barbara Waterhouse, Jocelyn Wagner, Tom and Ann Orwick, Leslie Darland, Dolores Ziedrich, and Roxanne McMillen gave me favorite pickle recipes. Muslehuddin and Rafia Ansari, Irina Sheykova, Vladic Kasperchik, and Mei Ow Waterhouse told me about the pickles their families make in their respective homelands. Sally White and Celestia Nelson lent me precious old cookbooks, and Shawn White brought me a big box of quinces to pickle. Ann and Rick Kaiser, Cheryl Ziedrich, Paul Smith, Matthew Cover, Mary Parkinson of the Albany (Oregon) *Democrat-Herald*, and, especially, Robert, Ben, Rebecca, and Sam Waterhouse all served as tasters. I thank them all.

Food preservation specialists also gave me invaluable support. Judy Burridge, Linn County home economist for Oregon State University Extension, was my teacher in an excellent Master Food Preservers' course. Nellie Oehler, Lane County home economist for Oregon State University

Extension, and Kenneth Hall, Ph.D., professor emeritus of food science at the University of Connecticut, provided their expert review of the manuscript. I'm most grateful for their help.

Finally, I thank the staff of the Harvard Common Press, especially Bruce Shaw, Dan Rosenberg, Christine Alaimo, and Laura Christman, for their resolute faith in the book and in me.

The
Joy of
Pickling

PICKLER'S PRIMER: READ THIS FIRST!

PICKLER'S PRIMER:
READ THIS FIRST!

IN CORVALLIS, OREGON, Chinese scientists arriving for a two-week stay opened suitcases full of pickles and dry noodles. In Hyderabad, India, pickle heaven for many, a Japanese businessman traveled with a heavy bag of pickles from home. In Knoxville, Tennessee, a Yugoslav friend took offense when I turned down one of her brined cucumber pickles, until she told me they were homemade, as essential to her transplanted life as slivovitz was to her husband's. Big kosher dills at the county fair, little dishes of fire on a Korean table, Middle Eastern turnips dyed scarlet with beet juice, intensely sour cornichons with French pâté—pickles come in a great variety of forms and flavors, sometimes mystifying or repellent to strangers. But people everywhere are passionate about the pickles of home, pickles that somehow represent satisfaction and safety.

In an age when fresh produce is flown around the world, so that few must survive the winter on preserved foods, pickles still retain their power of enticement. Salt and vinegar not only preserve foods, after all, but they sharpen flavors, and salt firms the texture of watery vegetables. The brine of fermenting pickles is as wonderfully aromatic as baking bread; in eastern Europe and elsewhere, pickle brine is a drink, a soup stock, and a skin conditioner. Pickle brine can purify vegetables of microorganisms that might make us sick. Besides preserving nutrients, fermentation can actually increase them. For those of us who raise our own food, pickling with salt brine or vinegar is still an excellent way to provide for our families through the seasons. And, since pickles travel well, they can serve as familiar, safe sustenance on short or long journeys.

Pickling is an international art with many schools, but the basic methods have been with us a long time. As early as 1000 B.C. in the Middle East, people were preserving crab apples, pears, plums, onions, and walnuts in vinegar and spices. Caesar's soldiers ate vinegar pickles, and so did Cleopatra, who believed they made her more beautiful. The Romans taught people throughout western Europe how to make vinegar pickles, and western Europeans brought this skill to America.

The practice of making pickles by fermentation—souring through the action of microorganisms—evolved further east. Laborers constructing the Great Wall of China in the third century B.C. were given mixed fermented pickles as part of their food rations. Later, the Tartars spread a taste for fermented pickles throughout eastern Europe, where brined cabbage and other fermented vegetables are still daily fare. Germany, on the culinary divide between east and west, still favors brined and vinegar pickles about equally.

In tropical lands, such as India, fermented pickles generally didn't catch on, since vegetables tend to spoil when brined at high temperatures. (Fermented pickles are popular in Malaysia, however, despite the high spoilage rate.) Indian pickles make use of some or all of various natural preservatives: not only vinegar (in minimal amounts) and salt, but also sunshine, for its antiseptic as well as evaporative properties; spices; oil, to help the seasonings adhere to the fruits and vegetables and to seal out air; and sugar.

In the Far East, where vinegar was made from rice wine instead of grape wine or hard cider, vinegar pickles came to share popularity with fermented pickles. Pickle preferences vary greatly from one Asian region to the next, however. Koreans, who may eat more pickles than any other people in the world, ferment most of theirs, although their famous pickled garlic is preserved with vinegar and soy sauce. The Japanese salt vegetables, too, but usually eat them before fermentation gets under way. They also pickle vegetables by immersing them in salty fermented foods—miso, fermented rice bran, and soy sauce.

In the United States and England, new sorts of pickles grew popular as imperialism supplied cheap cane sugar and trade with Asia brought new culinary ideas. Fruits were put up with vinegar, sugar, and spices, in a sort of cross between a preserve and a pickle. Chutneys, ketchups, and chowchows, all relishes with Asian roots, were transformed into ever more sugary concoctions.

In the meantime, brined pickles were also becoming part of American cuisine. German immigrants began teaching Americans to make sauerkraut even before 1700. Later, in the late 1800s and early 1900s, immigrants from eastern Europe shared their taste for fermented cucumbers.

After home canning came into fashion, a new sort of pickle arose. Before pickle jars could be hermetically sealed, fresh pickles were made with undiluted vinegar, and many pickles were further preserved with sugar and long cooking. Oil was often added to the top of the pickle jar to keep air out. Fermented cucumber pickles were made with a very strong brine, stored in the cellar, then soaked for days in fresh water before they became edible. Sauerkraut was stored in cool cellars or outdoors to slow fermentation through the winter.

Stored in vacuum-sealed jars, though, vegetables could keep for a long time in a dilute vinegar solution, even if salt and sugar were omitted entirely. When the jars were processed with heat after sealing, the pickles would keep even longer. Home canning reached a peak during World War II, when the U.S. government commandeered 40 percent of commercial pickle output for the armed forces. Extension agents promoted home food preservation along with Victory Gardens, even going so far as to divert steel from the munitions industry to pressure-canner production. "Novice canners using shoddy wartime equipment also produced a record number of disasters," writes Harvey Levenstein (*Paradox of Plenty*, 1993). "Innumerable stoves were ruined, kitchens were splattered, and victims were hospitalized with severe burns, cuts, and botulism." If U.S. Department of Agriculture (USDA) guidelines today seem to be based on the assumption that the typical home canner won't follow half of them, this history should explain the government's conservatism. Actually, even after their boiling-water baths, USDA-style pickles generally taste much fresher than their nineteenth-century predecessors.

Pickling Principles

THERE ARE TWO BASIC kinds of pickles, those preserved with vinegar (or, occasionally, lemon or lime juice or citric acid) and those preserved with salt. Vinegar pickles, also called fresh pickles because they aren't fermented, usually contain salt as well. Likewise, fermented pickles, which are always made with salt, sometimes include vinegar.

Although salt is not an essential ingredient in canned fresh pickles, a pickle is hardly a pickle without salt. By drawing off excess liquid from vegetables and fruits, salt firms the texture and concentrates the flavors. Salt also balances the flavor of the finished pickle, though the right flavor balance is a matter for each pickler to decide.

Most pickles made with salt are fermented. Others, like Japanese pressed pickles, are only briefly salt-cured, and therefore won't keep long, especially if they're not refrigerated. Fermented pickles keep longer for the same reason vinegar pickles do: They are acidic.

Fermented pickles fall into two types, dry-salted and brined. Sauerkraut is a dry-salted pickle; when mixed with salt, shredded cabbage makes its own brine, even before the cabbage is pressed or weighted. The brine protects the cabbage from air. Other pickles are made with a premixed brine: The salt is dissolved in enough water to cover the vegetables. In both dry-salted and brined pickles, salt helps control the fermentation process.

In general terms, fermentation is a controlled decomposition of food, involving yeasts, molds, or bacteria in an aerobic or anaerobic process. Whereas bread, beer, and wine making involve yeast fermentation, pickling involves fermentation by bacteria (although yeasts are usually present, too). The bacteria break apart sugars to create acid (mainly lactic acid), which preserves the food for some time in its partially decomposed form. This process is mainly anaerobic: The microorganisms that initiate it produce carbon dioxide, which replaces the oxygen in the pickling crock.

Vegetables crowded into a crock together will ferment with or without salt. Without the proper salt concentration, however, enzymes may soften the vegetables, and the wrong microorganisms may predominate, causing off-flavors or even putrefaction. Even without these problems, fermentation without salt is likely to progress too quickly, so that the vegetables never get sour enough to keep well for very long, and the seasonings haven't enough time to work their magic. The right amount of salt fosters the right progression of bacterial activity that produces firm, delicious pickles.

Just as vinegar pickles usually contain salt, fermented pickle brines often include some vinegar, partially for its flavor and partially to discourage the growth of the wrong microorganisms before fermentation gets under way. Too much vinegar, however, stops fermentation completely.

. . .

CUCUMBER VARIETIES FOR PICKLING

American—These traditional knobby cucumbers come in many varieties, some more disease-resistant than others, some with black spines, some with white. But American cucumbers of all varieties look and taste more or less alike. Although they make good gherkin pickles at 1 to 2 inches, they're typically pickled at 3 to 5 inches long. You can leave them whole, slice them crosswise for bread-and-butters or lengthwise for tongue pickles, or cut them into spears. When they grow longer than 5 inches, though, they become very wet and seedy in the middle. Seed the big ones before cutting them into chunks for pickles. You can get seeds of these cucumbers from any seed catalog or garden center.

Cornichons—These European cucumbers are also called gherkins (from *gurken*, Dutch for "cucumbers"), although they are unrelated to West Indian gherkins (see next page). Seed catalogs say that cornichons must be harvested at 1 to 2 inches long, but I find they make excellent pickles at up to 6 inches long. Even longer cornichons can be sliced for bread-and-butters, since these are skinny cucumbers, with very small seed cavities and tiny seeds. The tiny prickles come off easily with a light rubbing and are mostly absent on larger cornichons. The skins are thin, which means you must begin processing cornichons within a day of picking them; this is probably why they aren't grown commercially in the United States. But if I could grow only one cucumber variety in my garden, this would be it. Cornichon seeds are available from Nichols, Shepherd's, and PineTree (see page 367).

Asian pickling cucumbers—Not all Asian cucumbers are good for pickling, but last year my Mennonite neighbor grabbed up all my extra China Hybrid cucumbers for making bread-and-butters and chunk pickles. China Hybrids and Suyo Longs are knobby, over a foot long at pickling size, and suitable for trellising, though I let mine spread over the ground. The seeds and seed cavities are quite small. Orient Express is a smooth variety that's also good for pickling. My neighbors call all such long, slim cucumbers "burpless," though since no cucumber ever made me burp, I can't verify the accuracy of this term. China Hybrid and Orient Express cucumber seeds are available from Burgess; Suyo Long seeds are available from Johnny's and PineTree (see page 367).

West Indian Gherkins—Also called bur cucumbers, these are small, prickly fruits that grow on watermelon-like plants. I've never seen a West Indian gherkin in the flesh, but in pictures they look like North American wild cucumbers (which, by the way, are neither cucumbers nor edible). If you're growing gherkins, make them into gherkin pickles. You can buy gherkin seeds from PineTree (see page 367).

Salts

THROUGHOUT THIS BOOK, I call for "pickling salt." This is simply fine, pure granulated salt. In supermarkets, it's sold in five-pound bags as "canning and pickling salt." In natural foods stores, it's labeled "sea salt." Since the use of the term *sea salt* is unregulated, however, you may see it on supermarket bins of table salt. Table salt often contains iodide, and it always contains additives intended to prevent caking (according to the label, the table salt in my cupboard contains dextrose, sodium bicarbonate, and yellow prussiate of soda). You can identify table salt by stirring a little into a glass of water; it won't dissolve completely, but will form a whitish haze and sediment. The white stuff can't make you sick, but it can ruin the appearance of your pickles.

Beware of any sea salt that isn't white. European green, gray, and black salts, once cheap because they were contaminated with seaweed and other debris, are now sold at high prices in gourmet shops. They contain impurities that could adversely affect the pickling process.

Kosher salt is often used for pickling. Because its crystals are larger and therefore less densely packed than those of pickling salt, you need a greater volume of kosher salt—about one and a half times as much—if you're substituting it for pickling salt. A disadvantage of kosher salt is that it is slow to dissolve. To make a brine with kosher salt, you have to heat the water and salt together. This is why many pickling recipes call for heating a brine and then cooling it before pouring it over vegetables. If your water is clean and your salt fine, the heating step is unnecessary.

If you can't find pickling salt locally, you can still get it by mail-order (see page 367).

Vinegars

THROUGHOUT THIS BOOK, I assume you will use vinegar that is approximately 4 to 6 percent acetic acid, or 40 to 60 grain. Homemade vinegars vary a lot in acidity; if you want to use one, you must test its pH (see page 12). Commercial vinegars made in the United States, however, are all standardized within this range. Among these vinegars, you have several types from which to choose:

Distilled white vinegar is fermented from a solution of pure alcohol and diluted to 5 percent acidity. Although this vinegar has a harsh, uninteresting flavor, in the United States it is probably used more in pickling than any other vinegar. This is because distilled vinegar doesn't darken pickled foods, and, more important, it's cheap. I use it only in pickles that are very sweet or contain other strong flavors to balance the vinegar. Distilled vinegar is most useful, I think, in cleaning windows and floors.

Cider vinegar is fermented aerobically from hard cider, which is apple juice that has already undergone an anaerobic fermentation. This vinegar has a golden color and a mellow flavor, although the quality will vary somewhat depending on how the vinegar was made. The traditional pickling medium of early Americans and their English ancestors, cider vinegar can be used whenever you're unconcerned about the fruit or vegetable darkening a bit. Cider vinegar is sold in supermarkets in gallon jugs as well as smaller containers. Generally, it is standardized at 5 percent acidity.

"Apple cider-flavored" vinegar took the place of real cider vinegar in many markets in 1996. Fortunately, this fake cider vinegar must have sold poorly, at least in the Willamette Valley, because I haven't seen much of it since. Distilled white vinegar with flavorings and colorings added, it's priced a little cheaper than real cider vinegar.

Wine vinegar is the traditional pickling medium of France, Italy, Spain, and other countries where wine grapes are grown. Wine vinegar is used full strength for *cornichons à cru* and similar fresh pickles preserved without sugar or pasteurization. Like cider vinegars, wine vinegars vary in quality, but all tend to be sweeter and mellower than any distilled vinegar. Although most supermarkets sell wine vinegar only in small, expensive bottles, gallon jugs are available much more economically in Middle Eastern groceries and some restaurant-supply stores.

White wine vinegar isn't the only wine vinegar suitable for pickling. Splash a little red wine vinegar into a crock of brined pickles; the color won't be noticeable, and you may like the subtle effect of this full-flavored vinegar on the taste. In beet and prune pickles, red wine vinegar enhances both color and flavor. The French like red wine vinegar so much that they often pickle cornichons in it, despite its graying effect.

For its special flavor, you can even use dark, sweet balsamic vinegar in some pickles. Balsamic vinegar is usually standardized at 6 percent acidity, whereas other commercial wine vinegars are 5 percent acid.

Rice vinegar is the traditional vinegar of the Far East. Very mild in flavor, it comes in two types, brown and white, made from unpolished and polished rice, respectively. White rice vinegar is sold in supermarkets in small, expensive bottles, often with added sugar and salt. Some Asian groceries, however, carry more economically priced gallon jugs, without additives. Brown rice vinegar is available in natural foods stores and Korean markets. Rice vinegars are usually standardized at 4.3 percent acidity.

Malt vinegar, fermented from sprouted barley, is the sharp but pleasant vinegar used in English Pub–Style Pickled Onions (page 132). Brown in color, malt vinegar is sold in small bottles in some supermarkets. It is typically diluted to 5 percent acid.

For pickles to be canned or stored at room temperature without canning, use vinegar that is 5 percent acid. (For refrigerator pickles, feel free to use lower-acid rice vinegar.) Within this limit, there's no danger in changing the *type* of vinegar in a recipe. You shouldn't, however, reduce the proportion of vinegar in a recipe. This would lessen the acidity of the pickle, perhaps making it unsafe to eat. Although salt and sugar may combine with vinegar to inhibit microbial growth, fresh pickles generally should contain at least one part vinegar for each part water.

Take care also not to boil pickling liquid for a long time, since acetic acid evaporates faster than water does. Boil pickling liquid only as long as the recipe calls for.

If you dispense your own vinegar in a natural foods store, be aware that the vinegar probably won't be pasteurized. Unpasteurized vinegar will develop a "mother," a slimy translucent mass that can be transferred to wine or hard cider to speed its transformation to vinegar. To halt the biological activity in unpasteurized vinegar, bring it to a boil before using it.

WHAT'S YOUR PICKLE'S pH?

Pickles, both fresh and fermented, are preserved primarily by their acidity. Acidity can be measured according to pH. Pure water has a neutral pH, about 7.0. More acidic substances have lower pHs; more alkaline substances have higher pHs. To prevent the germination of *Clostridium botulinum* spores, food that is to be stored in airtight containers must be acidified to pH 4.6 or lower. Pickles are normally acidified within a range from 2.6 to 4.0.

If you're not sure you followed the recipe correctly—if, say, you may have added only half of the vinegar or used apple cider instead of apple cider vinegar—you can test the pH of one jar after the acid in the liquid has equilibrated with the vegetables or fruit (that is, the acidity has become equal throughout), which takes about three weeks. To test the pH of fresh or fermented pickles before they're stored, suggests Kenneth Hall, professor emeritus of food science at the University of Connecticut, purée the contents of one jar in a blender.

For both fresh and fermented pickles, the pH should be no higher than 4.0. Some people use litmus paper from the drugstore for testing pH, but I recommend the more accurate pH meters, such as those available from Cole-Parmer Instrument Company (see page 367). These meters are also useful in testing the pH of homemade vinegar.

Water

IF YOUR WATER tastes good and doesn't make you sick, it's probably suitable for pickling. If, however, it contains large quantities of minerals or chlorine, you may need to either purify your water or buy distilled or deionized water for pickling.

Hard water may cloud and discolor pickling liquid. If your water stains your toilet and sink with iron deposits, you definitely have a problem. Boil the water, and then let it sit for 24 hours before using it for pickling. Skim off the scum, and ladle off water from the top of the container, leaving any sediment undisturbed.

Be aware, too, that most public water supplies in the United States are treated with chlorine. If your shower often smells like the public swimming pool (when you haven't just cleaned it with chlorine products), your water may contain enough chlorine to delay the fermentation of brined pickles. Boiling the water for at least two minutes will vaporize the chlorine. Let the water cool overnight before combining it with the vegetables.

Aromatics

SPICES are sold in every supermarket, but some traditional pickling spices, such as juniper berries and mace, are usually missing from the shelves, and may even be hard to find in natural foods stores. You can leave out the juniper berries and substitute slivers of nutmeg for the mace, but if you'd like to send away for hard-to-find spices, see page 367.

Spices used in pickling may be whole, crushed, or ground. Although whole spices look attractive in pickle jars, they are often used only during brining or heating, then removed and discarded. Otherwise, the spices might darken the pickle over time, and their flavors might become overwhelming. For these reasons, whole spices are often tied in a spice bag or piece of cheesecloth, which can be easily removed before the pickles are put into jars. You can make spice bags from unbleached muslin, or buy some from Alltrista Corporation (see page 367). You can even use a thin cotton baby sock as a spice bag. But unless you're using very small seeds, such as celery seeds, a scrap of good cheesecloth, tied securely around the spices, works just as well.

For crushed spices, smash them with the side of a knife blade or pound them briefly in a mortar. The purpose is to crack them so they'll release their flavors faster, without grinding them to dust. This technique is very useful in making quick pickles.

Ground spices are used only when there is no concern about their clouding the pickling liquid—in thick relishes, for example, or Indian pickles. Since ground spices go stale rather quickly, especially if they're exposed to heat or sunlight, it's best to buy whole spices and grind them as you need them. Store all spices in a cool, dark place, preferably for no longer than a year.

. . .

You can buy mixed pickling spice at any supermarket, but you may prefer to mix up your own to suit your tastes. Here's an example:

Mixed Pickling Spice

One 4-inch cinnamon stick, broken up
6 bay leaves, torn into small pieces
6 small dried chile peppers, cut into small pieces
1 tablespoon black peppercorns
1 tablespoon yellow mustard seeds
1 teaspoon fennel seeds
2 teaspoons whole allspice
1 teaspoon whole cloves
2 teaspoons whole coriander
½ teaspoon blade (unground) mace or small pieces nutmeg
½ teaspoon fenugreek
1 tablespoon dill seeds

Makes about ½ cup

Although some people prefer to select just a few flavorings for each batch of pickles, others like the indefinable spiciness imbued by a blend of many aromatics. Commercial pickling spice mixtures vary, but they typically include a dozen or more flavorings. Whether you use a commercial blend or make your own (see the recipe on this page), be careful when measuring from the mixture, since little seeds such as dill and mustard will tend to fall to the bottom, and big ones such as allspice will tend to rise to the top.

Dill is one spice—and herb—that you should try to grow yourself. The seeds look prettiest when they are still attached to the umbels, and they taste mild and fresh before they ripen. The feathery leaves are milder still. Especially in rural areas, some stores occasionally sell uprooted dill plants, but these are usually old and shriveled, and they may be unavailable when you want them. To guarantee a supply of fresh dill throughout the cucumber harvest, plant some before the last spring frost date, and plant more every few weeks until midsummer.

. . .

The umbelliferous seed heads of cumin, fennel, and anise as well as dill make pretty and tasty additions to pickle jars.

Mustard seeds come in two types, yellow or white (*Sinapis alba*) and black or brown (*Brassica nigra*). American and European picklers have traditionally used yellow mustard seeds; Indians generally favor the more pungent but less bitter black or brown mustard seeds, which they sometimes grind. You can easily grind mustard seeds with a spice grinder or coffee grinder.

Peppers not only star in numerous pickling recipes, but they play compelling minor roles in many others.

For small dried hot peppers, use the Japanese (japonés, hontaka) type that is sold in both Mexican and Asian markets. In place of these peppers, you might use dried de árbol peppers, which are hotter and also strikingly elongated, or any other dried cayenne-type peppers. To extract the heat from a dried pepper faster, break it in half, slit it lengthwise, or crumble it. Hot pepper flakes—dried peppers crumbled with their seeds—decorate a pickle with bright red speckles. But be careful; pepper flakes pack more heat than you might expect.

Sometimes I call for ground dried hot pepper. You can use the kind traditionally labeled cayenne, which may or may not be made from cayenne peppers, but is typically very hot. Or you can use a less incendiary sort. The ground dried pepper sold in Korean markets, I've found, is generally much milder; this mild pepper is the type I prefer for kimchi. Mexican markets and even Mexican sections of supermarkets now stock pepper powders that are comparable to the Korean kind.

If you grow chile peppers in your garden, you may prefer to use them fresh in your pickles. You can slit, halve, or slice jalapeños, serranos, de árbols, or other small hot peppers before adding them to your pickles. Be careful, though, because they may be much hotter than dried peppers.

You may have learned to ignore the frequent warnings in cookbooks to wear rubber gloves when handling hot peppers. Some people do get rashes from working with peppers, but most of us can chop a chile or two with impunity. Wear gloves, though, if you're making a gallon of salsa or slicing two quarts of jalapeños. If you use your bare hands, they may burn for a day or two (or longer—a friend of mine put ice packs on her hands for three days after pickling sliced jalapeños). The burning sensation may not bother you much—unless you touch your eyes. If you wear contact lenses, avoid handling them for at least eight hours after chopping even a few hot peppers.

Fresh ginger is now almost universally available in supermarkets, so I use it liberally. When I call for a "thin slice" of ginger, I mean one about the thickness and diameter of a quarter. If the section you're cutting is wider or narrower, adjust the amount accordingly. In the store, look for plump ginger without a trace of mold.

Horseradish is a perennial plant in the mustard family grown for its pungent-tasting root. Pieces of the root are only very occasionally sold in supermarkets, so if you like horseradish it makes sense to grow your own. (Many mail-order seed companies sell small root pieces for planting.) For pickling, wash and scrape or peel the root, and slice, chop, or grate it. You can store horseradish in the freezer, scraped clean and wrapped in airtight plastic or foil. I recommend against buying commercially prepared horseradish, which is typically laden with adulterants. If you can't get fresh horseradish, or find you don't like it, you can leave it out of any pickle recipe.

Garlic, to most people, is what makes a kosher pickle kosher, but since garlic is now so widely used in pickling and American cooking generally we should probably leave the word *kosher* to its older, religious meaning. Anyway, make sure your garlic is fresh; it shouldn't be shriveled or soft or sprouting or have brown spots. Leave it whole or slice or chop it. Smaller pieces will spread their flavor faster, but garlic never wastes much time in making its presence known.

Firming Agents

BECAUSE PICKLES SOMETIMES soften during fermentation, and, especially, heating, people have discovered numerous additives that ensure their pickles stay crisp. If you follow recommendations in this book, soft pickles may never be a problem for you. Still, you may want to experiment with some of the following firming agents:

Lime used in pickling is calcium oxide, also called slaked lime or builder's lime. The calcium in pickling lime is absorbed into the tissue of a vegetable or fruit, where it combines with pectin to form calcium pectate. This makes the pickles—usually cucumber, melon, or green tomato—firm and crisp. Southerners, especially, have long loved limed pickles. In the 1970s and 1980s, when natural foods were in, pickling lime was out, at least among recipe writers. But commercial food processors never stopped using lime, for pickling and much more. They add lime to canned tomatoes, potatoes, green beans, peas, and many other foods.

Provided it is food-grade (*don't* buy it at a lumberyard or feed store), lime is a harmless food additive. As gardeners well know, however, lime is alkaline; it can raise the pH of a pickle just as it can raise that of your soil. The USDA therefore recommends soaking and rinsing limed vegetables or fruit three times before pickling them. Even when you do this, the pH of your pickle may be slightly increased, so use lime only in recipes that call for it.

If you don't have a local source for preserving supplies, you can probably find food-grade lime in a pharmacy, or, you can order it from Alltrista Corporation or Precision Foods (see page 367).

Alum, an aluminum compound that is used medicinally as an emetic and styptic, was a popular pickle ingredient in the 1950s and 1960s. Like lime, alum makes pickles crisp and crunchy. Its use went out of favor, however, when people began to worry about the health effects of aluminum in the diet. Since only a very little alum is needed to make pickles crisp, and since pickles play only a small part in the American diet, adding alum to your pickles probably won't hurt anyone if the recipe includes sufficient vinegar (alum, like lime, is alkaline). The astringent taste of alum is detectable, though, even when only a minimal amount is used. Many people like this taste. But, as my husband (with a grimace) described my alum-firmed fresh dills, "They taste like store-bought."

Alum is sometimes sold in the spice sections of supermarkets; you can also buy it at a pharmacy.

Horseradish is not only a traditional pickle flavoring, but it's also said to be a firming agent. From my limited trials, I suspect that horseradish may help prevent the softening of fermenting pickles by inhibiting yeast growth. The fresh pickles I made with horseradish, however, were noticeably softer than those I made with alum, grape leaves, and sour cherry leaves. Unfortunately, it seems that no scientist has done a proper study of horseradish in pickling. So I suggest using abundant amounts of grated or chopped horseradish with fermenting cucumbers, to see what happens (let me know!), but none at all with fresh cucumbers unless you happen to like the mustardy flavor.

Leaves of various kinds are also used as firming agents. Grape leaves are most popular, and they do seem to have a slight firming effect on both fermented and fresh cucumber pickles; they are also supposed to make pickles greener. The Russians like to use a variety of leaves, sometimes all at once. They recommend oak leaves and sour cherry leaves for their tannin (which is, like alum, astringent). One Polish author claims that peach leaves work as well as sour cherry leaves. Although I neglected to include oak and peach leaves in my fresh-pickle study, I found that sour cherry leaves firm pickles at least as well as grape leaves do, but not as well as alum does. Put a few washed leaves, if you like, into each jar of fresh pickles. If you're fermenting pickles in a crock, scatter or layer the leaves with the other ingredients, or put handfuls of leaves at the bottom and top of the crock.

Weighing Produce

YOU CAN USE a food-grade plastic bucket in place of a pickle crock, mayonnaise jars in place of canning jars, a knife in place of a kraut board. But I hope you won't try to do a lot of pickling or other preserving without a kitchen scale. Fruits and vegetables of a given kind—whether cucumbers, cabbages, or corn ears—tend to come in various sizes, so measuring them by either number or volume often isn't accurate enough. I therefore frequently call for produce by weight. If you buy your fruits and vegetables, of course, you can weigh them at the market before you bring them home. But having your own scale will make your preserving much easier and more successful.

Pots and Bowls

BECAUSE SALT AND vinegar react with most metals—sometimes with toxic results—the recipes in this book frequently call for *nonreactive* bowls, pots, and pans. Bowls used in pickling can be stainless steel, glass, or ceramic; pots and pans can be stainless steel, heatproof glass, or hard-anodized aluminum (such as those made by Calphalon). Other containers are not safe to use unless they are aluminum, copper, or tin lined with stainless steel. Even enameled metal containers are risky to use, since fine cracks and chips in the enamel could allow the metal to react with the acid in the pickling brine.

Canning Your Pickles

MANY PICKLES THAT are sufficiently acidified can be vacuum-sealed in mason jars—that is, "canned"—for longer keeping outside of the refrigerator. This includes cucumbers fermented in a medium-to-strong brine, sauerkraut, most of the fresh pickles in Chapter 3, and almost all of the relishes in Chapter 9. (Canning is unnecessary for pantry storage of *cornichons à cru* and similar very sour pickles.) Whenever a pickle is suitable for canning, I call for mason jars (in specific sizes) and two-piece caps, although you can dispense with these things if you'd rather store your pickles in the refrigerator.

If you've never canned food yourself or watched family members do it, the whole idea may intimidate you. Canning, after all, involves special equipment and a lot of heat and steam. Mason jars and lids, and the techniques required for using them, have changed over time, and so have the governmental guidelines that are meant to ensure that home-canned food is safe to eat. For these reasons, instructions from cookbooks, Mom, the neighbor, the canning-jar company, and the extension agent may conflict. Even recently published cookbooks may include outdated guidelines.

But canning your pickles is a sensible thing to do if you're making a lot and don't have several refrigerators, or if you'd like to give some jars to friends or relatives. When you understand the canning process, it is generally simple, quick, and safe.

Canning is a way of preserving food by sealing it hot in airtight containers, or by heating the containers after they're filled with the food. Heat raises the vapor pressure of the liquid inside the canning jar, or mason jar. As the vapor pressure rises, air is forced out of the jar. As the jar and its contents cool, a vacuum forms as the vapor pressure drops, and the softened adhesive on the rim of the lid creates an airtight seal.

Although a vacuum seal prevents oxidation and the growth of microorganisms such as mold, the anaerobic environment in the jar may enable growth of the scariest food-borne pathogen, *Clostridium botulinum*, if the food is low in acid and the jar is processed too briefly or at too low a temperature. This is why you must carefully follow established guidelines in canning such foods as beets or beans without vinegar.

But canning pickles is much less risky. *Clostridium botulinum* can't grow in high-acid foods; it needs a pH of over 4.6 to reproduce. (Nor need you worry about the notorious *Escherichia coli O157:H7*, bacteria that infect the intestinal tracts of warm-blooded animals. *E. coli* bacteria are killed by cooking, and all of the pickled meats in this book are thoroughly cooked.)

The equipment required for canning pickles demands much less expense and attention than that required for canning low-acid vegetables. In other words, you don't need a pressure canner to put up pickles. Not only is a pressure canner expensive to buy, but its gasket must be replaced and its gauge checked regularly. Steaming and rattling like some sort of bomb on the stove, it can also be frightening to operate, even for someone who has been using one for years.

I do, however, recommend boiling-water processing or low-temperature pasteurization for many of the pickles in this book. These heat treatments have two important advantages: They tend to produce a very tight vacuum seal, and they kill molds, yeasts, and bacteria that can grow in lower-acid pickles, particularly if the jars aren't well sealed. Heat treatment helps you avoid ever having to throw out pickles that have gone bad.

Many people hesitate to subject their pickles to a lot of heat for fear it will ruin the texture of the pickled food. Heating definitely can soften cucumbers and some other foods. For this reason a scientist at the University of California developed the low-temperature pasteurization method for home picklers. By this method you don't boil your jars, but just stand them in 180- to 185-degree F water for 30 minutes. The recipe instructions indicate when this method can be used.

If your mother or grandmother always canned pickles without a boiling-water or hot-water bath, you may wonder if you can safely do the same. In many cases, you can. By the now-maligned "open kettle" method, you boil first the jars, then the food you'll fill them with (the kettle isn't necessarily open during these processes, but the jars are). This method is in some ways more trouble than water-bath canning, however, since the jars, lids, and what's going into the jars must all be very hot if the jars are to seal. The jars, moreover, can't just be clean, as for water-bath canning, but they must be sterile, which is why you've got to boil them. And if the lids fail to seal, you may end up having to give your jars a water bath after all. The open-kettle method is dangerous with low-acid foods, because of the risk of contamination between the time the jar is removed from hot water and the time it's sealed. For all these reasons, the USDA no longer recommends the method. But many home preservers still use it for pickles and fruit preserves, especially when they're making small batches or want to ensure that their pickles stay firm. Generally the method works fine, but occasionally pickles at the top of a jar get soft and discolored or even moldy, or a lid comes loose after the jar has been put away in the pantry. Foregoing a water bath is safest with sweet pickles and relishes, those preserved with a lot of sugar as well as vinegar.

Because the processing instructions are abbreviated in the recipes, please read the following sections for information on the canning equipment you'll need and for a thorough explanation of boiling-water processing, low-temperature pasteurization, and the open-kettle method of processing.

Basic equipment for canning includes mason jars, which come in ½-cup (4-ounce), half-pint (8-ounce), 1½-cup (12-ounce), and 1-quart (16-ounce) sizes. Mason jars come in two mouth sizes, regular and wide; pint and quart jars are available in both widths. Most mason jars sold in the United States today are made by either of two companies, Ball and Kerr, which recently came under the possession of a single parent corporation, Alltrista. Alltrista also recently bought Canada's canning-jar company, Bernardin. All three of these companies make very similar jars and two-piece caps.

...

VOLUME EQUIVALENTS

1 bushel = 4 pecks
1 peck = 2 gallons
1 gallon = 4 quarts
1 quart = 4 cups

1 pint = 2 cups
1 cup = 16 tablespoons
1 tablespoon = 3 teaspoons

Mason jars can be used over and over for years; some of mine are older than I am. Before each use, though, check the glass for cracks and the rims for nicks. Even a tiny nick could prevent a good seal.

In place of mason jars you can use other jars, such as ones that held commercial mayonnaise, provided that the mouths fit the two-piece mason jar caps. If you use such jars, though, expect more failed seals and occasional jar breakage, since these jars are thinner. Some people use mayonnaise jars for pickles and jams, and reserve their mason jars for pressure canning, which puts more stress on the glass.

New mason jars come with two-piece caps—a flat lid, which is meant for one-time use only, and a ring, which you can reuse if it's not rusty. When a jar is well sealed, the lid is slightly depressed in the middle.

Kerr and Ball jars, rings, and lids can be used interchangeably. Many people, though, favor one brand over the other. Ball products are often a little cheaper, and I find that the sealing compound on Ball lids doesn't get sticky. Kerr lids seem to require more heat to seal well, so I don't recommend them for open-kettle canning. These differences may vanish, however, as the companies' common owner asserts control.

You may prefer to use European-style canning jars, with glass lids and separate rubber gaskets. Many home economists frown on these, because you can't check the seal by pressing on the lid. I see no danger in canning pickles in these jars, though, provided you use fresh rubber gaskets, follow the manufacturer's instructions, and make sure the jars are approximately the same size as those called for in the recipes. If the jars are larger, you may need to increase processing times slightly.

Boiling-water processing and low-temperature pasteurization require a large kettle with a rack at the bottom to protect the jars from overheating and breaking. Most cooks use an inexpensive enameled metal kettle made for the purpose, with a jar rack that you can raise or lower without putting your hands in the water. Until recently, though, these kettles weren't made tall enough for quart jars. Even the new ones are far from ideal, since the racks quickly get rusty.

But you can use any large kettle for boiling-water processing. Canning-supply stores and Alltrista Corporation (see page 367) sell jar racks that appear rust-resistant, at least, and may fit into your stainless-steel stockpot. I use my pressure canner for boiling-water processing; I just don't screw on the lid all the way. Made entirely of aluminum and quite tall enough for quarts, it works very well for me, although I have to remove the jars one at a time.

Many people use steam canners instead of boiling-water canners. Steam canners save water, energy, and time, and they don't boil over. But neither the USDA nor anyone else has determined safe processing times for foods canned with steam. The steamers tend to have cold spots, and the food in the jars generally doesn't get as hot as it would in a boiling-water bath. For these reasons I can't recommend steam canners.

Very helpful tools for canning include a jar lifter, a special kind of tongs for lifting hot jars safely; a canning funnel, which just fits into the mouth of a canning jar; a magnet on a stick, for lifting lids out of hot water; and a narrow plastic spatula, disposable plastic knife, or Japanese (pointed) wooden or plastic chopstick, for releasing air bubbles in a filled jar. An accurate thermometer is necessary when you're using the low-temperature pasteurization method (see page 29), and helpful when you're using a boiling-water bath. Canning tools are available at many department stores and supermarkets, and you can also order them from Alltrista Corporation (see page 367).

Boiling-Water Processing

BOILING-WATER PROCESSING proceeds this way: Fill the canner about halfway with water, and begin heating it. Heat some more water in a tea kettle, in case the water in the canner doesn't cover the jars adequately. Have ready clean, preferably hot jars in the size or sizes specified; I wash my jars in the dishwasher and leave them there until I'm ready to use them. (If the jars are going to be processed for fewer than 10 minutes, though, you should immerse them in boiling water for 10 minutes to sterilize them before filling them.) Immerse the lids in hot water.

Fill each jar with cold vegetables or fruit, and pour hot liquid over them (this is the "raw pack" method), or fill the jar with pickles and liquid that have been heated together (the "hot pack" method). For pickles such as sauerkraut, pack both the vegetables and the liquid cold (I call this the "cold pack" method). Don't overpack the jars; their contents should be at least 35 percent liquid to maintain the proper acidity. Leave the specified headspace—that is, the unfilled space at the top of the jar. Usually this is ¼ to ½ inch. (Headspace specifications tend to differ between the USDA and the canning-jar companies, and you may find that mine differ from instructions you have from another source. This isn't important; just remember that you need a little extra space for expansion of food as jars are processed, and for forming vacuums in cooled jars, but that you don't need the 1 to 1¼ inches required for pressure-canning. One-half inch is plenty for any pickle.)

After filling the jar, release air bubbles by inserting a narrow plastic spatula or similar tool between the pickles and the inner surface of the jar. Move the tool up and down while slowly turning the jar. Add more liquid if the level has dropped in this process, then wipe the rim with a clean, damp cloth or paper towel. Remove the lid from the hot water, and place it, gasket-down, on the jar. Firmly screw on the metal ring, but not as tight as possible. (Overtightening the ring could cause the lid to buckle or the jar to break, or could prevent air from venting during processing, so the pickle wouldn't keep as long.)

Remove the air bubbles from each jar.

Wipe the rim clean.

When the jar has cooled, remove the metal ring.

Put on the flat lid, then screw on the metal ring.

When the water in the canner is hot—about 140 degrees F if you've raw-packed the jars, about 180 degrees F if you've hot-packed them—load them into the canner. (If you drop cool jars into boiling water, they are likely to break.) Add as much extra hot water as you need to cover the jars by at least 1 inch. Bring the water to a boil over high heat, then reduce the heat, and gently boil the jars for the specified length of time.

If you're canning at an elevation of over 1,000 feet, you should process your jars longer than the recipes specify. The higher your elevation, the lower the temperature at which water boils. When the boiling temperature is lower, the boiling time must be increased. The USDA now publishes elaborate charts for figuring out processing times according to altitude, but I find these confusing. Generally, 5 minutes' time is added for each higher altitude range, although occasionally you can skip a range before you must add 5 minutes. I follow the simpler guidelines still recommended by Ball and displayed in the chart on this page.

. . .

ALTITUDE ADJUSTMENTS FOR BOILING-WATER PROCESSING

If your altitude (in feet) is—	Increase processing time—
1,001–3,000	5 minutes
3,001–6,000	10 minutes
over 6,000	15 minutes

When the boiling time is up, promptly remove the jars. Lift them straight out of the water (if you tilt the jars and the water on top runs off, the vacuum seal might break or, if the seal hasn't formed yet, sloshing liquid might keep it from doing so). Set the hot jars at least 1 inch apart on a rack, towel, or

Steps in Boiling-Water Canning:

- Fill the canner about halfway with water.

- Heat the water to about 140 degrees F for food packed cold, or about 180 degrees F for food packed hot.

- Lower the jars into the canner, all together on the canner rack or individually with a jar lifter.

- Add boiling water, if needed, so the water level is about 1 inch above the jar tops.

- Bring the water to a vigorous boil, and begin timing the processing. Put the lid on the canner, and lower the heat to maintain a gentle boil.

- When the processing time is up, remove the jars with a jar lifter. Set them to cool on a rack, towel, or hot pad.

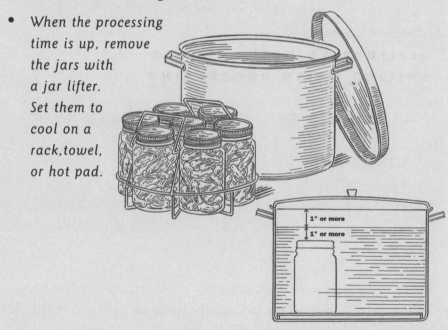

1" or more

1" or more

hot pad (if you set them directly on a tile counter, they'll probably crack). Leave the jars undisturbed until they're completely cool. As they cool, you may hear a *pang* as each vacuum seal forms, pulling the center of the metal lid downward.

When the jars are cool, test that the lids have sealed well by pressing in the center with a finger. If the center stays down, the seal is good. If the center pops up, store the jar in the refrigerator, or reprocess the jar after making sure the rim is clean and free of nicks and adding a new lid. A second processing should be done within 24 hours of the first, for the same amount of time. Reprocessing may soften the pickles more than you'd like, so refrigeration may be a better option.

If you like, you can remove the metal rings from the cooled jars. Most experienced preservers wash their rings after using them, dry them well, and store them in a dry place. This way the rings can be used over and over; they may last as long as the jars do. If left on the jars instead, rings often rust.

If you take a jar of pickles from the pantry only to find that the lid has come loose during storage, throw out the pickles.

Low-Temperature Pasteurization

THE LOW-TEMPERATURE PASTEURIZATION method has proven effective for many kinds of pickles, but is perhaps most valuable with fresh and fermented cucumber pickles, which tend to soften at high temperatures. By this method, you pack the vegetables and liquid into hot jars, seal the jars with hot lids, and place the jars in a canner filled halfway with water heated to 120 to 140 degrees F. Add hot water to cover the jars by at least 1 inch, and heat the water to 180 to 185 degrees F. Hold that temperature for 30 minutes. (You must be sure your thermometer is accurate. You can calibrate it by immersing its tip or bulb in boiling water; if your altitude is near sea level, water boils at 212 degrees F.) Check the temperature often; make only small adjustments in the flame level, because if you let the heat go over 185 degrees F the cucumbers may soften. I mention a flame here because I really don't think this method would work well with an electric stove; even with gas it takes a great deal of attention.

Open-Kettle Method

THE OPEN-KETTLE METHOD requires that you sterilize your mason jars and heat the lids thoroughly. Boil the jars in a kettle full of water for 10 minutes. Put the lids into a pan or dish, pour boiling water over them, and let them sit for several minutes so the sealing compound softens. Don't boil the lids, and don't leave them in water so long that it becomes cool. Ball lids may work better than Kerr lids for open-kettle canning.

Drain the jars very well, then fill them immediately with very hot pickles or relish. Leave the specified headspace, release the air bubbles, wipe the rims completely clean, and add the hot lids. Screw the rings on securely. If a lid hasn't sealed within 12 hours, store the jar in the refrigerator, or process it in a boiling-water bath for the specified length of time.

Storing Pickles

IF YOU'RE NOT canning your pickles, you can store them in any sort of glass jars. Do be sure, though, that the lids are nonreactive. Mason jar lids, even if they're used, fit this definition when their undersides aren't nicked or scratched. The metal rings can rust, however, and so can the outer edges of the rims, and the rust can spread to the inside of the jars. This is particularly likely to happen in pickles made with full-strength vinegar, such as *cornichons à cru*, especially if you fill the jar to the rim with vinegar (the best way to ensure that the vegetables stay immersed). Rusting can even occur with refrigerator pickles if the jars are placed, or if they fall, onto their sides, or if they're stored for a long time.

For all noncanned pickles, therefore, I like to use the all-plastic lids. In both regular and wide-mouth sizes, they are available in many supermarkets as well as from Alltrista Corporation (see page 367). When I can't find a plastic lid in the cupboard, I reuse a two-piece cap in good condition, but I line it with two layers of plastic wrap.

•••

CAPS THAT WILL NEVER RUST

All-plastic mason jar caps are useful even if you can your pickles. If all the pickles in a jar aren't eaten at once, you can replace the metal lid with a plastic cap for refrigerator storage. Plastic caps are much handier than separate lids and rings, which tend to lose each other in the kitchen and rust if refrigerated for too long. When you give canned pickles as gifts, you can fit a plastic cap over the flat metal lid, so that after the lid is removed the plastic cap can replace it.

For uncanned pickles to be stored at room temperature (such as *Cornichons à Cru* on page 90), or for pickles that will be stored at room temperature after undergoing less than 10 minutes of boiling-water processing, I recommend sterilizing the jars by immersing them in boiling water for 10 minutes just before filling them.

Pickle brine is not an embalming fluid; don't expect pickles left in a shed for several years to be fit to eat. Although canned pickles and cornichon-type pickles often keep well for over a year, you should try to use them within six months. Pickled cucumbers, especially, are likely to soften with longer storage. Lower-acid pickles designed for refrigerator storage will stay firm and appealing for a shorter period, about two months before oxidation damages their texture and flavor. (Some pickles should be eaten immediately, or within a week or two, but the recipes will alert you to this.) If, however, your pickling liquid contains at least one part vinegar for each part water, the pickles will keep in the refrigerator for much longer—perhaps a year or more if the jar is well sealed with a nonreactive lid and the liquid completely covers the vegetables or fruit. Pickles fermented in a medium-strength brine and refrigerated in their original containers may keep well for as long as six months, if any scum or mold is promptly removed. When I've strained and boiled the brine and refrigerated fermented pickles in clean jars, they have kept well for over a year. Generally, though, after the first several weeks pickles don't get better with age, so enjoy them while they're still young. Throw out any pickles that have become furry, slimy, or foul-tasting, no matter how they've been stored.

Fermented pickles are usually cured at room temperature or thereabouts, and so are Middle Eastern vinegar pickles. After their curing, though, all pickles that needn't be refrigerated should be stored in a cool, dry, dark place. Although I sometimes refer to "pantry storage," if your pantry is a cupboard near the kitchen stove or open shelves in front of a window, this is not the best place to store your pickles. A dry cellar is ideal; second best is an unheated room where the pickles are protected from light.

FERMENTED PICKLES

FERMENTED PICKLES

FRESH VEGETABLES, SALT, water, and some spices or fresh herbs are all you need to make fermented pickles. You don't really need a recipe, not any more than you need one for baking bread, provided you keep in mind the right proportion of salt to water. You don't have to limit yourself to cucumbers, either; other vegetables, such as cauliflower, snap beans, peppers, zucchini, peas, tomatoes, carrots, and brussels sprouts, are also very good brined. Among the world's pickles, brined cabbage—whether it's called sauerkraut, kimchi, or something else—is probably even more popular than brined cucumbers (see Chapter 4 for pickled cabbage recipes). You can even brine some fruits, as the Russians do, though the methods are a little different for these. Most fun of all, I think, is mixing vegetables, and this may be the most practical kind of pickling for you if your garden is small.

Although brining is slower than vinegar pickling, the process is remarkably simple and trouble-free. You just put your fresh, clean, unwaxed vegetables and aromatics into a clean crock or jar. Then you mix up a brine, stirring pure salt into water until the water first clouds and then clears again. You pour the brine over the vegetables to cover them well, then weight them so they stay immersed. Within three days, usually, fermentation will have begun. If you're using a clear jar, you'll see tiny bubbles rising inside. A yeasty scum may begin forming on top; you'll want to skim off most of this every day. The room will fill with an irresistible aroma, and if you taste the brine you'll find it quite tart. (You'll understand why some people prefer the brine to the pickles, and use it as a soup stock, a hangover remedy, or just a refreshing drink. For many women in eastern Europe, it is also a cosmetic.) Within a week, two weeks, four weeks, or six, fermentation will have slowed, and your pickles will be deliciously sour. If they are cucumber pickles, they will be olive-green throughout. They will be ready to eat.

If you're making kimchi or another Asian pickle, the fermentation time may be only a few days. In this case, the brine gets sour, but the vegetables don't completely ferment. These are pleasantly sour but still fresh-tasting pickles.

As you start experimenting with brine pickling, you'll want to keep several considerations in mind:

Containers. The cucumber pickle recipes are designed to suit containers of various sizes, from one quart to three gallons or larger. I don't recommend searching antique stores for an undamaged stoneware crock. You can get a brand-new one, American-made and identical to the old ones, for much less money, by mail-order (see page 367) if not from a local merchant. These crocks come in sizes as small as one gallon, and so are suitable even for a household of one or two.

Remember, though, that stoneware crocks are heavy. If you want to make a big batch of pickles and you're not very strong, you might want to use a food-grade plastic bucket. These are available from plastic-supply houses and sometimes from restaurants. (*Don't* use a laundry-soap container or plastic garbage can.)

To ferment smaller batches of pickles, I like to use glass jars, ranging in size from one gallon to as small as one quart. These are usually narrower at the top than in the middle, but a water-filled plastic bag can take the place of plate, weight, and cloth cover.

A cooking pot might do as a pickle crock, too, but only if it's made of stainless steel. Other metals react with the salt and acid in pickle brine.

Brine strength. This term refers to the weight of salt as a percentage of the weight of the solution. Brine strength is important because it affects the sourness of the pickle, the speed of the fermentation process, and how long the pickle will keep. Because pickling salt is of uniform density, you can easily translate between brine strength, salt weight, and salt volume for a given amount of water by using the charts on this page. In the recipes, I make life easier by specifying volume measurements only.

· · ·

BRINE STRENGTH, BY THE GALLON
Pickling salt added to 1 gallon of water at 68°F

Salt volume (in cups)	Salt weight (in ounces)	Brine concentration (percentage salt, by weight of solution)
⅓	3.3	2.4
½	4.9	3.5
⅔	6.5	4.7
¾	7.4	5.2
1	9.8	6.9

BRINE STRENGTH, BY THE QUART
Pickling salt added to 1 quart of water at 68°F

Salt volume	Salt weight (in ounces)	Brine concentration (percentage salt, by weight of solution)
1½ tablespoons	.9	2.7
2 tablespoons	1.2	3.5
3 tablespoons	1.8	5.4
¼ cup	2.5	6.9
⅓ cup	3.3	8.9

Source: Robert Waterhouse, personal communication, 1998.

Old-time picklers, though, couldn't rely on volume measurements, since there was no guarantee that the density of one year's salt matched that of the preceding year. Without kitchen scales, old-timers couldn't weigh their salt, either. So their recipes often called for "enough salt to float an egg." This meant a 10 percent brine, which resulted in very salty pickles that would keep all winter in the cellar, but would have to be soaked in fresh water for days before they became edible (after which they might be pickled anew in vinegar and sugar). Upon experimenting with pickles made in a 10 percent brine, I decided they were too awful to turn into a recipe for this book. You can make them if you want, though, by simply using about 1½ cups salt for each gallon of water.

If you don't like salty pickles at all, conversely, you can make them with a brine of only about 3½ percent, using ½ cup salt for each gallon of water. If you're fermenting cucumbers, you can call these pickles half-sours. They will be ready to eat within a week. They won't be suitable for canning, though, since they may not be sour enough to prevent the growth of harmful microorganisms.

If you want fully sour pickles that aren't overly salty, use a 5 to 6 percent brine; at room temperature the fermentation will last two to four weeks. Full-sours are suitable for canning.

If you like salty pickles and want a slower fermentation—of six to eight weeks, say—use a 7 to 8 percent brine. With stronger brines, though, lactic-acid fermentation happens slower, so more yeast and gas develop, and cucumber pickles often become "bloaters"—hollow, floating pickles. Mold is more likely to develop, too.

Fermentation temperature. You don't need a cold cellar to ferment vegetables, although cellars are useful for storing finished pickles. Traditionally, pickles are fermented in an out-of-the-way corner of the kitchen. Except when indicated in the recipes, temperatures anywhere between 55 and 80 degrees F are acceptable. The lower the temperature, though, the slower the fermentation; at 55 to 60 degrees F, fermentation in a 5 percent brine may take five to six weeks. Generally, a temperature of 70 to 75 degrees F is preferable, especially in the beginning, as fermentation gets under way.

Temperatures of more than 80 degrees F may encourage the growth of microorganisms that make the pickles soft. If you have very hot summers, you may prefer a stoneware crock to a plastic bucket, and a tile counter or cement floor to a wood or linoleum surface (which might be damaged, anyway, by dripping brine or condensation).

Weights. The vegetables in your crock or jar must be fully submerged in the brine, or they'll eventually get soft and off-flavored. One protruding pickle, in fact, may spoil the whole batch. Since you may be skimming off some of the brine with the yeast scum, you'll want to add plenty of brine at the beginning of the process. To keep the vegetables submerged, you might pack larger ones on top of smaller ones. Then add an inverted pie plate or dinner plate just a little 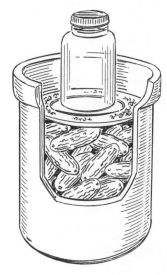 smaller than the opening of the crock, and weight it with tightly capped canning jars filled with water (two quart jars distribute the weight better than one half-gallon jar, which might crush the vegetables). Some people use well-scrubbed rocks instead of water-filled jars; other heavy objects may work as well if you enclose them in a leak-free, food-grade plastic bag.

Or you can omit the plate, and just use a brine bag—a leak-free, food-grade plastic bag, again, placed directly in the crock or jar, filled with extra brine, and well sealed. I use zipper-locked freezer bags, always fresh out of the box. If you're afraid your bag might leak, use two, one inside the other. You needn't worry much, though, since leaking brine won't hurt the pickles (fresh water would, of course, by weakening the brine).

Pickling with a brine bag is particularly undemanding, since no scum will develop if the bag completely covers the surface. Sometimes I use three one-gallon bags in my large crocks; if I set the bags in carefully, they work as well as one large bag.

Yeasts and molds. Unless a brine bag seals out all air, yeasts and molds can grow on the surface of a pickle brine. Usually indicated by white, foamy scum, yeasts are particularly common with fermenting cucumbers. Especially in eastern Europe, yeasts are often considered desirable for their effect on a pickle's flavor. But the growth of yeasts must be checked by regular skimming, or they may gradually cause softening, darkening, and off-flavors in the pickled food.

Molds appear less often, usually when fermentation is slowed by low temperatures, a high salt content, or both. Looking like tiny eyeballs floating on the brine, molds are harmless if they are promptly removed. Once fermentation gets under way, they are unlikely to develop provided the vegetables are well covered by brine. If they appear on the wall of the crock, wipe them off with a paper towel. You can limit the growth of molds by scalding your crocks before and after using them. A clean towel or pillowcase covering the crock during fermentation helps to keep out mold spores as well as dust and bigger pests.

I skim my pickle brines daily with a wide, shallow spoon. I don't try to remove all the yeast scum, since it tends to break up and float off most uncooperatively. I get rid of much of it, though, by rinsing off the brine bag or the plate and canning jars before replacing them. You might instead lay a clean piece of muslin or two or more layers of cheesecloth on top of the pickles (under a weighted plate), and lift the cloth off every day or two. Boil the cloth and reuse it, or replace it with a new one.

Leaves. Grape leaves, sour cherry leaves, and oak leaves are used to keep pickles firm. The Russians also use black currant leaves in pickling, for their subtle, smoky flavor and aseptic qualities; horseradish leaves, as well as horseradish roots, are said to have aseptic qualities, too.

You can scatter or layer leaves with other flavorings throughout your pickle crock, or even wrap each cucumber in a leaf. But most often people put handfuls of leaves at the bottom and top of the crock. This hints at other purposes: At the bottom of the crock, the leaves lift the vegetables out of the sediment that settles there and could perhaps cause softening. At the top of the crock, the leaves cushion the vegetables against the pressure of the plate and weight above, protect them from exposure to the air, and also collect the yeasty scum so that it doesn't settle on the vegetables. Cabbage and other vegetable leaves can be—and have been—used for these purposes. One recipe I found calls for daily replacement of the leaves on top of the crock. If fresh leaves are always handy, this is both more effective and easier than skimming the pickle liquid every day.

Storage. Fermented pickles should be stored in the refrigerator. You can leave them in their original containers, or, for longer storage, you can boil, skim, and cool the brine, rinse the vegetables, and refrigerate them in the cooled brine with fresh aromatics.

As indicated in the recipes, some fermented pickles are suitable for canning. Canned pickles will keep for over a year in a cool, dark, dry place, but are best eaten within six months or so. See Chapter 1 for basic canning instructions.

GROWING AND HARVESTING CUCUMBERS

You can start cucumbers in the ground, after the soil has warmed, or indoors a little earlier. Either way, you may want to stagger your plantings to fool the cucumber beetles, if these disease-spreading pests infest your garden.

I like to plant my cucumbers in hills—that is, clusters of two or three plants each—rather than in rows, which tend to spread until there's no place left to walk. I never trellis my plants, since I have more garden space than carpentry skill, but I suspect that long varieties will grow straighter if the vines can climb.

Water your cucumber plants regularly to avoid bitter or hollow fruits, but don't keep the soil soaked.

Harvest cucumbers at least every other day. Even with this schedule you'll find overgrown fruits, since young cucumbers are very adept at hiding. The big ones can be seeded for salads or "sunshine" pickles.

Harvest your cucumbers just before watering, not after. Cleaning mud from between tiny spines is aggravating work; besides, if you're fermenting your cucumbers you don't want to end up scrubbing off all the good bacteria. Mulching with straw will keep cucumbers cleaner, and perhaps help control the cucumber beetles, too.

Pick your cucumbers with a little bit of stem attached, if possible. This will help to keep them from shriveling, and many people think the stem makes an attractive little handle for a pickle. I brush off any remaining blossoms as I pick, since I suspect they can cause softening even before processing begins.

If you can't process your cucumbers immediately, keep them in a cool place—preferably not the refrigerator, which tends to dry out vegetables.

Half-Sours, by the Quart

HALF-SOURS AREN'T PICKLES taken prematurely from their brine; rather, they're cured quickly in a low-salt brine, which hastens the fermentation so the pickles never get very sour, no matter how long they remain in the brine. In *The Dill Crock* (1984), John Thorne describes half-sours as "cucumbers still, not pickles—little cucumbers who [have] died and gone to heaven."

¼ teaspoon black peppercorns, crushed

¼ teaspoon coriander seeds, crushed

1 bay leaf

1 garlic clove, chopped

1 quart 3- to 5-inch pickling cucumbers

1 dill head

1 chile pepper, slit lengthwise

1½ tablespoons pickling salt

3 cups water

1. Put the peppercorns, coriander, bay, and garlic into a quart jar. Gently wash the cucumbers, and remove the blossom ends. Pack the jar with the cucumbers, adding the dill head and chile pepper. Add the salt to the water, and pour the brine over the cucumbers, leaving 1½ inches headspace. Push a quart freezer bag into the mouth of the jar, and pour the remaining brine into the bag. Seal the bag. Keep the jar at room temperature, with a dish underneath if the seeping brine might do some damage otherwise.

2. Within 3 days you should see tiny bubbles rising in the jar; this means that fermentation has begun. If scum forms on top of the brine, skim it off daily, and rinse off the brine bag. If so much brine bubbles out that the pickles aren't well covered, add some more brine made in the same proportion of salt to water.

3. The pickles should be ready within a week, when they taste sour and when the tiny bubbles have stopped rising. Skim off any scum at the top of the jar, cap the jar, and store the pickles in the refrigerator for about 3 days, after which time they should be olive-green throughout. They are best eaten within about 3 weeks.

Makes 1 quart

• • •

PREPARING CUCUMBERS FOR PICKLING

Begin processing American-type pickling cucumbers within two days of picking, and cornichons within one day. The smaller the cucumber, the quicker it will soften and shrivel as it waits for its brine bath.

Wash the cucumbers gently, but do make sure you remove all dirt. Be sure to remove all traces of the blossoms, too; they may contain fungi, and enzymes and hormones that can soften pickles. The USDA recommends cutting $\frac{1}{16}$ inch off the blossom end of the cucumber, but I just scrape the end with my fingernail. Leave the spines, if you're using American-type cucumbers. Gently rub off the many tiny prickles on cornichons.

Many people prick or slit cucumbers before fermenting them; others slice off both ends. If you're using a low-salt brine—say, 2½ to 4 percent—any of these measures will promote even fermentation. For slow-fermented cucumbers, pricking, slitting, or stabbing allow gas to escape, which may reduce the number of bloaters. Bloating isn't normally a problem, though, if the cucumbers are of moderate size and the brine of moderate strength.

Hungarian Summer Pickles, by the Quart

THIS IS A pickle for the impatient. It's another half-sour, with a fermentation hastened by sunshine. Although most recipes tell you to ferment pickles in a cool, dark place, this isn't really necessary. Until recently, in fact, commercial picklers fermented cucumbers in open outdoor vats so that ultraviolet rays could control the growth of mold; some companies still make their pickles this way. In this recipe, using sunshine lets you do without a brine bag or other weight. (For insurance, though, use a narrow-mouth jar, and wedge the cucumbers in tightly to keep them from floating.)

Food scientists have found that cucumbers soften when temperatures rise above 80 degrees F during fermentation. This hasn't been a problem for me. Still, on very hot days you may want to move your pickle jar to a cooler place.

So that cucumbers ferment evenly during a brief cure and to reduce their tendency to float, eastern Europeans often poke or slit them. This recipe calls for slitting, but you might prefer to poke a bamboo skewer through one end of the cucumber and out the other.

June Meyer, who published a recipe like this one on the Internet, remembers the "sun pickles" of her childhood. "We kids would eat them like Popsicles," she writes. "The envy of all the neighborhood kids."

I quart 3- to 5-inch pickling cucumbers
I tablespoon pickling salt
2 tablespoons white or red wine vinegar
I fresh head and I frond of dill
About 2 cups water

---

1. Gently wash the cucumbers, and remove the blossom ends. Using a knife, slit the cucumbers through lengthwise, leaving their ends intact. Put the salt, vinegar, and dill into a narrow-mouth quart jar. Pack the cucumbers into the jar so they won't float, leaving 1 inch headspace. Cover the cucumbers with water. Cap the jar with a nonreactive lid, and give the jar a shake to dissolve the salt. Loosen the lid. Place the jar outdoors in the sun or in a sunny window, in a dish if seeping brine might do some damage. If you set the jar outdoors, bring it in at night.

2. Within 3 days you should see tiny bubbles rising in the jar; this means that fermentation has begun. The pickles should be ready within 5 days, when the tiny bubbles have stopped rising. Chill them, and eat. They will keep well in the refrigerator for a few weeks.

Makes 1 quart

. . .

TROUBLESHOOTING GUIDE: FERMENTED CUCUMBER PICKLES

Problem	Possible Causes
Hollow middle	The cucumbers grew this way, perhaps because of inadequate watering. (You can pick out cucumbers like this when you wash them—they float.) Or the cucumbers were held too long before brining. This is mainly a problem with larger, more mature cucumbers.
Pale skins	The cucumbers grew this way; perhaps they were sun-scalded (grape, sour cherry, or black currant leaves may help deepen the green of pale cucumbers). Or the pickles were exposed to light during storage.
Dark pickles	Your water contains a lot of iron or is alkaline, or your canning lids were corroded, or you used reactive metal pans or utensils in processing the pickles.

Shriveled pickles	The cucumbers were held too long before brining, or the brine was too strong at the beginning of the curing.
Small brown spots on pickles	The cucumbers were held too long before brining.
Slightly soft pickles	The cucumbers were held too long before brining, or the temperatures were too high during fermentation. Or the pickles were overheated during processing; try low-temperature pasteurization.
White sediment	Yeast grew on the brine and settled to the bottom of the container (yeast isn't a problem if it's regularly skimmed off during fermentation and if the pickles are heat-processed or refrigerated afterward), or table salt was used.
Slippery, mushy pickles	Undesirable microbes grew, for any of these reasons: Blossoms weren't removed before fermentation, too little salt was used, some cucumbers weren't completely submerged in the brine, the brine wasn't skimmed, or the pickles were canned without adequate heat treatment or an airtight seal. *Don't eat these!*
Off flavor	Undesirable microbes grew, for one or more of the reasons just above. But the pickles are safe to eat if they are sour, firm, and mold-free.

Robert's Tea Pickles

My husband, Robert, was inspired to suggest this recipe after he tasted my cucumbers pickled with black currant leaves. Currant leaves add a subtle smoky flavor, and he wanted even more smokiness. Lapsang souchong tea does indeed provide this. He liked the result so much that he's asking for more tea pickles. Earl Grey next time?

About 2 pounds 3- to 5-inch pickling cucumbers
1 fresh chile pepper, halved lengthwise
6 garlic cloves, sliced
2 teaspoons Sichuan peppercorns, crushed
2 teaspoons lapsang souchong tea
3 tablespoons pickling salt
4 cups water

1. Gently wash the cucumbers, and remove the blossom ends. Put the chile pepper, garlic, peppercorns, and tea into a 2-quart jar. Pack the cucumbers into the jar. Dissolve the salt in the water, and pour the brine over the cucumbers, leaving 1½ inches headspace. Push a freezer bag into the mouth of the jar, and pour the remaining brine into the bag. Seal the bag. Keep the jar at room temperature, with a dish underneath if seeping brine might do some damage.

2. Within 3 days you should see tiny bubbles rising in the jar. This means that fermentation has begun. If scum forms on top of the brine, skim it off daily, and rinse off the brine bag. If so much brine bubbles out that the pickles aren't well covered, add some more brine made in the same proportion of salt to water.

3. The pickles should be ready in 2 to 3 weeks; they will be sour and olive-green throughout. If you plan to eat them within a few weeks, remove the brine bag, skim off the scum, and cap the jar. Store it in the refrigerator.

4. If you want the pickles to keep for a few months, pour them with the brine into a colander set on top of a nonreactive saucepan. Discard the seasonings. Remove the colander from the pan, and transfer the pan to the stovetop. Bring the brine to a boil. Simmer it for 5 minutes, and skim off the scum that forms. Let the brine cool to room temperature. Rinse the pickles with cold water, pack them into a clean jar (with fresh garlic and Sichuan peppercorns, if you like), and cover them with the boiled and cooled brine before refrigerating them.

Makes 2 quarts

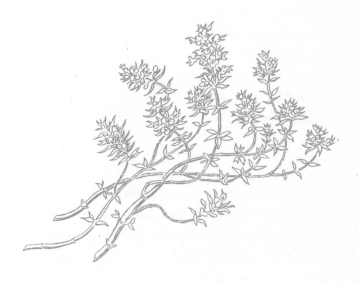

Mustardy Dill Pickles

HERE'S A ONE-GALLON recipe for those who love the flavors of mustard and horseradish. When I'm not buried in cucumbers, I love fermenting them in gallon glass jars, which are lighter than crocks and give me a clear view of what's happening inside.

---

1 handful grape or sour cherry leaves

About 4 pounds 3- to 5-inch pickling cucumbers

Tops of 4 celery stalks

1 large onion, sliced

½ cup chopped horseradish

¼ cup yellow mustard seeds

4 to 6 dill heads

6 tablespoons salt

2 quarts water

---

1. Lay half the leaves in the bottom of a 1-gallon jar. Gently wash the cucumbers, and remove the blossom ends. Put the cucumbers, celery tops, onion, horseradish, mustard seeds, and dill in layers in the jar. Dissolve the salt in the water, and pour enough brine over the cucumbers to cover them. Spread the remaining leaves on top. Push a freezer bag into the jar, and pour the remaining brine into the bag. If necessary, add more brine made in the same proportion of salt to water. Seal the bag. Store the jar at room temperature.

2. Within 3 days you should see tiny bubbles in the brine. This means that fermentation has begun. If scum forms on top of the brine, skim it off daily, and rinse off the brine bag.

3. The pickles should be ready in 2 to 3 weeks, when the bubbling has stopped and the pickles are sour and olive-green throughout. You can store the pickles in the refrigerator for up to 4 months without further processing.

For longer refrigerator storage or for pantry storage, pour the pickles and brine into a colander set on top of a nonreactive pot. Discard the leaves and spices. Remove the colander from the pot, and transfer the pot to the stove-top. Bring the brine to a boil, simmer it for 5 minutes, and skim off the scum that forms. Rinse the pickles with cold water, and drain them well.

If you're storing the pickles in the refrigerator, let the brine cool to room temperature. Pack the pickles into 2-quart jars or a clean gallon jar. If you like, add fresh dill, mustard, and horseradish. Pour enough cooled brine over the pickles to cover them. Cover the jars and refrigerate them.

For pantry storage, pack the pickles into quart or pint mason jars. Pour the hot brine over the pickles, leaving ½ inch headspace, and close the jars with hot two-piece caps. In a boiling-water bath, process pint jars for 10 minutes, quart jars for 15 minutes. Or pasteurize the jars for 30 minutes in water heated to 180 to 185 degrees F. When the jars have cooled, store them in a cool, dry, dark place.

Makes about 6 quarts

No-Dill Crock Pickles

I'M INCLUDING THIS RECIPE for two reasons—to show that a lot of flavors besides dill complement fermented cucumbers, and to provide a set of quantities to fit a two-gallon crock. Even if you wouldn't consider making pickles without dill, you may want to use the basic quantities here.

2 handfuls grape or sour cherry leaves

About 8 pounds 3- to 5-inch pickling cucumbers

2 tablespoons black peppercorns

1 tablespoon whole allspice

Zest of 2 lemons, in strips

8 fennel heads, or ¼ cup fennel seeds

8 fennel fronds

1 small bunch parsley

½ cup white wine vinegar

1 gallon water

¾ cup salt

1. Lay half the leaves in the bottom of a 2-gallon crock. Gently wash the cucumbers, and remove the blossom ends. Layer the cucumbers in the crock with the pepper, allspice, lemon zest, fennel, and parsley. Add the vinegar to the water, and dissolve the salt in the liquid. Pour enough brine over the cucumbers to cover them. Spread the remaining leaves on top. Keep the cucumbers submerged by weighting them down with a plate topped with a clean rock or a water-filled jar, or with a large freezer bag filled with leftover brine and sealed (if you need more brine, make it with the same proportion of salt to water, omitting the vinegar). Cover the crock with a pillowcase or towel, and store it at room temperature.

2. Within 3 days you should see tiny bubbles in the brine. This means that fermentation has begun. If a white scum forms on top of the brine, skim it off daily, and rinse off and replace the plate and weight or the brine bag.

3. The pickles should be ready in 2 to 3 weeks, when the tiny bubbles stop rising and the pickles are sour and olive-green throughout. Skim off any scum.

4. Pour the pickles and brine into a colander set on top of a nonreactive pot. Discard the leaves and spices. Remove the colander from the pot, and transfer the pot to the stovetop. Bring the brine to a boil, reduce the heat to low, and simmer the brine 5 minutes. Skim off the scum that forms. Let the brine cool to room temperature. Rinse the pickles with cold water, and drain them well.

5. For refrigerator storage, pack the pickles into 2-quart jars or a gallon jar. If you like, add fresh lemon zest, fennel, and spices. Cover the pickles with cooled brine. Cap the jar, and store it in the refrigerator for up to 6 months.

For pantry storage, pack the pickles into quart or pint jars, adding fresh aromatics, if you like. Cover the pickles with hot brine, leaving ½ inch headspace. Close the jars with hot two-piece caps. In a boiling-water bath, process pint jars for 10 minutes, quart jars for 15 minutes. Or pasteurize the jars for 30 minutes in water heated to 180 to 185 degrees F. When the jars have cooled, store them in a cool, dry, dark place.

Makes 6 quarts

. . .

"**I** once asked my grandmother, then seventy-two years old, how she kept her skin so wrinkle-free. The secret, she explained, was a daily dose of the fermented brine from the pickle barrel, rubbed into her skin. This treatment explained the unusual smell I'd always associated with my grandmother, but the astringent quality of the brine did seem to work wonders."

—*Darra Goldstein, A Taste of Russia (1983)*

Spicy Crock Pickles

THIS IS MY CHILDREN'S FAVORITE dill pickle recipe. The leaves keep the cucumbers firm and crunchy, and the mixed pickling spice renders them indefinably flavorful. I use a minimal amount of dill, but don't hesitate to use a lot if you like your pickles really dilly.

This recipe will fill a three-gallon crock.

2 handfuls grape leaves or sour cherry leaves

About 12 pounds 3- to 5-inch pickling cucumbers

2 tablespoons mixed pickling spice

1 garlic bulb, cloves separated and peeled

4 to 8 dill heads

6 quarts water

1 cup cider vinegar

1¼ cups pickling salt

1. Line the bottom of a 3-gallon crock with half the leaves. Gently wash the cucumbers, and remove the blossom ends. Layer the cucumbers, spice, garlic cloves, and dill heads in the crock. Combine the water and vinegar, and dissolve the salt in the liquid. Pour the brine over the cucumbers to cover, and lay the remaining leaves on top. Keep the leaves and cucumbers submerged by weighting them down with a plate topped with a clean rock or a water-filled jar, or with a large freezer bag filled with additional brine and sealed. Cover the crock with a pillowcase or towel, and store the crock at room temperature.

2. Within 3 days you should see tiny bubbles in the brine. This means that fermentation has begun. If a white scum forms on top of the brine, skim it off daily, and rinse off and replace the plate and weight or the brine bag.

3. The pickles should be ready in 2 to 3 weeks, when the tiny bubbles stop rising and the pickles are sour and olive-green throughout. Skim off any scum.

4. Pour the pickles and brine into a colander set on top of a nonreactive pot. Discard the leaves and spices. Remove the colander from the pot, and transfer the pot to the stovetop. Bring the brine to a boil, reduce the heat to low, and simmer the brine 5 minutes. Skim off the scum that forms. Rinse the pickles with cold water, and drain them well.

5. For refrigerator storage, let the brine cool to room temperature. Pack the pickles into 2-quart jars or gallon jars. If you like, add fresh dill and garlic. Pour enough cooled brine over the pickles to cover them. Cap the jar, and store it in the refrigerator for as long as 6 months.

For pantry storage, pack the pickles into quart or pint mason jars, adding fresh dill and garlic, if you like. Pour hot brine over the pickles, leaving ½ inch headspace. Close the jars with hot two-piece caps. In a boiling-water bath, process pint jars for 10 minutes, quart jars for 15 minutes. Or pasteurize the jars for 30 minutes in water heated from 180 to 185 degrees F.

When the jars have cooled, store them in a cool, dry, dark place.

Makes about 10 quarts

• • •

"**O**n a hot day in Virginia, I know of nothing more comforting than a fine spiced pickle, brought up troutlike from the sparkling depths of the aromatic jar below stairs in Aunt Sally's cellar."

—*Thomas Jefferson*

Russian Dill Pickles

IN EASTERN EUROPE, a slice of rye bread is often placed at the top of the pickle crock. All-wheat bread is never substituted, for rye attracts yeasts that contribute a desired flavor. The bread should not, of course, contain any preservatives.

Russians prefer to ferment their cucumbers in one-gallon oak barrels. But you can do without the barrel and just use oak leaves, for their tannin, or substitute sour cherry or grape leaves, which also help keep pickles firm. I've designed this recipe to fill a three-gallon crock.

These pickles are a little saltier than the Spicy Crock Pickles (page 54), with a 7 percent rather than a 5 percent brine. If you prefer a slightly less salty pickle, you can reduce the salt to 1 cup plus 2 tablespoons.

---

2 to 4 handfuls oak, sour cherry, or grape leaves

About 12 pounds 3- to 5-inch pickling cucumbers

3 handfuls dill heads and fronds

3 garlic bulbs, cloves separated and peeled

8 small dried chile peppers, slit lengthwise

8 bay leaves

1 tablespoon black peppercorns

1 tablespoon coriander seeds

2 teaspoons mustard seeds

1½ cups pickling salt

6 quarts water

1 thick slice rye bread

---

1. Spread a handful of leaves on the bottom of a 3-gallon crock. Gently wash the cucumbers, and remove the blossom ends. Layer the cucumbers in the crock with the dill, garlic, peppers, bay leaves, and spices, lining the crock with leaves if you have plenty. Dissolve the salt in the water, and cover the cucumbers with the brine. Lay the rye bread on top, and spread the leaves over it. Put a plate on top, and weight it with a clean rock or a water-filled jar. Cover the crock with a pillowcase or towel, and store it at room temperature.

2. Within 3 days you should see tiny bubbles in the brine. This means that fermentation has begun. If a white scum forms on top of the brine, skim it off daily, and rinse off and replace the plate and weight.

3. The pickles should be ready within 4 weeks, when the tiny bubbles have stopped rising and the pickles are sour and olive-green throughout. Skim off the scum.

4. Pour the pickles and brine into a colander set on top of a nonreactive pot. Discard the leaves and spices. Remove the colander from the pot, and transfer the pot to the stovetop. Bring the brine to a boil, reduce the heat to low, and simmer the brine 5 minutes. Skim off the scum that forms. Rinse the pickles with cold water, and drain them well.

5. For refrigerator storage, let the brine cool to room temperature. Pack the pickles into 2-quart or gallon jars. If you like, add fresh dill and garlic. Pour enough cooled brine over the pickles to cover them. Cap the jar, and store it in the refrigerator for as long as 6 months.

For pantry storage, pack the pickles into quart or pint jars, adding fresh dill and garlic, if you like. Cover the pickles with the hot brine, leaving ½ inch headspace. Close the jars with hot two-piece caps. In a boiling-water bath, process pint jars for 10 minutes, quart jars for 15 minutes. Or pasteurize the jars for 30 minutes in water heated to 180 to 185 degrees F.

When the jars have cooled, store them in a cool, dry, dark place.

Makes about 10 quarts

· · ·

"**S**o in our pride we ordered for breakfast an omelet, toast and coffee and what has just arrived is a tomato salad with onions, a dish of pickles, a big slice of watermelon and two bottles of cream soda."

—*John Steinbeck,* A Russian Journal

Brined Snap Beans

VINEGAR-PICKLED BEANS are justifiably popular, but if you want to enhance the delicate flavor of snap beans without disguising it, give this recipe a try. You won't want to use tough, overgrown store-bought beans, of course; use tender young ones from the garden instead.

2 pounds tender young snap beans, trimmed

6 small dried chile peppers

6 garlic cloves, chopped

12 black peppercorns, crushed

6 dill heads

½ cup pickling salt

3 quarts water

1. Layer the beans, chile peppers, garlic, peppercorns, and dill in a 1-gallon jar. Dissolve the salt in the water, and pour enough brine over the beans to cover them. Push a freezer bag into the mouth of the jar, and pour the remaining brine into the bag. Seal the bag. Store the jar at room temperature.

2. Within 3 days you should see tiny bubbles rising in the jar. If scum forms on top of the brine, skim it off daily, and rinse off the brine bag.

3. The pickles should be ready in about 2 weeks, when the bubbling has stopped and the beans taste sour. Remove the brine bag, skim off any scum, and cap the jar. Store it in the refrigerator.

Makes 1 gallon

Mixed Fermented Pickles

A PICKLE LIKE THIS is especially practical if your garden is small, so that you have only a handful of this, a handful of that, to ferment at any particular time. But I like to make mixed pickles, fermented and stored in glass gallon jars, because they're beautiful to look at and an adventure to eat. Vary the vegetables according to what you have on hand and where your whimsy takes you.

1 pound cauliflower or broccoli florets

2 sweet green or red peppers, cut into squares or strips

½ pound asparagus spears, cut into thirds, or whole young snap
    beans

½ pound shallots, peeled, or regular onions, cut into chunks or
    rings

¼ pound baby carrots (no larger than ½ inch in diameter), or larger
    carrots, cut into rounds or thin sticks

3 garlic cloves, slivered

2 or 3 tarragon sprigs

2 or 3 thyme sprigs

½ cup pickling salt

3 quarts water

2 tablespoons red wine vinegar

1. Toss all the vegetables together, and pack them into a gallon jar, distributing the garlic and herbs among them. Dissolve the salt in the water, and pour enough brine over the vegetables to cover them. Add the wine vinegar. Push a freezer bag into the mouth of the jar, and pour the remaining brine into the bag. Seal the bag. Store the jar at room temperature.

2. Within 3 days you should see tiny bubbles in the brine. This means that fermentation has begun. If a white scum forms on top of the brine, skim it off daily, and rinse off and replace the brine bag.

3. The pickles should be ready in 2 to 3 weeks, when the bubbling has stopped and the pickles are sour. Remove the brine bag, skim off any scum, seal the jar, and store it in the refrigerator.

Makes 1 gallon

Turkish Mixed Pickle

THIS IS A FERMENTED VERSION of pepper "mangoes," or pickled stuffed peppers (see page 139). It's my favorite mixed pickle—at the moment, at least—because all of the vegetables are permeated with the flavor of lemon. Although they're supposed to ferment for two to three weeks, I like them best when the lemon flavor is strongest, after about five days. Sometimes I slice all the vegetables instead of mincing some and stuffing them into the others.

2 cups chopped white head cabbage

¼ cup minced carrot

¼ cup minced red bell pepper

6 garlic cloves, minced

2 tablespoons minced dill fronds

2 green bell peppers, cored

1 red bell pepper, cored

Mixed prepared vegetables, to total 2 quarts when combined with the
    stuffed peppers, including any of the following: 1- to 2-inch pickling
    cucumbers, blossom ends removed; cauliflower florets; snap beans,
    trimmed, and cut in half if they're long; carrots, sliced into rounds;
    whole small sweet peppers; and small green tomatoes

1 small lemon, sliced

4 dill sprigs

4 small dried chile peppers

¾ cup white wine vinegar

3 cups water

2½ tablespoons pickling salt

For the brine bag: 2 teaspoons pickling salt dissolved in 1 cup water

1. In a bowl, mix together the cabbage, carrot, minced bell pepper, garlic, and dill. Stuff the mixture into the cored bell peppers. Arrange the peppers in a 2-quart jar, and fill the spaces between them with the mixed prepared vegetables, the lemon, the dill, and the chile peppers.

2. Combine the vinegar and water. Add the salt to the liquid, and stir until the salt dissolves. Pour this brine over the vegetables to cover them well. Push a freezer bag into the mouth of the jar, and pour in the brine made from 2 teaspoons pickling salt stirred into 1 cup water. Seal the bag.

3. Store the jar at room temperature for 2 to 3 weeks, or until the vegetables taste sour and the bubbling has stopped. Remove the brine bag, cap the jar, and store it in the refrigerator.

Makes about 2 quarts

Sichuan Soured Vegetables

ALTHOUGH THE CHINESE are expert at extending the gardening season, in Sichuan province and elsewhere people traditionally rely on dried, pickled, and salted vegetables to get through the cold winters. This is a mild Sichuan pickle, cured only long enough to sour the liquid; the vegetables don't actually ferment.

This recipe appeals to me particularly because it doesn't require mixing salt and water in a separate container. You make the brine right in your pickle jar, and then put in the vegetables, plus a little more salt so the vegetables on top add their own brine to the jar.

The Chinese don't throw out the brine when the pickles are gone; they just add a little more rice wine, salt, and sugar, and another batch of vegetables. If you do this, put the jar straight into the refrigerator; since the liquid is already sour, the fermentation isn't repeated.

1½ tablespoons Sichuan peppercorns, crushed

2 tablespoons rice wine

1½ tablespoons rice vinegar

1 tablespoon sugar

3 cups water

3 tablespoons pickling salt

2 quarts prepared vegetables, including any of the following: head of Chinese (napa) cabbage, cut into 2-inch squares; turnips, halved and sliced ³⁄₁₆ inch thick; 1- to 1½-inch-long pickling cucumbers, or larger ones, cut into chunks; snap beans, trimmed, and halved if long; summer squash, cut into chunks; whole baby carrots (up to ½ inch thick), or larger carrots cut diagonally ¼ inch thick, then lengthwise into ¼-inch-wide sticks; broccoli stems, peeled and halved lengthwise

10 small dried red chile peppers, some snipped in half for added heat

One 2-inch piece fresh ginger, sliced thin diagonally

1. In a 2-quart jar, combine the peppercorns, rice wine, rice vinegar, sugar, water, and 2 tablespoons salt. Stir well to dissolve the salt, or cap the jar and shake it. Pack the vegetables firmly into the jar, layering them with the chile peppers and ginger, and sprinkle the remaining 1 tablespoon salt on top. Cap the jar loosely. Let it stand at room temperature.

2. After about 3 days, the vegetables should be soured to your taste. Cap the jar tightly, and store it in the refrigerator.

Makes 2 quarts

A PERFECT PICKLE POT

Irene Kuo (*The Key to Chinese Cooking*) describes the beautiful and ingenious pickle jars once made in Kwangsi province. About 3 feet high and 1 foot in diameter, the vase-like porcelain urns each had a deep cup around the neck into which water was poured. "When the cover, shaped like a deep rice bowl, was placed over this cup its rim was submerged in about 2 inches of water, thereby preventing air from seeping in but allowing the gas of fermentation to escape through the water as the brine aged."

Sauerruben

THIS GERMAN FERMENTED turnip pickle is made almost exactly like sauerkraut (page 170). Make sauerruben in the fall or spring, using fresh, sweet young turnips or rutabagas. I've shredded turnips with the 2¼-inch-wide blade of an ordinary grater, but this is tiring work—and hazardous to the fingertips—so use a kraut board or food processor if you have one.

As with sauerkraut, you can add flavorings such as caraway seeds to sauerruben. I'm tempted to add chile pepper and garlic, but then I'd have a sort of kimchi, wouldn't I? Anyway, sauerruben is delicious without adornment. I like it even better than sauerkraut.

5 pounds turnips, peeled and shredded
3 tablespoons pickling salt

1. In a large bowl, mix the turnips with the salt. Pack the mixture firmly into a 3-quart to 1-gallon jar. Push a freezer bag into the mouth of the jar, and fill the bag with a brine made of 1½ tablespoons pickling salt to each quart water. Seal the bag. Set the jar in a place where the temperature remains between 60 and 75 degrees F.

2. After 24 hours, check to make sure that the turnips are well submerged in their own brine. If they aren't, add some fresh brine (1½ tablespoons pickling salt to 1 quart water) to cover them well. If the brine bag is large enough to seal out all air, you can leave the jar undisturbed. (Otherwise you may need to check for scum. Skim off any scum you may find, and rinse off and replace the brine bag.)

3. After 2 weeks, begin tasting the sauerruben. It will be fully fermented in 2 to 4 weeks at 70 to 75 degrees F, or within 4 to 6 weeks at 60 degrees F. When it's ready, remove the bag, cap the jar, and store it in the refrigerator or another very cool place (at about 38 degrees F).

4. For pantry storage, pack the sauerruben and juices into clean pint or quart mason jars, leaving ½ inch headspace at the top of each jar. Close the jars with hot two-piece caps. In a boiling-water bath, process pint jars for 20 minutes, quart jars for 25 minutes. (Make sure the water in the canner isn't too hot when you add the jars, or they may break.) Or pasteurize pint or quart jars for 30 minutes in water heated to 180 to 185 degrees F.

When the jars have cooled, store them in a cool, dry, dark place.

Makes 2 quarts

Korean Pickled Turnips

*S*UNMUKIMCHI, OR BRINED turnips, is a very popular and delicious Korean pickle.

1 pound small turnips, peeled
1 tablespoon plus 1½ teaspoons pickling salt
1 to 2 teaspoons hot pepper flakes
3 scallions, minced
8 garlic cloves, minced
1 teaspoon sugar

1. Halve the turnips lengthwise, if they are bigger than about 2 inches across. Slice them very thin crosswise. Put them into a bowl, and rub them with 1 tablespoon of the salt. Let them stand about 3 hours, occasionally turning the slices in their brine.

2. Drain and rinse the turnip slices, then drain them again. Add the remaining 1½ teaspoons salt and the other ingredients. Mix well. Put the mixture into a quart jar, and pour water over the contents so they are covered by about 1 inch. Cap the jar loosely, and let it stand at room temperature.

3. After about 6 to 8 days, when the turnips are as sour as you like, cap the jar tightly. Store it in the refrigerator.

Makes about 5 cups

Kakdooki

IN KOREA, HOUSEHOLDERS traditionally ferment vast quantities of vegetables every fall. They pack the vegetables into enormous ceramic jars, which they bury in the ground until needed. Modern food preservation methods and imports haven't weakened this tradition much, because Koreans *really* love their pickles. This is a simple version of Korean fermented daikon; for a slightly fancier one, see the next recipe.

1½ pounds daikon, peeled and cut into ¾-inch cubes
6 scallions, cut into thin rounds
8 garlic cloves, minced
2 teaspoons pickling salt
2 teaspoon sugar
2 teaspoons Korean ground dried chile peppers

1. In a bowl, mix all of the ingredients. Let the mixture stand for 6 to 12 hours.
2. Pack the mixture firmly into a quart jar, making sure the daikon cubes are covered with the brine. Cap the jar loosely. Let it stand at room temperature.
3. After 3 to 7 days, when the daikon is sour enough to suit you, tighten the cap. Store the jar in the refrigerator.

Makes 1 quart

Kakdooki with Shrimp and Apple

KOREANS OFTEN ADD dried shrimp, oysters, and anchovies to fermented vegetables, both for added nutrients and for enriched flavor. You can buy dried shrimp at many Asian markets.

2 pounds daikon, peeled and cut into ¾-inch cubes

4 teaspoons pickling salt

2 tablespoons Korean ground dried chile pepper

1 apple, peeled, cored, and coarsely grated

2 tablespoons dried shrimp

2 garlic cloves, minced

2 thin slices fresh ginger, peeled and minced

1 scallion, cut into thin rounds

1. Put the daikon cubes into a bowl, and toss them with the salt. Let the daikon stand for 1 hour.

2. Drain the daikon. Sprinkle the cubes with the chile pepper, and add the remaining ingredients. Mix well. Lay a piece of plastic wrap over the mixture, then lightly weight the mixture with a dish that just fits inside the bowl. Let the bowl stand at room temperature.

3. The pickles should be ready in about 3 days. Transfer them to a 3- to 4-cup jar. Cap the jar, and store it in the refrigerator.

Makes about 3 cups

. . .

"In the summer [my mother] festooned our house with strings of drying cabbages and turnips; whatever other vegetables we couldn't eat fresh were laid down in big earthenware jars with brine and aromatic spices. In the winter the jars would be opened and we ate pickled vegetables every day. For breakfast we had rice or congee sprinkled with dried, pickled, or salted vegetables, and pickled vegetables were often served at lunch and dinner as well. We ate pickles for snacks, and my mother added them to some dishes, like soups, for pungent flavoring."

—Mrs. Chiang, Mrs. Chiang's Szechwan Cookbook *(1976)*

Chinese Fermented Daikon

THIS CHINESE COUSIN of kakdooki uses whole rather than ground peppers.

1 pound daikon
4 thin slices fresh ginger, peeled
2 small dried chile peppers, slit lengthwise
1½ tablespoons pickling salt
2 cups water

1. Cut the daikon into quarters or eighths lengthwise (the strips should be about ½ inch thick), then crosswise into 1½-inch lengths. Layer the daikon, ginger, and chile peppers in a 1-quart jar. Dissolve the salt in the water, and pour enough brine over the vegetables to cover them. Push a freezer bag into the mouth of the jar, and pour the remaining brine into the bag. Seal the bag. Let the jar stand at room temperature.

2. After 2 to 3 days, when the daikon is as sour as you like, remove the brine bag and cap the jar. Store the daikon in the refrigerator.

Makes 1 quart

Vietnamese Pickled Bean Sprouts

THESE MILD-FLAVORED, lightly fermented sprouts are a lovely complement to spicy or rich foods. According to Bach Ngo and Gloria Zimmerman, authors of *The Classic Cuisine of Vietnam* (1986), pickled bean sprouts are traditionally served with pork cooked in coconut water or simmered with five-spice powder. Because pickled sprouts are so mild in flavor, you can use them in many ways that you might use fresh sprouts. My kids like them in soft tacos.

3 cups water

1 tablespoon pickling salt

½ teaspoon sugar

1 pound mung bean sprouts, rinsed and drained

1 medium carrot, shaved with a vegetable peeler into thin strips

1. Bring the water, salt, and sugar just to a boil in a saucepan. Immediately remove the brine from the heat, and let it cool to room temperature.

2. Toss the prepared vegetables together in a bowl. Pack them into a 2-quart jar, and cover the vegetables with the brine. It will not cover them completely at first, but within an hour or so the levels of liquid and vegetables should be about equal. Press the vegetables down with a spoon, if necessary, to cover them completely with the brine. Let the jar stand at room temperature.

3. After about 3 days, the sprouts should be sour enough. Cap the jar, and refrigerate it. The sprouts will keep well for several weeks, at least.

Makes about 1½ quarts

Vietnamese Soured Mustard Greens

Lᴵᴷᴇ Vɪᴇᴛɴᴀᴍᴇsᴇ ᴘɪᴄᴋʟᴇᴅ bean sprouts (see the preceding recipe), this pickle is mild and refreshing.

1½ pounds mustard greens (leaves and tender stems),
    cut into 2-inch lengths
6 scallions, cut into 2-inch lengths
5½ teaspoons pickling salt
1½ teaspoons sugar
1 quart water

1. Spread the mustard greens and scallions on a tray, and dry them in the sun (I put them in the greenhouse) for several hours, or set the tray in a very slow oven until the vegetables are quite wilted.

2. Dissolve the salt and sugar in the water. Pack a handful of the greens into a 2-quart jar, add enough brine to cover them, and repeat this process until all the greens are in the jar and well-covered with brine. Push a freezer bag into the mouth of the jar, and pour the remaining brine into the bag. Seal the bag. Let the jar stand at room temperature.

3. After 3 to 4 days, the greens should be sour enough. Remove the brine bag, cap the jar, and store it in the refrigerator.

Makes about 6 cups

Stuffed Cucumber Kimchi

THIS IS A MILD and very pretty kimchi. Serve the cucumber pieces separated and sprinkled with the stuffing.

2 cups water

5 teaspoons pickling salt

¾ pounds (about 8) 4-inch pickling cucumbers

½ pound daikon, sliced thin crosswise, then cut into matchsticks

3 scallions, cut into 1-inch lengths, then slivered

One 2-inch-long piece of a medium carrot, halved crosswise and
    slivered

2 garlic cloves, slivered

2 teaspoons slivered fresh ginger

1 teaspoon hot pepper flakes

1 teaspoon sugar

1. Pour the water into a medium bowl, and stir in 4 teaspoons salt until it dissolves. Gently wash the cucumbers, and make 3 deep diagonal slashes in each, cutting three-quarters of the way through. Put the cucumbers into the brine, and let them stand for 2 to 4 hours.

2. Drain the cucumbers, reserving the brine. Squeeze each cucumber gently to remove excess water.

3. In a bowl, mix the remaining 1 teaspoon salt and the other remaining ingredients. Stuff the slits of the cucumbers with the mixture, and put the stuffed cucumbers into a bowl. Add any remaining stuffing. Cover the bowl loosely, and let it stand 6 to 10 hours.

4. Pack the stuffed cucumbers into a 1- to 1½-quart wide-mouth jar, and push the extra stuffing down between them. Pour some of the reserved soaking liquid over the cucumbers to cover. Cap the jar loosely, and let it stand at room temperature.

5. After 2 to 3 days, the cucumbers should be sour enough. Cap the jar tightly, and store it in the refrigerator.

Makes 1 quart

> • • •
>
> **"S**upper that night began with water glasses of vodka, with pickles and home-baked black bread. . . . And at two-thirty in the morning we had the following meal: glasses of vodka, and pickles again, and fried fish which had been caught in the village pond."
>
> —*John Steinbeck,* A Russian Journal

Brined Cherry Tomatoes

TOMATOES MAY BE BRINED at any stage of ripeness. The red ones have a sweeter flavor, of course, but they get mushy when they're fermented. Very green tomatoes keep their appealing firm texture, and you might also like their bitterness. Partially ripe tomatoes, just beginning to turn red, are perhaps best of all for brining; after fermentation, they're a little bitter, a little sweet, and still quite crisp. As important as the stage of ripeness, though, are the aromatics that accompany the tomatoes. Be generous with the dill, garlic, horseradish, and herbs, and you'll be rewarded with a very satisfying pickle.

This recipe comes from Russia.

1¾ pounds half-ripe cherry tomatoes
About 6 dill heads
¼ cup coarsely grated or chopped horseradish

4 or 5 garlic cloves, halved

Tops of 2 celery stalks

3 parsley sprigs

3 tarragon sprigs

½ fresh chile pepper, such as jalapeño, seeded

Several dill fronds

2 tablespoons pickling salt

1 quart water

1. Put the tomatoes into a 2-quart jar, interspersing the aromatics among them. Curl some dill fronds on top. Dissolve the salt in the water, and pour enough of the brine over the tomatoes to cover them well. Push a freezer bag into the mouth of the jar. Pour the remaining brine into the bag, and seal it. Let the jar stand at room temperature for about 1 week, until fermentation has slowed.

2. Remove the brine bag, and cap the jar tightly. Store the jar in the refrigerator for about 1 week before eating the tomatoes. Refrigerated, they will keep for about 3 weeks more.

Makes about 2 quarts

• • •

"**A**t the markets, white tubs filled with brined apples interspersed with cranberries lined the long counters, and a Moscow student chomped a cold, golden apple unreservedly, showing with pride his affiliation: eating brined apples during the Butterweek had been a time-honored tradition among students in Moscow."

—*Aleksandr Kuprin*, The Cadets

Pickled Apples

ANOTHER RUSSIAN SPECIALTY, brined apples retain their crispness but acquire a flavor like that of sparkling wine.

3 quarts water

¼ cup honey

8 teaspoons pickling salt

2 or 3 handfuls sour cherry leaves

4 to 6 tarragon sprigs

3 pounds small, tart apples, such as Gravensteins

1. In a nonreactive pot, bring to a boil the water, honey, and salt, stirring to dissolve the salt. Let the brine cool.

2. Spread some of the cherry leaves and 1 or 2 tarragon sprigs on the bottom of a 1-gallon jar. Add a layer of apples placed on their sides; 3 should just fit. Layer more leaves, tarragon, and apples, and then repeat again for a third layer. Top with the rest of the leaves and tarragon. Pour enough of the brine over the apples to cover them well. Push a freezer bag into the mouth of the jar, and pour the remaining brine into the bag. Seal the bag. Let the jar stand at room temperature for 5 to 6 days, until fermentation slows.

3. Remove the brine bag, cap the jar tightly, and set it in a dark place where the temperature doesn't rise above 50 degrees F (I have used a refrigerator with good results). Let the jar stand for 30 to 40 days before eating the apples.

After you open the jar, the apples will keep well for at least 1 week if you store them in the refrigerator.

Makes 1 gallon

Russian Brined Lemons

THE RUSSIANS SERVE these lemons in thin slices with fish and game. You might also try them with pork chops, rice dishes, stewed chickpeas, or thin-sliced raw red onion.

The quantities here will depend not only on how many lemons you wish to brine, but also on which container you'll use, and this may depend partly on what you can use to keep the lemons immersed. When I wanted to brine just three lemons, I used a narrow 12-ounce jelly jar, and kept the lemons immersed by stacking plastic milk-jug caps between the top lemon and the jar lid. If you want to brine more lemons, you might use a quart jar, and weight the lemons with a plastic bag filled with brine and sealed. Or you might use a crock, and weight the lemons with a plate on top of which you have placed a clean rock or jar filled with water.

Thin-skinned whole lemons, washed and dried
Brine, made of 1 tablespoon salt to each cup water

1. Put the lemons into a jar or crock, and cover them with the brine. Weight them down in whichever way is practical so that the lemons are fully submerged in the brine. If you're not using a brine bag as the weight, cap the jar loosely, or cover the crock and weight with cloth.
2. Store the jar or crock in the refrigerator or another cool place. The lemons will be ready to eat in 2 to 3 weeks.

Serve the lemons sliced thin. Refrigerated in their brine, they will keep for about 1 month.

FRESH PICKLES

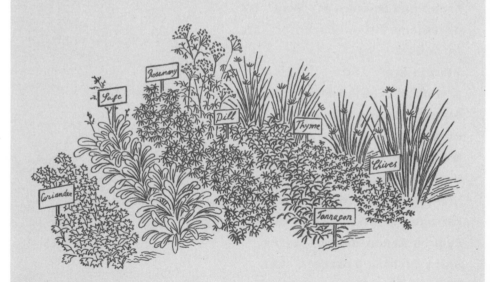

FRESH PICKLES

CUCUMBERS ARE JUST the beginning in this very large category of pickles. In this chapter you'll find recipes for pickled peppers, cauliflower, mushrooms, eggplant, artichokes, baby corn, okra, mixed vegetables, and much more.

These pickles are all "fresh" in that they're not fermented. The acid that preserves the vegetables and fruits comes from vinegar, usually, or from citrus juice or citric acid. The chapter includes canned pickles, which typically aren't very sour, since the vinegar is usually cut with about an equal amount of water. Other pickles here are truly fresh—in the sense that they're not cooked at all—but very sour, since they're preserved in pure vinegar. A third type of fresh pickle, typically packed in dilute vinegar, is intended for short or long storage in the refrigerator.

Pickles normally canned can be stored in the refrigerator instead, if you're making a small batch or simply don't want to bother with a boiling-water bath and two-piece caps. Use jars of any size, and any caps that won't react with salt and vinegar.

After the jars are opened, all of these pickles should be stored in the refrigerator.

Short-Brined Dill Pickles

BEFORE I STARTED fermenting cucumbers, I made these pickles every summer. The recipe is very flexible; as long as you stick with the proportions of vinegar, water, salt, and sugar given here, you can vary the seasonings as you like. Add yellow mustard seeds, for example (about 2 teaspoons per quart), grated or sliced horseradish, bay leaves, or more hot peppers. Or be a little more daring: Try adding some black currant leaves or shallots, or even leave out the dill and use fennel or cumin instead. Grape or sour cherry leaves can help keep the pickles firm, but they aren't essential, either.

12 pounds 3- to 5-inch pickling cucumbers

1½ cups pickling salt

2 gallons plus 2 quarts water

7⅓ cups cider vinegar or distilled white vinegar

¼ cup sugar

16 garlic cloves, sliced

24 dill heads

32 black peppercorns

8 small dried chile peppers (optional)

24 to 32 grape leaves or 48 to 64 sour cherry leaves (optional)

1. Gently wash the cucumbers, and remove the blossom ends. Halve or quarter the cucumbers lengthwise, if you like, or leave them whole. In a large bowl or crock, dissolve ¾ cup pickling salt in 2 gallons water. Add the cucumbers. Let them stand in the brine 8 to 12 hours.

2. Drain the cucumbers. If you like less salty pickles, rinse them, and drain them well again.

3. In a nonreactive pot, bring to a boil the remaining ¾ cup pickling salt, the remaining 2 quarts water, the vinegar, and the sugar, stirring to dissolve the sugar and salt. While the mixture heats, divide the garlic, dill, and peppercorns—and the chile peppers and grape or cherry leaves, if you're using them—among 8 quart or 16 pint mason jars. Pack a portion of the cucumbers into each jar.

4. Pour the hot liquid over the cucumbers, leaving ½ inch headspace. Close the jars with hot two-piece caps. In a boiling-water bath, process pint jars for 10 minutes, quart jars for 15 minutes. Or pasteurize the jars for 30 minutes in water heated to 180 to 185 degrees F.

5. Store the cooled jars in a cool, dry, dark place for at least 1 month before eating the pickles.

Makes about 8 quarts

···

TROUBLESHOOTING GUIDE: FRESH CUCUMBER PICKLES

Problem	Possible Causes
Hollow middle	The cucumbers grew this way, perhaps because of inadequate watering (you can pick out cucumbers like this when you wash them—they float). Or the cucumbers were held too long before processing.
Pale skins	The cucumbers grew this way, perhaps because they were sun-scalded (grape, sour cherry, or black currant leaves added to the jars may help deepen the green of pale cucumbers). Or the pickles were exposed to light during storage.
Dark pickles	Your water contains a lot of iron, or the canning lids were corroded, or you used reactive metal pans or utensils in processing the pickles. Or you used loose ground spices.

Shriveled pickles	The cucumbers were held too long before processing, or you overcooked the cucumbers or heat-processed the jars for too long. Or you used too much salt, sugar, or vinegar in the liquid at the beginning of the pickling process.
Small brown spots on pickles	The cucumbers were held too long before processing.
White sediment	You used table salt.
Soft pickles	The cucumbers were held too long before processing, or overheated during processing. Try low-temperature pasteurization next time.

Really Quick Dill Pickles

BECAUSE CUCUMBERS intended for fresh pickling are traditionally brined for a day first, I was surprised to find that I really like pickles made by this no-brine method. For firmer pickles, add two or three grape leaves or six to eight sour cherry leaves for each quart of pickles. You can of course double or triple this recipe to suit the size of your harvest.

4 pounds 4-inch pickling cucumbers
24 black peppercorns
1 garlic bulb, cloves peeled and chopped
6 small dried chile peppers (optional)
6 dill heads, with fronds
2¾ cups cider vinegar, white wine vinegar, or distilled white vinegar
3 cups water
¼ cup pickling salt

1. Gently wash the cucumbers, and remove the blossom ends. Halve or quarter the cucumbers lengthwise, if you like, or leave them whole. Divide the peppercorns, garlic, and chile peppers, if you're using them, among 6 pint or 3 quart mason jars. Pack equal portions of the cucumbers and dill heads and fronds into each jar.

2. In a nonreactive saucepan, bring the vinegar, water, and salt to a boil, stirring to dissolve the salt. Pour the liquid over the cucumbers, leaving ½ inch headspace. Close the jars with hot two-piece caps.

3. In a boiling-water bath, process pint jars for 10 minutes, quart jars for 15 minutes. Or pasteurize the jars for 30 minutes in water heated to 180 to 185 degrees F.

4. Store the cooled jars in a cool, dry, dark place for at least 1 month before eating the pickles.

Makes 3 quarts

···

FRIED DILL PICKLES

Northerners may laugh when they first hear of this favorite Southern snack, but fried dill pickles are a real delicacy. This recipe, from Pickle Packers International, produces a thin, crisp, tempura-like coating that complements the intense flavor of the hot pickle. Try these pickles with Hot Orange Ketchup (page 320).

Although the recipe calls for sliced pickles, I fry small ones whole.

1 cup all-purpose flour
¼ cup cornstarch
1 teaspoon baking powder
¼ teaspoon salt
1 cup ice water
1 egg yolk
2 tablespoons pickle brine
8 medium to large dill pickles, sliced ¼ inch thick (about 4 cups)
Vegetable oil for deep-frying

1. In a bowl, stir together the flour, cornstarch, baking powder, and salt. Make a well in the center, and add the water, egg yolk, and pickle brine. Whisk the ingredients together to form a smooth batter. Cover the bowl, and refrigerate it for 30 minutes.

2. In a heavy pot, heat at least 2 inches of oil to 375 degrees F. In batches, dip the pickle slices in the batter, slip them into the oil, and fry them without crowding until the coating is crisp and golden, 1½ to 2 minutes. Drain the pickle slices on paper towels, and serve them immediately.

. . .

BEYOND DILL

If you're not crazy about dill, or if you just want to try some different flavorings in your fresh pickles, here are some ideas. For each quart of pickles, use ½ teaspoon mixed pickling spice, ½ teaspoon cumin seeds, 2 bay leaves, or a fennel head or two in place of the dill. For mildly sweet, spicy pickles, omit the dill and add 1 teaspoon mixed pickling spice and 2 tablespoons white sugar.

Sandwich-Sliced Dill Pickles

COMMERCIAL PICKLE PACKERS have recently discovered old-fashioned "tongue pickles," which have been reborn as "stuffers" and "sandwich builders." These are all, of course, simply names for cucumber pickles sliced lengthwise into slabs.

5 pounds 4-inch pickling cucumbers
6 tablespoons pickling salt
2 quarts plus 3 cups water
12 garlic cloves, coarsely chopped
1½ teaspoons hot pepper flakes
24 black peppercorns
6 dill heads
2¾ cups cider vinegar

1. Gently wash the cucumbers, and remove the blossom ends. Cut the cucumbers lengthwise ³⁄₁₆ inch thick, discarding a narrower slice at either side.

Put the cucumbers into a bowl. Dissolve 3 tablespoons salt in 2 quarts water, and pour the brine over the cucumbers. Let them stand 12 hours.

2. Drain the cucumbers. Divide the garlic among 6 pint or 3 quart mason jars. Distribute the pepper flakes and peppercorns equally among the jars. Loosely pack a portion of the cucumber slices and the dill heads into each jar.

3. In a nonreactive saucepan, bring to a boil the vinegar, the 3 cups water, and the remaining 3 tablespoons salt, stirring to dissolve the salt. Pour the hot liquid over the cucumber slices, leaving ½ inch headspace. Close the jars with hot two-piece caps.

4. In a boiling-water bath, process pint jars for 10 minutes, quart jars for 15 minutes. Or pasteurize the jars for 30 minutes in water heated to 180 to 185 degrees F.

5. Store the cooled jars in a cool, dry, dark place for at least 1 month before eating the pickles.

Makes 6 pints

• • •

PICKLE LOVERS' PARADISE

The little town of Atkins, Arkansas, holds a Pickle Fest every spring. Dean's Pickles, the local pickle-packing plant, gives free tours; the VFW booth sells fried dill pickles; and fair-goers compete in both pickle-eating and pickle juice-drinking contests.

Cornichons à Cru

BECAUSE THEIR THIN skins make them quite perishable, the very small cornichons (European gherkins) or American-type pickling cucumbers you will need for this recipe should be processed the same day they are harvested, whether you have grown them yourself or are lucky enough to have found them in a produce market or farmers' market.

Recipes for this classic French pickle vary a lot, so don't feel you must follow this one religiously. Common additions are garlic, cloves, and thyme, and I have sometimes added mustard, coriander, allspice, or even cinnamon. The French often use red wine vinegar, which makes for a delicious if less pretty pickle. I sometimes use cider vinegar, and once I pickled cornichons with ginger, hot pepper, garlic, and rice vinegar, to create what I called Cornichons à l'Orientale, a pungent, clean-tasting pickle.

Traditionally, these cornichons accompany pâté. My husband loves them with fried ham.

About 1¼ pounds 1½- to 2-inch cornichons or 1- to 1½-inch
American-type pickling cucumbers
3 tablespoons pickling salt
4 shallots, peeled
1 bay leaf
2 tarragon sprigs
10 black peppercorns
2 small dried chile peppers
About 2 cups white wine vinegar

1. Wash the cucumbers gently, rub off the tiny spines if you're using cornichons, and remove the blossom ends. In a bowl, mix the cucumbers with the salt. Let the cucumbers stand 24 hours.

2. Drain the cucumbers. Rinse them in cold water, and pat each one dry with a clean towel. Pack the cucumbers into a sterile 1-quart jar, interspersing among them the shallots, bay leaf, tarragon, peppercorns, and chile peppers, and leaving at least 1 inch headspace. Fill the jar to the brim with vinegar. Cover the jar tightly with a nonreactive cap, preferably one that is all plastic. Store the jar in a cool, dry, dark place.

3. The cornichons will be ready to eat in 1 month, and will keep well, unopened, for about 1 year.

Makes 1 quart

Olive Oil Pickles

THIS RECIPE IS really four in one. You can use small whole cucumbers or sliced medium ones. In either case, you can add mustard seeds, if you like, or leave them out. All of these versions have been popular in this country since the days of Mary Randolph (*The Virginia Housewife*, 1824) or earlier. The olive oil not only provides a floating barrier against spoilage, but also deliciously coats each pickle as it's drawn from the jar. The pickles are uncooked, uncanned, and very tasty.

About 1¼ pounds pickling cucumbers, preferably small
2 small onions, sliced thin
4 teaspoons pickling salt
½ teaspoon hot pepper flakes
2 tablespoons yellow mustard seeds (optional)
About 1½ cups white wine vinegar or cider vinegar
2 tablespoons olive oil

1. Gently wash the cucumbers, and remove the blossom ends. If the cucumbers are 2 to 3 inches long, leave them whole; if they are 4 to 5 inches long, slice them into 3/16-inch-thick rounds. In a bowl, toss the cucumbers and onions with the salt. Let them stand 3 to 5 hours.

2. Drain the vegetables well. Layer them in a sterile 1-quart jar with the pepper flakes and, if you like, the mustard seeds. Leave at least 1 inch headspace. Cover the vegetables well with vinegar, almost to the rim, then cover the surface with the olive oil. Cover the jar with a nonreactive cap, preferably one that is all plastic. Store the jar in a cool, dry, dark place.

3. The pickles will be ready to eat in about 3 weeks, and will keep well, unopened, for at least 6 months.

Makes 1 quart

Dutch Lunch Spears, by the Quart

THIS IS MY VARIATION on an old Mennonite recipe. I've cut the vinegar and sugar substantially, but these pickles will still please people who like strong flavors.

If you'd like to put some of these pickles on the pantry shelf, multiply the quantities by four. Give the jars a 10-minute boiling-water bath, or pasteurize them for 30 minutes in water heated to 180 to 185 degrees F.

> 1¼ pounds 3-inch pickling cucumbers
>
> 3 tablespoons plus 2 teaspoons pickling salt
>
> 1 quart plus ¾ cup water
>
> 1 garlic clove, peeled
>
> 1 small onion, peeled
>
> 1 dill head
>
> 2 grape leaves (optional)
>
> ¾ cup cider vinegar

¼ cup sugar

1 teaspoon mixed pickling spices

1. Gently wash the cucumbers, and remove the blossom ends. Quarter the cucumbers lengthwise, and put them into a bowl or crock. Dissolve 3 tablespoons salt in 1 quart water, and pour the brine over the cucumbers. Top the cucumbers with a heavy plate that just fits inside the crock or bowl. Let the cucumbers stand for 8 to 12 hours.

2. Drain and rinse the cucumbers, then drain them again. Pack the cucumbers, garlic, onion, and dill head into a 1-quart jar. Add the grape leaves if you have them; they will help keep the cucumbers firm and green.

3. In a nonreactive saucepan, bring to a boil the ¾ cup water, the 2 teaspoons salt, and the vinegar, sugar, and spices, stirring to dissolve the salt and sugar. Pour the hot liquid over the cucumbers. Cap the jar tightly, and let it cool.

4. Store the jar in the refrigerator for at least 1 week before eating the pickles. Refrigerated, they will keep for several months, at least.

Makes 1 quart

. . .

"There never was a more indefatigable preserver, pickler, curer, spicer, or canner than the Dutch housewife. Very little escapes her expert touch—and as a consequence she got in the habit centuries ago of loading every table with many 'sweet and sours.'

To such an extent that over the centuries it became a fixed tradition of Dutch hospitality for her to put on the table (especially for 'company') *precisely seven sweets and seven sours*. The 'company' would often count them! indeed would gaily demand them if missing."

—*J. George Frederick*, Pennsylvania Dutch Cook Book *(1935)*

Honeyed Sunshine Pickles

OVERSIZED, YELLOWED, hard-skinned cucumbers can still make good pickles if you peel and seed them. (Until late in the summer, however, gardeners should avoid letting any cucumbers ripen, or the plants may stop fruiting prematurely.) Ripe cucumbers are often pickled like watermelon rind. For this mildly sweet, pretty yellow pickle I use crescents of ripe lemon cucumbers—which look much like navel oranges—but you might use chunks of ripe pickling cucumbers instead.

7 pounds ripe lemon or pickling cucumbers
I pound onions, halved and sliced
¼ cup pickling salt
21 thin slices fresh ginger
3½ cups cider vinegar
I cup water
I cup honey
¼ cup seeded and minced chile peppers
2 tablespoons yellow mustard seeds
I teaspoon celery seeds
I teaspoon ground turmeric
I cup golden raisins

1. Peel, halve, and seed the cucumbers. Cut lemon cucumbers into crescents, pickling cucumbers into 1-inch chunks. Toss the cucumbers and onions with the salt, and cover the vegetables with ice cubes from 2 ice trays. Let the vegetables stand 3 to 5 hours.

2. Drain the vegetables. Rinse them in cold water, and drain them well again. Put 3 ginger slices into each of 7 pint mason jars.

3. In a large nonreactive pot, bring the remaining ingredients to a boil, stirring to dissolve the honey. Add the drained vegetables, and slowly bring the mixture to a boil. Ladle the hot vegetables and liquid into the jars, leaving ½ inch headspace. Close the jars with hot two-piece caps.

4. To ensure a good seal, process the jars for 10 minutes in a boiling-water bath.

5. Store the cooled jars in a cool, dry, dark place for at least 3 weeks before eating the pickles.

Makes 7 pints

Old-Fashioned Bread-and-Butters

BREAD-AND-BUTTER PICKLES have gone upscale, it seems. At a benefit for Citymeals-on-Wheels at Rockefeller Center in New York City, Alice Waters, chef and owner of Chez Panisse in Berkeley, served bread-and-butter pickles with smoked salmon and watercress on toasted walnut bread. (Afterward, though, she said she regretted not choosing miniature hamburgers instead of the salmon to go with the pickles.)

These bread-and-butters are a little less sweet than most; you can increase the sugar, if you like. Some people also add a little ground cloves, and you might try some diced red pepper in place of some of the onions.

6 pounds 4- to 5-inch pickling cucumbers

2 pounds small onions, sliced into thin rounds

½ cup pickling salt

4½ cups cider vinegar

3 cups sugar

1½ teaspoons ground turmeric

1 teaspoon celery seeds

2 teaspoons yellow mustard seeds

1. Gently wash the cucumbers, and remove the blossom ends. Slice the cucumbers crosswise ³⁄₁₆ inch thick. In a large bowl, toss the cucumbers and onions with the salt. Cover the vegetables with ice cubes from 2 ice trays. Let the vegetables stand 3 to 4 hours.

2. Drain the vegetables. In a large nonreactive pot, bring the remaining ingredients to a boil. Add the vegetables, and slowly bring the contents to a boil. Using a slotted spoon, pack the vegetables loosely in 8 pint or 4 quart mason jars, leaving ½ inch headspace. Divide the liquid evenly among the jars. Close the jars with hot two-piece caps.

3. To ensure a good seal, process the jars for 10 minutes in a boiling-water bath.

4. Store the cooled jars in a cool, dry, dark place for at least 3 weeks before eating the pickles.

Makes about 4 quarts

Bread-and-Butters My Way

BECAUSE I FIND traditional bread-and-butter pickles cloying, I've developed a lighter version, using only a quarter as much sugar as usual, some water to cut the vinegar, and a little chile pepper for zing.

About 3½ pounds 3- to 5-inch pickling cucumbers
¼ cup pickling salt
4 teaspoons yellow mustard seeds
1 teaspoon celery seeds
1 teaspoon hot pepper flakes
3 cups cider vinegar
1 cup water
½ cup sugar
1 teaspoon ground turmeric

1. Gently wash the cucumbers, and slice them crosswise 3/16 inch thick. You should have 2 quarts. In a large bowl, toss the cucumber slices with the salt. Cover the cucumbers with ice cubes from 2 ice trays. Let the cucumbers stand 3 to 4 hours.

2. Drain the cucumbers well. Toss them with the mustard seeds, celery seeds, and pepper flakes. Pack the cucumbers loosely into 4 pint mason jars.

3. In a saucepan, bring the vinegar, water, sugar, and turmeric to a boil. Pour the hot liquid over the cucumber slices, leaving ½ inch headspace. Close the jars with hot two-piece caps. Process the jars for 10 minutes in a boiling-water bath, or pasteurize them for 30 minutes in water heated to 180 to 185 degrees F.

4. Store the cooled jars in a cool, dry, dark place for at least 3 weeks before eating the pickles.

Makes 4 pints

Bread-and-Butter Zucchini

ZUCCHINI STANDS IN well for cucumbers in bread-and-butter pickles.

About 4 pounds zucchini, 1 inch in diameter
¾ pound small onions, sliced into thin rounds (about 2 cups)
½ cup pickling salt
2 cups cider vinegar
1 cup sugar
2 tablespoons yellow mustard seeds
1 tablespoon celery seeds
1 teaspoon ground turmeric

1. Slice the zucchini into ³⁄₁₆-inch rounds. You should have 2 quarts. Put the zucchini and onions into a bowl, and toss the vegetables with the salt. Cover the vegetables with ice cubes from 2 ice trays. Let the vegetables stand for 2 hours.

2. Drain the vegetables well. In a nonreactive pot, bring to a boil the vinegar, sugar, and spices. Add the vegetables, and slowly bring them to a boil, stirring frequently. Reduce the heat to low, and simmer them 5 minutes. Ladle the vegetables and liquid into pint mason jars, packing the vegetables loosely and leaving ½ inch headspace. Close the jars with hot two-piece caps.

3. To ensure a good seal, process the jars for 10 minutes in a boiling-water bath.

4. Store the cooled jars in a cool, dry, dark place for at least 3 weeks before eating the pickles.

Makes 8 to 9 pints

Jardinière

THIS PICKLE IS a glorious way for the gardeners among you to show off your fresh produce—little cornichons, tiny patty pans, and real baby carrots. But you needn't stick with the vegetables here; alternative ingredients might include cauliflower florets, onion chunks, green beans in 2-inch lengths, zucchini in sticks or thick rounds, and celery pieces. You'll need 5 pints of prepared vegetables.

1¼ pounds 1- to 3-inch pickling cucumbers

2 medium red bell peppers, cut into squares or strips

½ pound shallots, peeled

¼ pound carrots, cut into thin sticks

½ pound 1-inch-wide patty pan squashes, or slightly larger ones, halved

5 large garlic cloves

1¼ teaspoons black peppercorns

20 allspice berries

5 tarragon sprigs

5 thyme sprigs

5 small fresh chile peppers (optional)

2¾ cups white wine vinegar

2 cups water

1 tablespoon pickling salt

1. Gently wash the cucumbers, and remove the blossom ends. Combine the prepared vegetables in a large bowl. Into each of 5 pint jars, put 1 garlic clove, ¼ teaspoon peppercorns, and 4 allspice berries. Pack the jars with the vegetables. Add a tarragon sprig and a thyme sprig, and a chile pepper if you like, and shake the jars to settle the vegetables.

2. In a nonreactive saucepan, bring to a boil the vinegar, water, and salt, stirring to dissolve the salt. Pour the hot liquid over the vegetables, leaving ½ inch headspace. Close the jars with hot two-piece caps, and process them for 20 minutes in a boiling-water bath.

3. Store the cooled jars in a cool, dry, dark place for at least 3 weeks before eating the pickles.

Makes 5 pints

Giardiniera

THIS IS AN ITALIAN VERSION of the French jardinière. Again, you can vary the ingredients. You'll need a total of 3 quarts prepared vegetables.

½ pound pickling cucumbers, about ¾ inch in diameter

2 celery stalks, cut crosswise into ¾-inch lengths

5 teaspoons pickling salt

½ small cauliflower head, broken and cut into florets

1 large carrot, cut into ³⁄₁₆-inch rounds

1 cup peeled whole shallots or very small onions

½ pound Italian sweet peppers, seeded and cut into ¾-inch rings, or
    whole sweet cherry peppers, left whole but slit twice lengthwise

6 bay leaves

12 garlic cloves

1½ teaspoons black peppercorns

6 oregano sprigs

2¾ cups white wine vinegar

2½ cups water

6 tablespoons olive oil

1. Gently wash the cucumbers, and remove the blossom ends. Cut the cucumbers crosswise into ½-inch-thick rounds. In a bowl, toss the cucumbers and celery with 1 teaspoon of the salt. Let the mixture stand 1 to 2 hours.

2. Drain the cucumbers and celery well. Combine them in a large bowl with the remaining vegetables.

3. Into each of 6 pint jars, put 1 bay leaf, 2 garlic cloves, and ¼ teaspoon peppercorns. Pack the jars with the vegetables, adding an oregano sprig to each jar, and shaking the jar to settle the vegetables.

4. In a nonreactive saucepan, bring to a boil the vinegar, water, and remaining 4 teaspoons salt, stirring to dissolve the salt. Pour the hot liquid over the vegetables, leaving ½ inch headspace. Top each jar with 1 tablespoon olive oil. Close the jars with hot two-piece caps, and process them for 20 minutes in a boiling-water bath.

5. Store the cooled jars in a cool, dry, dark place for at least 3 weeks before eating the pickles.

Makes 6 pints

Armenian Pickled Mixed Vegetables

Here's a beautiful, hot-pink mixed pickle to put up in a big jar in the refrigerator.

2 quarts mixed vegetables, including any or all of the following:
  2- to 3-inch pickling cucumbers; green bell peppers, cut into wide
  strips; small carrots, cut into thin 3- to 4-inch-long sticks; whole
  green cherry tomatoes; cauliflower florets; and small radishes,
  halved or quartered if larger than 1 inch in diameter
1 small raw beet, peeled and sliced
2 large garlic cloves, sliced
8 basil sprigs
8 cilantro sprigs
8 tarragon sprigs
1 cup white wine vinegar
3 cups water
3 tablespoons pickling salt
6 black peppercorns
3 bay leaves
One 1-inch cinnamon stick

1. Gently wash the cucumbers, and remove the blossom ends. Pack the vegetables, including the beet, into a 2-quart jar, interspersing the herbs and half the garlic. Shake the jar to settle the vegetables.

2. In a nonreactive saucepan, bring the remaining ingredients to a boil. Cover the vegetables well with the hot liquid, and cap the jar.

3. When the jar has cooled, store it in the refrigerator. The pickle will be ready to eat after 1 month, and will keep for at least another month thereafter.

Makes 2 quarts

Gingery Sweet
Pickled Vegetables

I FIRST TASTED this Cantonese pickle in a commercial version that I bought in Seattle's International District. The pickle contained stem ginger, in thick pieces so tender that you could eat them right along with the other vegetables. If you happen to grow your own ginger, by all means use the stems in this recipe. Otherwise, include the ginger just as a flavoring.

The children who have tasted this pickle love it just as much as the adults do.

½ pound 2- to 3-inch pickling cucumbers

1 teaspoon pickling salt

½ cup peeled, thin-sliced fresh ginger

2 small dried chile peppers

1½ cups rice vinegar

1½ cups water

1½ cups sugar

2 cups diagonal carrot slices (⅛ inch thick)

1 large bell pepper, cut into 1-inch squares

¾ pound onions (1 large or 2 medium), cut into 1-inch chunks

1. Gently wash the cucumbers, and cut them into 1-inch lengths, discarding a thin slice from each end. Toss the cucumbers with ½ teaspoon salt in a bowl. Let the cucumbers stand for 1 to 2 hours.

2. In a large nonreactive saucepan, bring to a boil the ginger, chile peppers, vinegar, water, sugar, and remaining ½ teaspoon salt, stirring to dissolve the sugar and salt. Remove the pot from the heat, and add the carrots. Let the mixture cool.

3. Drain and rinse the cucumbers, and drain them again. Add the cucumbers, pepper, and onion to the saucepan. Mix well, then transfer the vegetables and liquid to a 2-quart jar. Cover the jar with a nonreactive cap, and refrigerate it.

The pickles will be ready to eat after about 3 days. Refrigerated, they will keep for at least 2 months.

Makes 2 quarts

Pickled Asparagus

THIS PICKLE IS so much the rage now that you can even buy it in warehouse stores. But you can save money by making your own, even if you don't have an asparagus patch.

I pickle asparagus in 12-ounce jelly jars, which are a little taller than pint jars—just right for the tender portion of an asparagus stalk.

Some people like to pack asparagus into jars with the tips down, so that the spears are easy to remove without breaking them, but others think that asparagus looks more attractive with the tips up. Pack your pickles either way.

5 large garlic cloves, sliced

15 allspice berries

30 black peppercorns

20 coriander seeds

5 small pieces of mace or nutmeg

½ teaspoon hot pepper flakes (optional)

About 3 pounds asparagus, trimmed to fit into 12-ounce jelly jars

2½ cups white wine vinegar

2½ cups water

2½ teaspoons pickling salt

2 tablespoons sugar

1. Divide the garlic, allspice, peppercorns, coriander, mace or nutmeg, and pepper flakes (if you're using them) among 5 12-ounce jelly jars. Pack the asparagus vertically in the jars, tips down or up.

2. In a nonreactive saucepan, bring to a boil the vinegar, water, salt, and sugar, stirring to dissolve the salt and sugar. Pour the hot liquid over the asparagus, leaving ½ inch headspace. Close the jars with hot two-piece caps. Process the jars for 10 minutes in a boiling-water bath, or pasteurize the jars for 30 minutes in water heated to 180 to 185 degrees F.

3. Store the cooled jars in a cool, dry, dark place for at least 3 weeks before eating the asparagus.

Makes 5 12-ounce jars

Marinated Artichoke Hearts

ALTHOUGH ALMOST ALL of the artichokes sold in the United States come from California's central coast region, artichokes will grow well wherever summers are cool and winters mild. In Seattle, Angelo Pellegrini raised all the artichokes his family could eat, and shared extra shoots with any friends, neighbors, or strangers who expressed interest in the plants. In *The Unprejudiced Palate* (1948), he recommended freezing artichokes, after trimming them, halving them, and blanching them for three to four minutes.

I haven't yet divided my single artichoke plant, so I used canned artichoke hearts to develop this recipe (a can weighing 13¾ ounces holds one pint artichoke hearts). If you can't grow artichokes yourself, frozen artichoke hearts are preferable to tinned ones, though hard to find. Boil frozen artichoke hearts for 5 minutes and drain them well before proceeding with the recipe.

1 pint canned or cooked fresh or frozen artichoke hearts
⅓ cup white wine vinegar

⅓ cup water

6 black peppercorns, crushed

1 garlic clove, sliced

1 sprig thyme

1 sprig marjoram or oregano

1 teaspoon pickling salt

1 pinch hot pepper flakes

⅓ cup olive oil

1. Pack the artichoke hearts into a pint jar. In a nonreactive saucepan, bring the vinegar, water, peppercorns, garlic, herbs, salt, and pepper flakes to a boil. Pour the hot liquid over the artichokes, then add the olive oil. Cover the jar tightly with a nonreactive cap, and let it cool.

2. Store the jar in the refrigerator for 1 week or longer before eating the artichokes; turn over the jar occasionally from top to bottom to mix the seasonings.

Refrigerated, the artichokes will keep well for several weeks.

Makes 1 pint

Basic Pickled Beets

FOR SOME FAMILIES I know, pickled beets are a must at every special dinner. This is a typical recipe, except that I use brown sugar for extra flavor, and cider vinegar instead of harsher-tasting distilled vinegar. Pickle very small beets whole, and slice larger ones.

7 pounds beets, with their rootlets and 2 inches of tops

2 cinnamon sticks, broken

1 tablespoon allspice berries

1 teaspoon whole cloves

1 cup sugar

1 cup brown sugar

2 teaspoons pickling salt

4 cups cider vinegar

2 cups water

1. Scrub the beets. Put them into a large pot, and cover them with boiling water. Return the water to a boil, and boil the beets 15 to 35 minutes, depending on their size, until they are just tender.

2. Drain the beets, and cover them with cold water. When they are cool, trim them, and slip off their skins. If they are large, halve or quarter them—or, if you like, slice all the beets into ¼-inch-thick rounds.

3. Tie the spices in a spice bag or scrap of cheesecloth. Combine the sugars, salt, vinegar, and water in a nonreactive pot, and add the spice bag. Bring the contents to a boil, stirring to dissolve the sugar. Reduce the heat, and simmer the liquid, uncovered, for 10 minutes.

4. While the liquid simmers, pack the beets into pint or quart mason jars. If you've sliced the beets, pack the slices loosely. Pour the hot liquid over the beets, leaving ½ inch headspace. Close the jars with hot two-piece caps. Process the jars for 30 minutes in a boiling-water bath.

5. Store the cooled jars in a cool, dry, dark place for at least 3 weeks before eating the beets.

Makes about 8 pints

Pickled Beets with Red Wine

THESE HAVE NONE of the harshness of typical pickled beets. Even people who usually scorn beets may like these.

6 pounds beets, with rootlets and 2 inches of tops
1 teaspoon whole cloves
Two 4-inch cinnamon sticks, broken
One 1-inch piece fresh ginger, sliced thin
3 cups sugar
2 cups red wine
3 cups red wine vinegar
1 tablespoon pickling salt

1. Scrub the beets. Put them into a large pot, and cover them with boiling water. Return the water to a boil, and boil the beets 15 to 35 minutes, depending on their size, until they are just tender.
2. Drain the beets, and cover them with cold water. When they are cool, trim them and slip off their skins. If they are large, halve or quarter them— or, if you prefer, slice all the beets into ¼-inch-thick rounds.
3. Tie the cloves, cinnamon, and ginger in a spice bag or scrap of cheese-cloth. Put the spice bag, sugar, wine, vinegar, and salt into a nonreactive pot. Bring the contents to a boil, stirring to dissolve the sugar and salt. Simmer the syrup, uncovered, for 10 minutes.
4. While the syrup simmers, pack the beets into pint mason jars. If you've sliced the beets, pack the slices loosely. Pour the hot syrup over the beets, leaving ½ inch headspace. Close the jars with hot two-piece caps.

5. Process the jars for 30 minutes in a boiling-water bath.

6. Store the cooled jars in a cool, dry, dark place for at least 3 weeks before eating the beets.

Makes about 7 pints

Tarragon or Basil Green Beans

I LIKE TO PICKLE slender little French beans or Cherokee Wax beans. Sometimes I combine the two in a single jar.

---

6 garlic cloves, sliced

36 black peppercorns

3 pounds young, tender snap beans, trimmed, if necessary, to 4 inches

6 tarragon sprigs or 12 basil sprigs

3½ cups white wine vinegar

3½ cups water

2 tablespoons pickling salt

---

1. Into each of 6 sterile pint mason jars, put 1 sliced garlic clove and 6 peppercorns. Pack the beans vertically into the jars, adding 1 tarragon sprig or 2 basil sprigs to each jar.

2. In a nonreactive saucepan, bring to a boil the vinegar, water, and salt. Pour the hot liquid over the beans, leaving ½ inch headspace. Close the jars with hot two-piece caps. Process the jars for 5 minutes in a boiling-water bath, or pasteurize them for 30 minutes in water heated to 180 to 185 degrees F.

3. Store the cooled jars in a cool, dry, dark place for at least 1 month before eating the beans.

Makes 6 pints

Zydeco Green Beans

LES HARICOTS VERTS are here pickled with the flavors of Louisiana—garlic, mustard, and especially chile peppers. You can, of course, omit one or both peppers. For traditional dilly beans, omit the mustard.

6 garlic cloves, sliced

6 teaspoons yellow mustard seeds

3 pounds haricots verts or other young, tender, very thin snap beans,
    trimmed, if necessary, to 4 inches

6 to 12 small fresh or dried chile peppers

6 dill heads (optional)

3½ cups white wine vinegar

3½ cups water

2 tablespoons pickling salt

1. Into each of 6 sterile pint mason jars, put 1 sliced garlic clove and 1 teaspoon mustard seeds. Pack the beans vertically into the jar, adding 1 or 2 chile peppers, and, if you like, a dill head to each jar.

2. In a nonreactive saucepan, bring to a boil the vinegar, water, and salt. Pour the hot liquid over the beans, leaving ½ inch headspace. Close the jars with hot two-piece caps. Process the jars for 5 minutes in a boiling-water bath, or pasteurize them for 30 minutes in water heated to 180 to 185 degrees F.

3. Store the cooled jars in a cool, dry, dark place for at least 1 month before eating the beans.

Makes 6 pints

Spicy Pickled Broccoli

ALTHOUGH THIS PICKLE has Indian roots, it's not heavily spiced. The seasonings enhance the broccoli flavor without disguising it at all.

1½ pounds broccoli florets and peeled, sliced stems
2 tablespoons chopped garlic
1 tablespoon coarsely grated fresh ginger
1 tablespoon dill seeds
1 tablespoon yellow mustard seeds
1 tablespoon vegetable oil
2½ cups white wine vinegar
2½ cups water
1 teaspoon pickling salt

1. In a large bowl, toss the broccoli with the garlic, ginger, dill, mustard, and oil. Pack the mixture into a 2-quart jar.

2. Combine the vinegar and water, and dissolve the salt in the liquid. Pour the liquid over the broccoli. Cap the jar.

3. Store the jar in the refrigerator for at least 1 week before eating the broccoli. Refrigerated, the pickle will keep well for at least several weeks.

Makes 2 quarts

Pickled Cauliflower

THIS IS A LOVELY PICKLE for an antipasti platter. The same recipe works well with brussels sprouts.

1 teaspoon cumin seeds

2 teaspoons coriander seeds

2 teaspoons fennel seeds

1 medium cauliflower, broken and cut into florets
    (you should have 7 cups)

½ cup diced red bell pepper or a combination of red bell pepper
    and red chile peppers

½ cup diced green bell pepper or a combination of green bell pepper
    and green chile peppers

2 cups white wine vinegar

2 cups water

2 tablespoons pickling salt

1. Put ¼ teaspoon of cumin and ½ teaspoon each of coriander and fennel into each of 4 pint mason jars. Toss the cauliflower and peppers together, and pack the vegetables firmly into the jars (the brine will loosen the vegetables).

2. In a nonreactive saucepan, bring the vinegar, water, and salt to a boil. Pour the liquid over the cauliflower, leaving ½ inch headspace. Close the jars with hot two-piece caps, and process them for 10 minutes in a boiling-water bath.

3. Store the cooled jars in a cool, dry, dark place for at least 3 weeks before eating the cauliflower.

Makes 4 pints

Indian-Style Pickled Cauliflower

BECAUSE MY FAMILY demands this pickle so often, I've increased the quantities of vinegar and water to avoid having to shake the jar daily, as is required with most Indian pickles.

This recipe calls for only a very little oil.

I medium cauliflower head, broken and cut into florets

2 fresh chile peppers, such as jalapeños, seeded and chopped

6 to 8 garlic cloves, chopped

I teaspoon ground turmeric

I teaspoon cumin seeds

One 2-inch piece fresh ginger, peeled and grated

I tablespoon vegetable oil

2½ cups white wine vinegar

2½ cups water

2 teaspoons pickling salt

---

1. In a bowl, toss together the cauliflower, peppers, garlic, turmeric, cumin, ginger, and oil. Pack the mixture into a 2-quart jar. Combine the vinegar and water, and stir in the salt until it dissolves. Pour the liquid over the cauliflower. Cap the jar.

2. Store the jar in the refrigerator for at least 1 week before eating the cauliflower.

Refrigerated, the pickle will keep well for at least several weeks.

Makes 2 quarts

Pink Pickled Cauliflower and Cabbage

THE PEOPLE OF the Middle East love to tint their pickles pink. This pickle, a favorite of that region, is colored here by the red cabbage, but you can also make the pickle with green cabbage if you add a few slices of raw or pickled beet.

½ small red cabbage (about ¾ pound)
1 small cauliflower, broken and cut into florets
1 or 2 small dried chile peppers, slit lengthwise
1 teaspoon caraway seeds
1 large garlic clove, sliced
1 bay leaf
2¼ cups white wine vinegar
2¼ cups water
3 tablespoons pickling salt

1. Cut the cabbage head lengthwise and crosswise to make 1-inch squares. In a sterile 2-quart jar, mix the cabbage, cauliflower, chile pepper(s), caraway seeds, garlic, and bay leaf. Combine the vinegar and water, and dissolve the salt in the liquid. Pour the liquid over the vegetables. Cap the jar with a nonreactive cap, and let it stand at room temperature.
2. After 10 days, the pickle will be ready. If you don't eat it right away, refrigerate the jar. The pickle will keep well in the refrigerator for 4 to 6 weeks, after which the vegetables may lose their crispness.

Makes 2 quarts

SAVE YOUR 2-QUART JARS

Ball and Kerr stopped making 2-quart mason jars in 1997, since the USDA had no guidelines for canning with them. Many people, however, still use these jars for storing dry and refrigerated foods. Two-quart jars are also handy for making refrigerator pickles and small batches of fermented pickles. For the recipes in this book that call for 2-quart jars, you can use any jars of approximately the same volume.

Spicy Pickled Baby Corn

FARMERS SAY THAT you can make this pickle with any field corn or sweet corn, if you pick it at the right stage of maturity. But special varieties are available for pickling; I've been using one from Nichols (see page 367) called simply "baby corn." I plant the seeds close together, and pick the ears when the silks just begin to show. I get four ears on most stalks.

---

1 bay leaf, crumbled

8 allspice berries

8 black peppercorns

20 coriander seeds

½ teaspoon mustard seeds

1 quart husked baby corn (each ear about 3 inches long)

4 small dried chile peppers

1 teaspoon pickling salt

2 teaspoons sugar

1 cup cider vinegar

1 cup water

---

1. Put the bay leaf, allspice, peppercorns, coriander seeds, and mustard seeds into a 1-quart jar. Add the corn ears, interspersing the chile peppers among them.

2. In a nonreactive saucepan, bring to a boil the salt, sugar, vinegar, and water. Pour the hot liquid over the corn, and cap the jar.

3. Store the jar in the refrigerator for at least 1 week before eating the corn.

Makes 1 quart

Sweet Pickled Daikon

THE STRONG ODOR of this Japanese pickle makes it especially fun to serve to friends. It tastes much, much better than it smells.

The sun-drying is traditional, and it preserves the daikon longer, but I have skipped this step with good results.

¾ pound daikon, dried in the sun until limp (3 to 4 days)
¼ cup rice vinegar
½ cup water
½ cup sugar
1½ tablespoons pickling salt

1. Cut the daikon in half lengthwise, then slice it crosswise as thin as you can. Put the daikon into a pint jar.
2. In a nonreactive saucepan, bring to a boil the remaining ingredients, stirring to dissolve the sugar and salt. Pour the hot syrup over the daikon, and cap the jar tightly.
3. Store the jar in the refrigerator for at least 3 days before eating the pickle. Refrigerated, it will keep for several weeks. Keep the jar tightly covered to prevent the aroma from escaping.

Makes 1 pint

• • •

GROW YOUR OWN DAIKON

In cookbooks, daikon is often called long white radish or Chinese turnip, but I use the Japanese term because that's what we've become used to seeing in supermarkets. Although daikon is rather expensive in stores, it's almost as easy to grow as any other radish. Since daikon has a long growing period, however, most cultivars tend to bolt when planted in spring. I've been growing one called April Cross, sold by Nichols (see page 367), that seldom goes to seed prematurely. In hot places, though, daikon should be planted in mid- to late summer for fall or winter harvest.

Pickled Eggplant Cubes

"AUBERGINES CERTAINLY are indigestible," writes Patience Gray in *Honey from a Weed* (1986), "especially when conserved in vinegar." She is partially right: For some people, aubergines—that is, eggplants—usually don't go down without discomfort. But such people are delighted with this pickle, which they find they can eat with impunity. Serve it in salads or on toasted bread with hummus.

3 cups white wine vinegar
2¼ pounds slender eggplants, peeled and cut into ⅜- to ½-inch cubes
2 tablespoons chopped garlic
¼ cup loosely packed small basil leaves
2 teaspoons pickling salt

1. Bring the vinegar to a boil in a nonreactive saucepan. In 3 or 4 batches, blanch the eggplant in the vinegar for 2 minutes. Transfer the eggplant to a bowl with a slotted spoon.

2. Add the garlic, basil, and salt to the bowl, and toss the mixture. Pack the eggplant and seasonings into pint mason jars. Return the vinegar to a boil, and pour it over the eggplant, leaving ½ inch headspace. Close the jars with hot two-piece caps. To ensure a good seal, process the jars for 10 minutes in a boiling-water bath.

3. Store the cooled jars in a cool, dry, dark place for 1 week or longer before eating the eggplant.

Makes 3 pints

Italian Pickled Raw Eggplant

RAW EGGPLANT, PRESSED to remove excess moisture and marinated with basil, garlic, and hot pepper, makes a tasty antipasto.

---

1 ½ pounds slender eggplants, peeled

2 teaspoons pickling salt

¼ cup red wine vinegar

3 garlic cloves, peeled and sliced

½ teaspoon hot pepper flakes

8 basil leaves, each torn in half

About ¼ cup olive oil

---

1. Slice the eggplants crosswise into 1-inch pieces, then lengthwise into pieces ³⁄₁₆ inch thick. In a bowl, toss the eggplant strips with the salt, and put them into a colander. Let them drain 12 hours.

2. Press each eggplant slice between your palms to remove any remaining excess moisture. Put the slices into a bowl, and toss them with the vinegar. Let them stand 1 hour.

3. In a pint jar, layer the eggplant with the garlic, pepper flakes, and basil, pressing the eggplant down to fit. Pour over the eggplant enough olive oil to cover it well. Cover the jar with a nonreactive cap, and refrigerate the jar.

After several hours, add more olive oil if the eggplant isn't well covered.

4. The eggplant will be ready after several days, but will keep well, refrigerated, for several months. Bring it to room temperature before serving it.

Makes 1 pint

• • •

EGGPLANTS: BIG AND LITTLE, FAT AND THIN

The idea of pickling whole eggplants may seem strange if the only eggplants you know are the enormous ones sold in American supermarkets. But eggplants were so named because many varieties resemble bird eggs in both size and shape (and even color—some are white rather than purple). Our giant eggplants would be novelties in much of the world, where little eggplants are the norm. Fruits of the smaller varieties, I've found, generally have a firmer texture and less bitter flavor, and so are well worth seeking out in seed catalogs and farmers' markets.

For stuffed eggplant pickles, small round eggplants are most common, but I use the elongated Little Fingers variety, available from Shepherd's (see page 367).

Lebanese Pickled Eggplant Stuffed with Garlic

IN LEBANON, THESE pickles are traditionally eaten as part of the *maza*, an assortment of hot or cold appetizers. The maza usually includes olives and yogurt cheese, and always includes spearmint leaves and flatbread.

1¼ pounds 3- to 4-inch-long eggplants

1 garlic bulb, separated into cloves, the cloves peeled and crushed

1 tablespoon plus 1 teaspoon pickling salt

½ teaspoon cayenne

1½ cups red wine vinegar

¾ cup water

1. Steam the eggplants 5 to 7 minutes, or until they are tender but not mushy. Let them cool.

2. Slit each eggplant once lengthwise, cutting most of the way through. Mix the garlic with the 1 tablespoon salt and the cayenne, and stuff the eggplants with this mixture. Pack the eggplants into a sterile 1-quart jar.

3. In a nonreactive saucepan, bring to a boil the vinegar, water, and remaining 1 teaspoon salt, stirring to dissolve the salt. Let the liquid cool.

4. Fill the jar to the brim with the cooled liquid (top the jar off with a little more vinegar, if necessary). Cover the jar with a nonreactive cap, preferably one that is all plastic. Let the jar stand in a cool place for 1 to 2 weeks.

5. If you don't eat the pickles right away, store the jar in the refrigerator. The pickles will keep for at least several weeks.

Makes 1 quart

Armenian Pickled Eggplant Stuffed with Peppers and Parsley

THIS ARMENIAN RECIPE is much like the preceding Lebanese one, except that parsley, hot peppers, and sweet bell peppers take the place of the garlic.

1¼ pounds 3- to 4-inch-long eggplants

¼ cup coarsely chopped red bell pepper

2 tablespoons coarsely chopped green bell pepper

1 tablespoon minced red chile pepper

2 tablespoons chopped parsley

1 small garlic clove, minced

1 tablespoon plus ¼ teaspoon pickling salt

1½ cups white wine vinegar

½ cup water

2 tablespoons sugar

---

1. Steam the eggplants 5 to 7 minutes, or until they are tender but not mushy. Put them into a colander, and set a heavy dish on top. Press them 4 to 10 hours.

2. Slit each eggplant once lengthwise, cutting most of the way through. In a small bowl, mix together the peppers, parsley, garlic, and ¼ teaspoon salt. Stuff each eggplant with some of this mixture, and squeeze the eggplant gently to close the slit. Pack the eggplants into a sterile 1-quart jar.

3. In a nonreactive saucepan, bring to a boil the vinegar, water, sugar, and 1 tablespoon salt, stirring until the sugar and salt have dissolved. Let the liquid cool.

4. Fill the jar to the brim with the cooled liquid (top the jar off with a little more vinegar, if necessary). Cover the jar with a nonreactive cap, preferably one that is all plastic. Let the jar stand in a cool place for 1 to 2 weeks.

5. If you don't eat the pickles right away, store the jar in the refrigerator. The pickles will keep for at least several weeks.

Makes 1 quart

Turkish Pickled Eggplant Stuffed with Cabbage and Dill

BECAUSE THE STUFFING in this recipe is bulkier than that in the preceding two recipes, the eggplants are tied shut. If you find dill stems or quartered celery stalks too awkward to use for tying, you can substitute cotton kitchen string.

1 pound 3- to 4-inch-long eggplants
3 celery stalks or 6 or more dill stems
2¼ cups red wine vinegar
1 tablespoon plus ¼ teaspoon pickling salt
½ cup shredded cabbage
1 small sweet pepper, such as bell or pimiento, minced
¼ cup minced dill fronds
1½ tablespoons minced garlic
1 tablespoon minced celery leaves

1. Steam the eggplants 5 to 7 minutes, or until they are tender but not mushy. Put them into a colander, and set a heavy dish on top. Press them 4 to 10 hours.

2. Steam or boil the celery stalks or dill stems until they are quite tender. Let them cool. Quarter the celery stalks lengthwise.

3. Slit each eggplant once lengthwise, cutting most of the way through. In a small bowl, mix together the cabbage, pepper, dill, garlic, celery leaves, and ¼ teaspoon salt. Stuff each eggplant with some of this mixture. Tie each eggplant closed with 1 or 2 celery strips or dill stems. Pack the eggplants into a sterile 1-quart jar.

4. In a nonreactive saucepan, bring to a boil the vinegar and 1 tablespoon salt, stirring until the salt has dissolved. Let the liquid cool.

5. Fill the jar to the brim with the cooled liquid (top the jar off with a little more vinegar, if necessary). Cover the jar with a nonreactive cap, preferably one that is all plastic. Let the jar stand in a cool place for 1 to 2 weeks.

6. If you don't eat the pickles right away, store the jar in the refrigerator. The pickles will keep for at least several weeks.

Makes 1 quart

Pickled Jerusalem Artichokes

THIS IS A FAVORITE Southern pickle. Native to North America, the Jerusalem artichoke plant is a perennial sunflower grown for its edible tubers. (The Italian word for sunflower, *girasole*, sounded like "Jerusalem" to English speakers.) It was once hoped that these tubers would prove as useful as potatoes, and many people still eat Jerusalem artichokes cooked and mashed. They are, however, difficult to digest, and so they came to be used mainly as hog feed. Now, however, they're widely available in produce markets under the new name "sunchokes." Jerusalem artichokes are pleasant to eat, for their crunchy texture if not their bland flavor, and they produce no uncomfortable aftereffects if eaten in small quantities. So don't let the hogs have them all—pickle a couple of jars for yourself.

1½ pounds Jerusalem artichokes
¼ cup plus 1 teaspoon pickling salt
1 quart water
4 thin slices fresh ginger
2 large garlic cloves, sliced
2 small dried chile peppers
½ teaspoon coriander seeds
1 teaspoon cumin seeds
2 cups cider vinegar
¼ cup brown sugar

1. Scrub the artichokes, and slice them ¼ inch thick. Put the artichokes into a bowl. Stir the ¼ cup salt into the water until the salt dissolves, and pour the brine over the artichokes. Let them stand 12 to 18 hours.

2. Drain and rinse the artichokes, and drain them again. Into each of 2 pint jars, put 2 slices of ginger, 1 sliced garlic clove, 1 chile pepper, ¼ teaspoon coriander seeds, and ½ teaspoon cumin seeds. Add the artichokes, packing them loosely. In a nonreactive saucepan, bring to a boil the vinegar, the sugar, and the 1 teaspoon salt, stirring until the sugar and salt are dissolved. Pour the hot liquid over the artichokes, leaving ½ inch headspace. Close the jars with hot two-piece caps. Process the jars for 15 minutes in a boiling-water bath.

3. Store the cooled jars in a cool, dry, dark place for at least 3 weeks before eating the artichokes.

Makes 2 pints

Polish Pickled Mushrooms

THIS MUSHROOM PICKLE, my favorite, is also the least trouble to make. I fell in love with the recipe after trying it with some fried-chicken mushrooms (*Lyophyllum decastes*) that I found growing near the house one day. If you can't find fried-chicken mushrooms or identify them with certainty, use button or other firm-fleshed mushrooms.

This spicy pickle would be very good with game.

1 pound mushrooms, wiped clean with a damp cloth
½ cup chopped onion
2 bay leaves
2 teaspoons black peppercorns
1 teaspoon whole allspice
2 teaspoons pickling salt
½ cup water
¼ cup white wine vinegar

1. In a nonreactive saucepan, bring all of the ingredients to a boil. Reduce the heat, and simmer for 15 minutes. Pack the mushrooms and their liquid into a pint jar. Let the jar cool.

2. Cap the jar. Store it in the refrigerator for several days before eating the mushrooms.

Refrigerated, the mushrooms will keep about 3 weeks.

Makes 1 pint

Pickled Mushrooms with Ginger and Red Wine

FRESH GINGER GIVES these mushrooms an unexpected, delightful flavor. They make an appealing side dish for lamb or game.

1 pound small button mushrooms, wiped clean with a damp cloth

2 teaspoons pickling salt

6 tablespoons red wine vinegar

⅔ cup red wine

½ teaspoon sugar

4 whole cloves

8 black peppercorns

One 1-inch piece of fresh ginger, sliced thin

1 bay leaf

1. In a bowl, toss the mushrooms with the salt. Put them into a flat-bottomed dish, and cover the dish with plastic wrap. Let the mushrooms stand for 8 to 12 hours.

2. Put the mushrooms and their juice into a nonreactive saucepan. Cook them over medium heat until all the juice has evaporated, about 8 to 10 minutes. Add all the remaining ingredients. Simmer the mixture 5 minutes. Remove the pan from the heat, and let the mushrooms cool.

3. Pack the mushrooms into a 2- to 3-cup jar. Pour the liquid over the mushrooms, and cap the jar. Refrigerate the jar for at least 2 days before eating the mushrooms.

The mushrooms will keep for about 2 months in the refrigerator.

Makes 1 pint

Herbed Marinated Mushrooms

SHIITAKES INTENSIFY the mushroom flavor of this pickle. I use dried shiitakes, which are quite inexpensive in Chinese markets, rather than the high-priced fresh ones sold in supermarkets.

Neither too sour nor too salty, this pickle makes a fine antipasto to serve along with cheese and pickled peppers.

---

12 dried shiitake mushrooms

½ cup olive oil

1 pound small button mushrooms, wiped clean with a damp cloth

2 garlic cloves, sliced

2 shallots, minced

¼ cup balsamic vinegar

Leaves from 2 thyme sprigs, or ½ teaspoon dried thyme

3 fresh sage leaves, chopped, or ½ teaspoon crumbled dried sage

4 teaspoons chopped parsley

1 bay leaf, crumbled

½ teaspoon pickling salt

---

1. Put the shiitake mushrooms into a bowl, and pour boiling water over them. Let them soak for 5 minutes, and then drain them (save the liquid to add to soup).

2. In a skillet, heat 2 tablespoons of the olive oil. Add the shiitake and button mushrooms, and sauté them over medium-low heat until the mushrooms are tender, about 15 minutes. Transfer the mushrooms to a bowl.

3. In a small nonreactive saucepan, simmer the garlic, shallots, and vinegar. Add the herbs, bay, salt, and remaining olive oil, and heat the mixture briefly. Pour the mixture over the mushrooms, and toss them.

4. Pack the mushrooms and their liquid into a pint jar. Cap the jar, and let it cool. Store the mushrooms in the refrigerator for about 1 week before eating them. Refrigerated, they will keep for several weeks, at least. Bring the jar to room temperature before serving the mushrooms.

Makes 1 pint

Lemony Pickled Mushrooms in Olive Oil

THIS MAY SEEM a very extravagant recipe, since the pickling liquid is discarded before the mushrooms are put into jars and a great deal of precious olive oil is then required to cover the mushrooms. But the marinated mushrooms are really delicious. Besides, you can use the vinegar solution for making a quick pickle, and the olive oil for dressing salads or for sautéing.

This recipe is based on one developed by Dr. George York, a microbiologist at the University of California, Davis.

½ cup lemon juice
1 quart plus 1 cup water
1½ pounds (about 6 cups) very small button mushrooms, wiped clean
   with a damp cloth
2 garlic cloves, sliced
4 thyme sprigs
4 marjoram sprigs
1 cup white wine vinegar
1½ teaspoons pickling salt
2 bay leaves, torn in half
About 1¾ cups olive oil

1. In a large nonreactive saucepan, combine the lemon juice and 1 quart water. Add the mushrooms, garlic, and herbs. Bring the mixture to a boil, reduce the heat, and simmer the mushrooms for 5 minutes.

2. Drain the mushrooms, and put them into a bowl. Combine the vinegar, the remaining 1 cup water, and the salt. Pour the liquid over the mushrooms, and let them stand for 10 to 12 hours.

3. Drain the mushrooms, saving the liquid, if you like. Pack the mushrooms into half-pint mason jars, dividing the herb sprigs and bay leaves among the jars. Cover the mushrooms with the olive oil, leaving ½ inch headspace. Seal the jars with hot two-piece caps (make sure the rims are free of oil, which could prevent a good seal). Process the jars for 20 minutes in a boiling-water bath, or pasteurize the jars for 30 minutes in water heated to 180 to 185 degrees F.

4. Store the cooled jars in a cool, dry, dark place for at least 1 week before eating the mushrooms.

Makes 4 half-pints

Pickled Okra

ALTHOUGH OKRA IS easy to grow in the South, I've had little luck with this vegetable in my garden in Oregon's Willamette Valley, not so much because of the relatively short growing season as because of the cucumber beetles, which ravage the plants. Supermarket okra won't do; it's usually shriveled and turning brown. I made this pickle last year, though, after coming upon fresh green okra pods at an Asian market in Portland.

4 large garlic cloves, sliced

2 to 4 small dried or fresh chile peppers

2 teaspoons dill seeds

2 quarts (about 2 pounds) fresh small okra pods, stems trimmed

4 cups cider vinegar

4 cups water

2 tablespoons pickling salt

1. Into each of 4 pint mason jars, put 1 sliced garlic clove, ½ or 1 whole chile pepper, and ½ teaspoon dill seeds. Pack the okra into the jars.

2. In a saucepan, bring to a boil the vinegar, water, and salt, stirring to dissolve the salt. Ladle the hot liquid over the okra, leaving ½ inch headspace. Close the jars with hot two-piece caps. Process the jars for 15 minutes in a boiling-water bath.

3. Store the cooled jars in a cool, dry, dark place for at least 3 weeks before eating the okra.

Makes 4 pints

English Pub–Style Pickled Onions

THIS PICKLE IS made the traditional way, with a short brining to keep the onions crisp, and with cool rather than hot vinegar. If you'd like to can the onions, though, use two one-pint or four half-pint mason jars instead of a quart jar, and pour the spiced vinegar over the onions while the vinegar is hot. Seal the jars immediately with hot two-piece caps, and process the jars for 10 minutes in a boiling-water bath.

Sharp-tasting, brown malt vinegar is available at some supermarkets. If you can't find it, or if you'd like a milder pickle, use white wine vinegar.

½ cup pickling salt

2 quarts water

1½ pounds very small onions or shallots

2 tablespoons brown sugar

2 cups malt vinegar

1 teaspoon black peppercorns

¼ teaspoon whole allspice

¼ teaspoon hot pepper flakes

1 bay leaf, crumbled

1. In a bowl, dissolve ¼ cup salt in 1 quart water. Add the onions. Weight them gently with a plate that fits inside the bowl. Let them stand 8 to 12 hours.

2. Drain the onions, and peel them. Return them to the bowl. Make a brine with the remaining salt and water, pour it over the onions, and weight them gently again. Let them stand 2 days.

3. In a nonreactive saucepan, bring the sugar and vinegar to a boil. Let the liquid cool.

4. Drain and rinse the onions, and drain them well again. In a 1-quart jar, layer the onions, peppercorns, allspice, pepper flakes, and bay leaf. Cover them with the cooled, sweetened vinegar. Cover the jar with a nonreactive cap, preferably all plastic.

5. Refrigerate the jar for at least 1 month before eating the onions. They will keep for at least 6 months.

Makes 1 quart

Pickled Sugar Snap Peas

THE BEST WAY to eat sugar snap peas is right off the vine. This recipe ranks a close second, though. I pickle any sugar snap peas that the kids don't eat right away, and continue to enjoy them for weeks after the pea vines have wilted away.

1¼ cups white wine vinegar

1¼ cups water

1 tablespoon pickling salt

1 tablespoon sugar

1 pound sugar snap peas, stemmed and strung

4 garlic cloves, sliced

1 or 2 small dried chile peppers, slit lengthwise

2 tarragon sprigs

1. In a nonreactive saucepan, bring to a boil the vinegar, water, salt, and sugar, stirring to dissolve the salt and sugar. Let the liquid cool.

2. Pack the peas, garlic, chile peppers, and tarragon into a 1-quart jar. Pour the cooled liquid over the peas, and cover the jar with a nonreactive cap.

3. Store the jar in the refrigerator for at least 2 weeks before eating the peas. Refrigerated, they will keep for several months.

Makes 1 quart

Pickled Sweet Green Pepper Strips

THESE SWEET, SOUR, crunchy strips are a wonderful addition to salads or a great accompaniment for dips such as hummus and baba ghanoush.

---

4 thin slices fresh ginger

4 small garlic cloves

2 teaspoons pickling salt

2 pounds green bell or pimiento peppers, cut into ½-inch lengthwise strips

2 cups white wine vinegar or distilled white vinegar

2 cups water

1 ¼ cups sugar

---

1. Put 1 ginger slice, 1 garlic clove, and ½ teaspoon pickling salt into each of 4 pint mason jars. Pack the pepper strips snugly into the jars.

2. In a nonreactive saucepan, bring to a boil the vinegar, water, and sugar, stirring to dissolve the sugar. Reduce the heat, and cover the pan. Simmer the liquid, covered, for 5 minutes.

3. Pour the hot liquid over the pepper strips, leaving ½ inch headspace. Close the jars with hot two-piece caps. In a boiling-water bath, process the jars for 10 minutes.

4. Store the cooled jars in a cool, dry, dark place for at least 3 weeks before eating the peppers.

Makes 4 pints

Marinated Sweet Peppers

IN THIS RECIPE the peppers are softened by blanching, not roasting, so no peeling is necessary. The pickling liquid makes a good salad dressing.

2¼ pounds pimiento or bell peppers (red, yellow, green, or a mix of
    colors), cored and seeded
3 small garlic cloves
3 sprigs thyme, marjoram, or oregano
1 cup white wine vinegar
1½ teaspoons pickling salt
1 cup olive oil

1. Put the peppers into a bowl, and cover them with boiling water. Let them stand 3 minutes.

2. Drain the peppers, and cover them with ice water. When they have thoroughly cooled, drain them well. Put a garlic clove and an herb sprig into each of 3 pint mason jars. Add the peppers.

3. In a nonreactive saucepan, bring the vinegar and salt to a boil. Add the olive oil, and bring the contents to a boil again. Pour the hot liquid over the peppers, leaving ½ inch headspace. Close the jars with hot two-piece caps. Process the jars for 10 minutes in a boiling-water bath.

4. Store the cooled jars in a cool, dry, dark place for at least 3 weeks before eating the peppers.

Makes 3 pints

Short-Brined Pickled Peppers

BRINING PEPPERS BEFORE PICKLING them in vinegar intensifies their flavor. Use this recipe to pickle whole small peppers, to serve as appetizers, or large peppers, cut into pieces, to use in stews, salsas, pasta sauces, and so on. The peppers can be green or ripe, sweet or hot.

4 pounds peppers

1¼ cups pickling salt

1 gallon plus 1½ cups water

2 tablespoons sugar

2 garlic cloves, chopped

1 tablespoon coarsely grated horseradish

5½ cups white wine vinegar or distilled white vinegar

1. If you're using whole small peppers, slit them twice lengthwise. If you're using large peppers, core, seed, and halve or quarter them. In a large bowl, crock, or nonreactive pot, stir the salt into the 1 gallon water until the salt dissolves. Add the peppers. Let them stand in the brine for 12 to 18 hours.

2. Drain and rinse the peppers, and drain them again. In a nonreactive saucepan, bring to a boil the sugar, garlic, horseradish, vinegar, and 1½ cups water. Cover the pan, and reduce the heat. Simmer the liquid, covered, for 10 minutes.

3. Pack the peppers into 6 pint mason jars. Pour the hot liquid over the peppers, leaving ½ inch headspace. Close the jars with hot two-piece caps. Process the jars for 10 minutes in a boiling-water bath.

4. Store the cooled jars in a cool, dry, dark place for at least 3 weeks before eating the peppers.

Makes 6 pints

Refrigerator Pickled Peppers

FLAVORED WITH FENNEL, celery, and bay, this is a delightfully unusual pepper pickle.

---

2 pounds bell or pimiento peppers, preferably of mixed colors, cut into
*   strips or 1- to 1½-inch squares*
1 large celery stalk with leaves, chopped
3 garlic cloves, chopped
1 tablespoon fennel seeds
1 bay leaf
3 cups water
1½ cups white wine vinegar
2½ tablespoons pickling salt

---

1. In a large bowl, toss the peppers with the celery, garlic, and fennel seeds. Pack this mixture with the bay leaf into a 2-quart jar.
2. Combine the water and vinegar, and dissolve the salt in the liquid. Pour the brine over the vegetables. Cap the jar, and refrigerate it. The peppers will be ready in about 8 days, and will keep well for 6 to 8 weeks in the refrigerator.

Makes 2 quarts

Pickled Roasted Peppers

IN THIS PICKLE, the bittersweet flavor of roasted peppers is undisguised, even heightened, by the full-strength vinegar.

1¾ cups white wine vinegar or distilled white vinegar
1 tablespoon sugar
2 tablespoons pickling salt
1 garlic clove, chopped
3½ pounds bell, pimiento, or Anaheim peppers (red, yellow, green, or a
   mix of colors), roasted, peeled, cored, and seeded

1. In a nonreactive saucepan, bring to a boil the vinegar, sugar, salt, and garlic. Reduce the heat, and simmer the liquid, covered, for 10 minutes.
2. Pack the peppers into pint or half-pint jars. Pour the hot liquid over the peppers, leaving ½ inch headspace. Close the jars with hot two-piece caps, and process the jars for 10 minutes in a boiling-water bath.
3. Store the cooled jars in a cool, dry, dark place for at least 3 weeks before eating the peppers.

Makes 2½ pints

HOW TO ROAST PEPPERS

To roast and peel peppers, put them under a broiler or on a screen or fork over a gas flame. Turning them frequently, let them blacken. As soon as their skins are charred and blistered over most of the surface, remove the peppers from the heat, and either put them into a plastic bag or lay a damp cloth on top of them. When they have cooled, their skins will come off easily under running water.

Pepper "Mangoes"

MANGOES—NOT THE TROPICAL FRUIT but any fruit or vegetable stuffed with cabbage and seasonings and then pickled in vinegar—were popular in the United States and England in the nineteenth century. These pickles were most often made with melons—small, thin-skinned, white-fleshed melons that were pickled green, and so were more like plump cucumbers than like the muskmelons, honeydews, and casabas we know today. Although melons of the mango type are still popular in places such as Japan and Italy, even their seeds are hard to come by in the United States. Also delicious, however, are pepper mangoes, or pickled cabbage-stuffed peppers, and these are easy to make with modern produce.

To make a pepper mango, some cooks cored and stuffed the pepper through a slit in the side, leaving the stem end intact. Others cut off the stem end like a jack-o'-lantern top, then fastened it back on with toothpicks after stuffing the pepper. My technique is easier: Just cut out the stem and core, stuff the pepper, and leave the opening alone. These pickles make a pretty accompaniment to a winter meal.

1 gallon water

1 cup plus 1 teaspoon pickling salt

12 small to medium green bell or pimiento peppers, cored and seeded

1½ pounds cabbage (about 1 small head), cored and shredded

2 tablespoons minced garlic

2 tablespoons minced dill fronds

2 teaspoons yellow mustard seeds

2 small dried chile peppers

2 small bay leaves

About 2 cups cider vinegar

1. Pour the water into a large bowl, crock, or nonreactive pot, and stir 1 cup of the salt into the water until the salt dissolves. Submerge the bell or pimiento peppers in the brine. Let them stand 12 to 18 hours.

2. Drain and rinse the peppers, and drain them again thoroughly. In a large bowl, mix the cabbage with the 1 teaspoon salt, the garlic, the dill, and the mustard. Stuff this mixture into the peppers.

3. Put a chile pepper and a bay leaf into each of 2 sterile quart jars. Pack 6 of the peppers into each jar. Cover the peppers by 1 inch or more with the cold vinegar, and cover the jars tightly with nonreactive, preferably all plastic caps.

4. Store the jars in a cool, dry, dark place. They'll be ready to eat in about 1 week.

Makes 2 quarts

Honeyed Jalapeño Pepper Rings

I LOVE JALAPEÑO peppers because they're meaty and usually mild—mild, that is, compared with really hot peppers, such as serrano, cayenne, and, especially, habanero. You can use this pickle as a table condiment, to spoon right into your tacos or black bean soup.

This pickle will be particularly appealing if you mix green and red jalapeños. Remember, though, that jalapeños get soft and mushy if left on the plant after ripening; pick the red ones when they're still quite firm.

You can seed the peppers or not, as you wish. After I cut the peppers into rings, I take out most of the seeds with the help of a grapefruit spoon. Then I put the rings into a colander and rinse off the seeds still clinging to the peppers.

Be sure to wear rubber gloves while you're handling the peppers.

---

24 black peppercorns

8 small garlic cloves, sliced

2¼ pounds jalapeño peppers, cut into ³⁄₁₆-inch rings and, if you like,
   seeded

4 cups cider vinegar

2 tablespoons honey

2 teaspoons pickling salt

2 tablespoons mixed pickling spice

¼ cup olive oil

---

1. Divide the peppercorns and garlic among 8 half-pint mason jars. Add the pepper rings.

2. Combine the vinegar, honey, and salt in a nonreactive saucepan. Add the pickling spice, tied in a spice bag or scrap of cheesecloth. Bring the mixture to a boil.

3. Immediately pour the hot liquid over the peppers in the jars, leaving a little more than ½ inch headspace. Pour about 1½ teaspoons olive oil into each jar, and close the jars with hot two-piece caps. Process the jars for 10 minutes in a boiling-water bath, or pasteurize the jars for 30 minutes in water heated to 180 to 185 degrees F.

4. Store the cooled jars in a cool, dry, dark place for at least 3 weeks before eating the peppers.

Makes 8 half-pints

Pickled Whole Hot Peppers

FOR THIS PICKLE I prefer Cascabella peppers, in their glorious colors of yellow, orange, and red. But you can use any small, hot pickling pepper, such as Floral Gem (a similar wax-type pepper), jalapeño, or hot cherry.

Give a jar of these pickled peppers to some chile-head friends, and stick around to watch them expire.

> 2 pounds small chile peppers
> 8 small garlic cloves
> 8 whole allspice berries
> 16 black peppercorns
> 2 small bay leaves, torn in half
> 2 cups cider, white wine, or distilled white vinegar
> 2 cups water
> 4 teaspoons pickling salt
> ¼ cup olive oil

1. Rinse the peppers, slit them twice lengthwise, and trim the stems to about ¼ inch. Divide the garlic and dry spices among 4 pint mason jars. Add the peppers. In a nonreactive saucepan, bring to a boil all of the remaining ingredients except the olive oil. Pour the hot liquid over the peppers, leaving slightly more than ½ inch headspace, then pour 1 tablespoon olive oil into each jar. Close the jars with hot two-piece caps. Process the jars for 10 minutes in a boiling-water bath.

2. Store the cooled jars in a cool, dry, dark place for 3 weeks or more before eating the peppers.

Makes 4 pints

• • •

PRETTY PEPPERS FOR PICKLING

Developed in California, Cascabella peppers are aptly named, for their skins (*cáscaras*) are truly beautiful (*bella*). These small, waxy, conical peppers start out light yellow, then turn orange before ripening red. They grow prolifically on bushy plants, which are such a pretty sight that you may want one for its ornamental value alone.

Cascabella peppers are available from Nichols and Shepherd's (see page 367). Don't confuse them with cascabel ("jingle bell") peppers, which are round, red Mexican chiles.

If you don't pickle all your Cascabellas, Shepherd's catalog suggests, try coring some, stuffing them with cheese, and serving them "with cold beer and a slice of lime at the end of a sizzling Indian summer day."

Pickled Purslane

EVEN IF YOU'VE never heard the word *purslane*, you probably know this plant; it's a succulent, ground-hugging weed that seems to find a home in most vegetable gardens. In Italy, France, and other European countries, it's also a well-loved vegetable.

Frankly, I don't much like the invasive form of purslane. Better, I think, are the upright, thick-stalked varieties whose seeds are available from mail-order companies, including Shepherd's and Territorial (see page 367). These purslanes are tart and crunchy, and they are said to be excellent sources of vitamin E and omega-3 fatty acids.

Popular in eighteenth-century England and America, pickled purslane stalks deserve to come back in style. Don't discard the leaves—they're very good in salads.

About ½ pound purslane stalks, cut to fit vertically in a pint jar
1 dill head
1 small fresh or dried chile pepper, split lengthwise (optional)
10 tablespoons white wine vinegar
10 tablespoons water
1½ teaspoons pickling salt
1 garlic clove, sliced
4 black peppercorns

1. Pack the purslane stalks vertically in a pint jar, slipping the dill head and chile pepper, if you're using it, down the side. In a nonreactive saucepan, bring to a boil the vinegar, water, salt, garlic, and peppercorns, stirring to dissolve the salt. Pour the hot liquid over the purslane. Cover the jar with a nonreactive cap.

2. Store the jar in the refrigerator for 1 week before eating the purslane. It will keep, refrigerated, for several months or longer.

Makes 1 pint

Pickled Green Cherry Tomatoes

THESE CRUNCHY, SLIGHTLY BITTER pickled tomatoes have a taste that may grow on you. They will soften if processed with heat, so store them in the refrigerator.

1 to 2 dill sprigs
1 garlic clove, sliced
One ½-inch-square piece of horseradish, sliced thin
½ teaspoon yellow mustard seeds
½ teaspoon mixed pickling spice
1 small dried chile pepper
1 pint green cherry tomatoes
½ cup cider vinegar
½ cup water
½ teaspoon pickling salt

1. Put the seasonings into a pint mason jar. Fill the jar with the tomatoes. Combine the vinegar and water, and stir in the salt until it dissolves. Pour the liquid over the tomatoes, right to the brim of the jar. Close the jar with a non-reactive cap (you can use a two-piece mason jar cap if you line it with two layers of plastic wrap).
2. Store the jar in the refrigerator. The tomatoes will be ready to eat in about 1 week, and will keep, refrigerated, for 2 months or longer.

Makes 1 pint

Limed Green Tomato Pickle

WHEN FROST THREATENS and you rush to the garden to rescue the last of the tomatoes, take the yellowish and pink ones to ripen indoors, but don't leave behind the very green ones. They are the ones you want for this pickle.

This is a Southern-style green tomato pickle: The tomato slices are treated with lime so they stay very crisp. They are also sweet—but not too sweet, since I've called for less sugar than is traditional. This pickle complements baked beans, burgers, and pork chops and roasts.

Be sure to soak and rinse the limed tomatoes in fresh water three times, as the recipe directs, so the lime doesn't neutralize the acid in the pickle.

---

4 pounds green, preferably plum tomatoes

½ cup pickling lime (see page 17)

2 quarts water

I quart cider vinegar

I cup brown sugar

I cup sugar

I½ tablespoons pickling salt

2 teaspoons yellow mustard seeds

I teaspoon allspice berries

I teaspoon whole cloves

One I-inch cinnamon stick, broken up

¾ pound onions, sliced into rounds (about 2 cups)

---

1. Cut the tomatoes crosswise into ¼-inch slices, discarding a narrow slice from each end. In a large bowl, stir the pickling lime into the water, and add the tomatoes. Let them soak in the limewater for 12 to 24 hours.

2. Drain the tomatoes, rinse them, and cover them with cold water. Let them soak 1 hour, then drain, rinse, and soak them 1 hour again. Repeat this process a third time, then drain the tomatoes.

3. In a large nonreactive pot, combine the vinegar, sugars, salt, and mustard seeds. Tie the other spices in a spice bag or scrap of cheesecloth, and add this to the pot. Bring the mixture to a boil again, stirring to dissolve the sugars and salt. Add the tomatoes and onions. Bring the contents to a boil, then reduce the heat. Simmer the pickle for 15 minutes, occasionally stirring the vegetables and pushing them under the liquid.

4. Ladle the vegetables and pickling liquid into 6 pint jars, leaving ½ inch headspace. Close the jars with hot two-piece caps. To ensure a good seal, process the jars for 10 minutes in a boiling-water bath.

5. Store the cooled jars in a cool, dry, dark place for at least 2 weeks before eating the pickle.

Makes 6 pints

• • •

"**G**randmother lived to be ninety, she thought, and she never missed a dinner without the proverbial 'seven sours.'"

—*Mary Emma Showalter,*
Mennonite Community Cookbook *(1957)*

Curried Green Tomato Pickle

THIS GREEN TOMATO PICKLE, with its unusual spices, is one of my favorites. According to an old Mennonite cookbook, the recipe is French in origin.

2½ pounds green plum tomatoes, sliced ³⁄₁₆ inch thick (about 2 quarts tomato slices)

1 medium onion, sliced thin

2 tablespoons pickling salt

2 cups cider vinegar

½ cup brown sugar

1½ teaspoons curry powder

1 teaspoon ground turmeric

½ teaspoon dry mustard

½ teaspoon ground cinnamon

½ teaspoon ground ginger

½ teaspoon ground allspice

1. Combine the green tomatoes and onion in a large bowl or a crock. Add the salt, and mix gently. Let the mixture stand 8 to 12 hours.

2. Drain and rinse the vegetables, and drain them again. In a large nonreactive pot, bring to a boil the vinegar, sugar, and spices. Add the vegetables. Bring the contents to a boil again, then reduce the heat. Simmer the vegetables, stirring occasionally, about 3 minutes, or until the vegetables are just heated through. Pack the mixture into 3 pint mason jars, leaving ½ inch headspace. Close the jars with hot two-piece caps. To ensure a good seal, process the jars for 10 minutes in a boiling-water bath.

3. Store the cooled jars in a cool, dry, dark place for at least 3 weeks before eating the pickle.

Makes 3 pints

Marinated Dried Tomatoes

DRIED TOMATOES ARE wonderful when briefly rehydrated, then packed in olive oil. If you add fresh garlic or herbs, however, you've got to keep the jar refrigerated and finish off the tomatoes within three weeks, or risk contracting botulism. Olive oil, of course, solidifies in the refrigerator, which means you must bring the jar to room temperature before eating the tomatoes. My solution is to acidulate the tomatoes—that is, to pickle them. Pickled dried tomatoes taste extra tart, but they are a delicious addition to salads.

1 ½ cups dried tomatoes

1 tablespoon whole small basil leaves

¼ teaspoon pickling salt

2 large garlic cloves, slivered or minced

6 tablespoons red wine vinegar

2 tablespoons olive oil

1. Put the tomatoes into a small bowl, cover them with boiling water, and let them stand for 5 minutes.

2. Drain the tomatoes. Toss them in the bowl with the basil, salt, garlic, and vinegar. Let the mixture stand for 1 hour.

3. Pack the mixture into a sterile half-pint jar. Top with the olive oil. Cover the jar tightly with a nonreactive cap, and store it in a cool, dry, dark place. For long-term storage, keep the jar in the refrigerator.

Makes about 1 cup

Pickled Tomatillos

A LOT OF GARDENERS both love and hate tomatillos. These fruits are lovable in that they're easy to grow; you plant them once, and they come up on their own year after year. But a plant that acts like a weed is no joy to a vegetable gardener unless the fruits get eaten, and most gardeners can't think what to do with tomatillos besides turning them into salsa. How much salsa can you eat? they ask.

Here's another great use for tomatillos. Enjoy these pickles with grilled meat or fish, or with tacos or tostadas and beans. Once you try them, you may eat them up faster than salsa.

1 pound husked green tomatillos, washed
2 sweet or mild peppers, such as bell, pimiento, or Anaheim, cut into
     strips or 1-inch squares
2 to 3 jalapeño peppers, seeded and sliced into rings
3 large garlic cloves, sliced
3 oregano sprigs
1 cup white wine vinegar
1 cup water
2 teaspoons pickling salt
1 teaspoon sugar
½ teaspoon cumin seeds

1. Halve the tomatillos if they're small; quarter them if they're large. In a 1-quart jar, combine the tomatillos, peppers, garlic, and oregano. Bring the remaining ingredients to a boil in a nonreactive saucepan, and pour the hot liquid over the vegetables. Let the contents cool.

2. Cover the jar tightly with a nonreactive cap, and refrigerate the pickles for about 1 week before eating them. They will keep, refrigerated, for at least 2 months.

Makes 1 quart

• • •

"**M**y father has told me that when he was a child visiting relatives in Syria he remembers that the women of the family devoted their time to pickling and to making jams and syrups whenever they had no parties, feasts, or other household activities to occupy them. Large glass jars were filled with turnips, onions, cucumbers, lemons, cauliflowers, eggplants, and peppers. The family could hardly wait to start eating them, and often did so before the pickles were quite ready. A visit to the cellar or store cupboard to see how they were maturing and mellowing to soft pinks, saffrons, mauves, and pale greens was a mouth-watering expedition."

—*Claudia Roden, A Book of Middle Eastern Food (1980)*

Pink Pickled Turnips

I NEVER LIKED TURNIPS until I tried this Middle Eastern pickle, which is now one of my favorites. In their pink brine, colored by the beet, the turnips are as pretty as they are delicious.

When I don't have a fresh beet on hand, I use a pickled one in this recipe.

2 pounds small turnips, peeled and quartered

Tops of 2 or 3 celery stalks

4 garlic cloves

1 small raw beet, peeled and sliced

2 cups white wine vinegar

2 cups water

3 tablespoons pickling salt

1. Pack the turnips, celery tops, garlic, and beet into a sterile 2-quart jar. Combine the vinegar and water, and stir in the salt until it dissolves. Pour the liquid over the turnips, and cover the jar tightly with a nonreactive cap. Let it stand at room temperature.

2. After 10 days, the pickle will be ready. If you don't eat the turnips right away, refrigerate the jar. The pickle will keep well in the refrigerator for about 1 month.

Makes about 2 quarts

Japanese Pickled Ginger

USE VERY FRESH YOUNG GINGER for this pickle, a traditional garnish for sushi.

4 ounces fresh ginger, peeled and sliced paper-thin
2 cups water
½ teaspoon plus a sprinkle of pickling salt
½ cup rice vinegar
1½ tablespoons sugar
½ teaspoon light Japanese soy sauce

1. Put the ginger slices into a bowl, and cover them with cold water. Let them stand 30 minutes.

2. Drain the ginger. Bring the water to a boil in a saucepan, and add the ginger. Bring the water back to a boil, then drain the ginger. Let it cool.

3. Put the ginger into a bowl. Sprinkle it lightly with salt. In a saucepan, bring to a boil the vinegar, sugar, salt, and soy sauce, stirring to dissolve the sugar and salt. Pour the hot liquid over the ginger, and mix well. Let the ginger stand at least 1 hour before using it.

4. Store the ginger in the refrigerator in a container tightly covered with a nonreactive cap. It will keep several months, at least.

Makes 1 cup

Chinese Pickled Garlic

THIS RECIPE MAKES a wonderfully hot, crunchy condiment; it's also a good way to preserve garlic for the times when you've run out of fresh bulbs or are just in a hurry. Although the recipe is Chinese, it includes no soy sauce, so the pickled garlic is suitable for use in all sorts of dishes. The garlicky vinegar is good in dressings and sauces, too.

Pickle garlic in the summer or fall, when the cloves are plump, white, and sweet-smelling.

1 cup peeled fresh garlic cloves
½ cup rice vinegar, white wine vinegar, or distilled white vinegar
½ teaspoon sugar
½ teaspoon pickling salt

1. Put the garlic into a half-pint jar. Stir together the vinegar, sugar, and salt, and pour the liquid over the garlic. Cover the jar tightly with a nonreactive cap.

2. Store the jar in the refrigerator for at least 1 month before using the garlic. It will keep well for a year or more.

Makes 1 cup

French Pickled Garlic

MELLOWED BY BRIEF cooking and wine, this pickled garlic is very mild in flavor. Slice it to add to salads or use as a garnish. Or top off the jar with olive oil, and serve the whole cloves as an appetizer.

½ cup white wine vinegar
½ cup dry white wine
1 small dried chile pepper
1 small thyme sprig
1 small rosemary sprig
1 small bay leaf
10 black peppercorns
2 teaspoons sugar
½ teaspoon pickling salt
1 cup peeled fresh garlic cloves

1. Put all of the ingredients except the garlic into a nonreactive saucepan. Bring the contents to a boil, and gently boil them for 5 minutes. Add the garlic. Return the contents to a boil, then cover the pan, and remove it from the heat. Let it stand at room temperature for 24 hours.

2. Bring the contents of the saucepan to a boil again, then transfer them to a half-pint jar. Let the jar cool, and cover it tightly with a nonreactive cap.

3. Store the jar in the refrigerator. The garlic will be ready to eat in about 5 days, and will keep well for about 1 year.

Makes 1 cup

Pickled Nasturtium Pods

STOPPING HIS TRUCK in my driveway to ask directions, an old man was distracted by the sight of nasturtiums growing around the dogwood tree. "Excuse me—do you mind?" he said, as he reached down to pluck a vermilion blossom. Munching the flower, he reached for a couple of the saucer-like leaves. "Do you know," he asked, chewing them with relish, "that every part of this plant is edible? Even the seeds." He knelt on the ground to search out several that were still green and plump. "They're hot as peppers," he declared, eating them one at a time. "Here, try one."

As we stood there munching nasturtium seeds, I asked the old man if he'd ever had them pickled. He had not, preferring to eat them right in the garden, warm from the summer's sun. But the old man didn't know what he was missing. Despite the unpleasant, sulfurous smell the plump seeds release when brined, pickled nasturtium seeds (or pods, or buds, as they are variously called) taste very much like pickled capers, except that they are crunchier and a bit peppery. "Nasturtium buds make better capers than capers do," noted Euell Gibbons. My family likes them in pasta sauces; they are also good in salads.

Nasturtium pods need no seasoning besides salt and vinegar, but they're even better with a little spice. Here I use the seasonings Eliza Smith called for, in her 1739 cookbook *The Compleat Housewife*.

4½ tablespoons pickling salt

3 cups water

I pint fresh, green, plump nasturtium pods

4 whole cloves

I pinch blade (unground) mace

¼ whole nutmeg

I slice horseradish (about 1½ inches in diameter by ³⁄₁₆ inch thick), cut
    into thin strips

1 shallot, peeled

About 1 cup white wine vinegar

1. Dissolve 1½ tablespoons salt in 1 cup water, and pour this brine over the nasturtium pods. Let them stand 1 day.

2. Drain the pods. Make a fresh brine the same way as before, and pour it over the pods. Let them stand 1 day. Do the same on the third day.

3. On the fourth day, drain the pods, put them into a sterile pint jar with the cloves, mace, nutmeg, horseradish, and shallot, and cover all well with the vinegar. Cover the jar tightly with a nonreactive cap, and let the jar stand at room temperature for at least 1 week.

After 1 week, store the jar in the refrigerator or a cool, dry, dark place. The pickled pods will keep well for a year or more.

Makes about 1¾ cups

Pickled Walnuts

THIS WAS A VERY popular nineteenth-century pickle. Here's the basic method: You pick green English walnuts (not black walnuts, which are native to America) between late June and mid-July, soak the walnuts in brine for some days, let them blacken in the sun, and then cover them with spiced vinegar. My recipe is based on that of Mary Randolph (*The Virginia Housewife*, 1824).

Unfortunately, I have little information about how this pickle was used, but I like the chewiness of the young nut meats inside the soft, sour skins. I suspect the pickled walnuts were sliced or pounded, then added to stews and sauces or used to garnish roast meat.

2 pounds green English walnuts

6 tablespoons pickling salt

2 tablespoons black peppercorns

1 tablespoon whole allspice

½ teaspoon whole cloves

1 teaspoon yellow mustard seeds

2 garlic cloves, sliced

4 thin slices fresh ginger

4 to 5½ cups white wine vinegar or cider vinegar

1. Pierce each nut about 6 times with a large needle, and put the nuts into a 2-quart jar. Dissolve 2 tablespoons of the salt in 1 quart boiling water, and pour the salted water over the nuts. Cover them, and leave them at room temperature for 3 days.

2. Drain off the water. Dissolve another 2 tablespoons salt in 1 quart boiling water, and pour this over the nuts. Repeat the process 3 days later.

3. Nine days after first putting the nuts in the jar, drain them, and leave them in a colander in the sun for 2 to 3 days to blacken. Bring them in at night and in wet weather, and turn them occasionally.

4. Pack the nuts and spices into a sterile 2-quart jar, or divide them among smaller jars. Pour the vinegar over the nuts to cover them by 1 inch or more. Cover the jar tightly with a nonreactive cap, preferably all plastic, and store the jar in a cool, dry, dark place. The pickled walnuts will be ready to eat in 3 months, and they will keep well for about 1 year.

Makes about 2 quarts

Preserved Grape Leaves

IF YOU LIKE to make *dolma*, stuffed grape leaves, you may be glad to know that you can easily preserve your own leaves for this purpose. And since they won't be salty, you won't have to soak them before stuffing them. Use tender, light-green leaves picked early in summer, from any variety of grapevine.

You can buy citric acid at a canning or brewing supply store, or order it from Alltrista Corporation or Precision Foods (see page 367). Citric acid is a harmless substance that occurs naturally in foods, especially citrus fruits.

---

2 teaspoons pickling salt

1 quart water

About 30 grape leaves, stemmed

1 cup water plus ¼ cup lemon juice, or 1¼ cups water plus ½ teaspoon
     citric acid

---

1. Bring the salt and the 1 quart water to a boil in a large saucepan. Add the leaves, and blanch them for 30 seconds. Drain them.

2. Stack the leaves in small piles of about 6 each, and roll the stacks loosely from the side (not from the stem end or tip). Pack the rolls into a pint mason jar, folding over the ends if necessary.

3. In a small nonreactive saucepan, bring to a boil 1 cup water and the lemon juice, or 1¼ cups water and the citric acid. Pour the hot liquid over the rolled leaves, leaving ½ inch headspace. Close the jar with a hot two-piece cap, and process the jar for 15 minutes in a boiling-water bath. Or cover the jar with a nonreactive cap, and store it in the refrigerator.

M a k e s   1   p i n t

Crisp Pickled Pumpkin or Squash

THIS MILDLY SWEET PICKLE may especially please people who like the flavor but not the mushy texture of cooked pumpkin or squash. Here the texture of the pumpkin remains firm and crisp, and the pumpkin flavor is enhanced but undisguised.

3½ pounds pumpkin or winter squash, peeled, seeded, and cut into
    ¾-inch cubes (about 9 cups)
2 tablespoons pickling salt
4 whole cloves
8 black peppercorns, crushed
I bay leaf, crumbled
2 cups cider vinegar
I cup sugar
4 thin slices fresh ginger, slivered
3 garlic cloves, chopped

1. In a bowl, toss the pumpkin or squash cubes with the salt. Let the cubes rest for 2 to 3 hours.

2. Drain and rinse the cubes, and drain them again. Pack them into pint mason jars.

3. Tie the cloves, peppercorns, and bay leaf in a spice bag or scrap of cheese-cloth. In a nonreactive saucepan, combine the spice bag with the vinegar, sugar, ginger, and garlic. Bring the mixture to a boil, stirring to dissolve the sugar. Reduce the heat, cover the pan, and simmer the liquid for 10 minutes.

4. Remove the spice bag from the pan, and pour the hot liquid over the pumpkin or squash cubes, leaving ½ inch headspace. Close the jars with hot two-piece caps. Process the jars for 10 minutes in a boiling-water bath.

5. Store the cooled jars in a cool, dry, dark place for at least 3 weeks before eating the pickle.

Makes 4 pints

Apple and Onion Pickle

I FOUND THIS RECIPE in an interesting old cookbook, Marion Harris Neil's *Canning, Preserving, and Pickling*, published in 1914. The sweet, tart, and spicy apple and onion slices make a delightful relish for a holiday feast. I pack the slices into a wide, .75-liter European canning jar, perfect not only for its broad shape but for its glass lid, which won't react with the vinegar.

1 firm-fleshed apple (about ½ pound), peeled, cored, and sliced thin
1 large sweet onion (about ¾ pound), sliced thin
2 teaspoons slivered fresh ginger
One 3-inch cinnamon stick, broken
6 allspice berries, crushed
¼ teaspoon blade mace, preferably, or small pieces of nutmeg
1 generous pinch hot pepper flakes
About 1¾ cups cider vinegar

1. Choose a jar that will hold the apple and onion slices horizontally. Sterilize the jar. Pack alternate layers of apple and onion into the jar, distributing the aromatics among the layers. Cover the apple and onion by 1 inch or more with vinegar, and cover the jar with a nonreactive cap or lid.

2. Store the jar in a cool, dry, dark place. The pickle will be ready to eat in about 2 weeks, but will keep well for several months.

Makes about 3 cups

Sour Grapes

MORE TART THAN SWEET, this pickle is more like *cornichons à cru* than like the fruit pickles in Chapter 6. If you grow your own table grapes, put some up this way for gifts; they'll look beautiful in their jars, ornamented by tarragon sprigs. This recipe is based on one created by Helen Witty (*Fancy Pantry*, 1986).

Serve the pickled grapes with pâté or cold meat, or in main-dish salads.

3½ cups red or green vinifera table grapes (such as Red Flame or
      Thompson), or a combination of the two, stemmed
4 tarragon sprigs
3 tablespoons sugar
1½ teaspoons pickling salt
1¾ cups white wine vinegar, or a little more

---

1. Rinse and drain the grapes, and pat them dry. Pack them into a sterile 1-quart jar, slipping the tarragon sprigs in along the side. Stir the sugar and salt into 1¾ cups vinegar until the sugar and salt dissolve, then pour this liquid over the grapes. If the grapes are not well covered, add a little more vinegar. Cover the jar tightly with a nonreactive cap, preferably one that is all plastic.
2. Store the jar in a cool, dry, dark place for at least 1 month before eating the grapes. They will keep for at least 1 year.

Makes 1 quart

Mango Pickle I

MOST INDIAN MANGO PICKLES are made with the green fruit of a variety that has no noticeable sweetness until it ripens. Since these mangoes are virtually unavailable in the United States, I haven't included any recipes that call for them. This recipe and the next one, however, use the mangoes commonly available in U.S. supermarkets; when underripe, their flesh is firm but bright orange and quite sweet.

This pickle is delectably hot. Have it with curry, with grilled or roasted meat, or even with plain rice.

---

3 slightly underripe mangoes, peeled and sliced lengthwise

3 fresh green chile peppers, such as serrano or jalapeño, 1 cut into thin
    lengthwise strips, the other 2 minced

1½ teaspoons pickling salt

½ cup white wine vinegar

1 teaspoon coriander seeds

¾ teaspoon fenugreek seeds

1 teaspoon cumin seeds

1½ teaspoons black mustard seeds

⅓ cup mustard oil or other vegetable oil

2 tablespoons grated fresh ginger

1 tablespoon minced garlic

1 teaspoon yellow mustard seeds

---

1. In a bowl, mix the mango slices, chile pepper strips, salt, and vinegar. Grind the coriander, fenugreek, cumin, and black mustard seeds in a spice or coffee grinder.

2. In a skillet, heat the oil. Fry the minced chile peppers, ginger, and garlic for 2 to 3 minutes. Remove the skillet from the heat, and stir in the ground spices and the whole mustard seeds. Mix the seasonings with the mango slices and pepper strips. Transfer the mixture to a sterile 3- to 4-cup jar, and let the mixture cool.

3. Cover the jar tightly with a nonreactive cap, preferably one that is all plastic. Refrigerate the jar for at least 4 days before you eat the pickle. During this period, shake the jar at least once a day.

Refrigerated, the pickle will keep for at least 2 months.

Makes about 3 cups

• • •

THE LOWDOWN ON MUSTARD OIL

The oil extracted from mustard seeds is available at Indian groceries and many natural foods stores, but it is always labeled "for external use only." This is because the U.S. Food and Drug Administration (FDA) has banned the sale of mustard oil for culinary use, since it contains erucic acid, which "in laboratory studies with test animals . . . has been associated with nutritional deficiencies as well as cardiac lesions" (FDA Alert, September 9, 1989). Canola oil, which is extracted from a rapeseed cultivar, also contains erucic acid, although in much smaller amounts; so, of course, do mustard seeds and prepared mustard, on whose use and sale the government poses no restrictions. For centuries Indians have favored mustard oil for their oil-based pickles, and in much of India this oil is also used for deep-frying. Without the unique, strong flavor of mustard oil, your Indian-style pickles will still taste good, but not quite authentic.

Mango Pickle II

THIS RECIPE IS much like the preceding one, but the seasonings are different enough that I couldn't leave either recipe out of the book. Try both pickles, and see which you like best.

4 slightly underripe mangoes (about 4 pounds), peeled and sliced
    lengthwise
4 whole small fresh chile peppers, such as serrano or jalapeño, cut into
    thin lengthwise strips
4 teaspoons pickling salt
1⅓ cups cider vinegar
2 large garlic cloves, chopped
2 teaspoons ground coriander
2 teaspoons black mustard seeds
1 teaspoon hot pepper flakes
2 teaspoons ground dry mustard
½ cup mustard or vegetable oil
2 bay leaves

1. Toss the mango slices, pepper strips, and salt together in a bowl. Let the mixture stand 6 to 12 hours.

2. Drain the mangoes and peppers. Add the remaining ingredients, and stir well. Pack the mixture into a sterile 1-quart jar, and cover the jar tightly with a nonreactive cap, preferably one that is all plastic. Refrigerate the jar for at least 4 days before you eat the pickle. During this period, shake the jar at least once a day.

3. Refrigerated, the pickle will keep for at least 2 months.

Makes about 1 quart

Moroccan Preserved Lemons

VARIATIONS ON THIS RECIPE are popular in much of North Africa, the Middle East, and India. Sometimes the lemon segments are separated rather than kept attached at the base. Paprika may be added for color as well as flavor; in India turmeric is sometimes used in the same way. Whole bay leaves, cinnamon sticks, and peppercorns may also be added to the jar.

Before using preserved lemons, Moroccans often remove and discard the pulp; do so or not, as you like. Then rinse the rind (or rind and pulp), and chop it into small pieces. Add the pieces to soups, stews, salads, or steamed potatoes, or sprinkle them on roast poultry.

---

3 small lemons (about ½ pound), rinsed and well dried
5 teaspoons pickling salt
Juice of 1 to 2 lemons
2 tablespoons olive oil

---

1. With your palms, roll the lemons on your work surface until they feel soft; this will help to release their juices. Cut the lemons lengthwise into eighths, leaving ¼ inch intact at the stem end. Squeeze the lemons over a bowl to extract as much juice as possible. Rub 1 teaspoon salt into the interior of each lemon. Pack the lemons into a sterile narrow 12-ounce jelly jar, wedging the last one in so it won't float.

2. Add the juice of another lemon to the juice in the bowl, and stir in the remaining 2 teaspoons salt. Pour this mixture over the lemons. If it doesn't cover them, add the juice of 1 more lemon. Top with the olive oil. Cover the jar tightly with a nonreactive cap, and let it stand at room temperature for 3 weeks, shaking the jar occasionally and turning it over once or twice during this period.

3. After 3 weeks, the lemons will be ready to eat. Store them in a jar in the refrigerator, where they will keep well for months.

Makes 1½ cups

Sweet Pickled Lemons

PLENTY OF SUGAR and strong spices balance the bitterness of lemon peel in this Indian pickle, making it a good choice for people who have never tasted pickled lemon. I suggest chopping the lemons before serving them.

3 small lemons (about ½ pound), rinsed and well dried
1 ½ teaspoons fennel seeds
1 ½ teaspoons cumin seeds
1 ½ teaspoons black peppercorns
1 ½ tablespoons pickling salt
6 tablespoons lemon juice
1 ½ cups brown sugar
2 small dried chile peppers

1. Cut the lemons lengthwise into eighths, leaving ¼ inch intact at the stem end. In a spice or coffee grinder, grind the fennel, cumin, and black pepper. Mix the spices with the salt, and stuff the mixture into the lemons. Put the lemons into a sterile narrow 12-ounce jelly jar. Cover them with the lemon juice, and cap the jar tightly with a nonreactive lid. Let the jar stand for 7 days, preferably in a sunny window.

2. On the eighth day, pour the juices from the jar into a nonreactive saucepan, pressing the lemons to extract more liquid. Add the sugar to the pan. Over low heat, bring the mixture to a simmer, stirring to dissolve the sugar. Add the lemons, and boil them gently for 10 minutes or until they are tender. Stir in the chile peppers.

3. Pack the lemons into a sterile pint jar, and cover the jar tightly with a non-reactive cap. Let the jar stand at room temperature for at least 1 month, then refrigerate the pickle if you don't eat it right away. Refrigerated, it will keep for months.

Makes 2 cups

Chapter 4

SAUERKRAUT, KIMCHI, AND OTHER CABBAGE PICKLES

SAUERKRAUT, KIMCHI, AND OTHER CABBAGE PICKLES

THIS CHAPTER CELEBRATES CABBAGE, that humble cool-weather vegetable that keeps people healthy through much of the world. Easy to grow and cheap to buy, cabbage comes in countless varieties. Whereas the other favorite pickling vegetable, the cucumber, has little nutritional value beyond its high water content, cabbage has fairly high levels of vitamin C—high enough to prevent scurvy in sailors—and some Asian cabbages are very rich in vitamin A.

When brined, cabbage is much more digestible than when fresh. Pickled cabbage assists in the digestion of other foods, too, and can be just as rich in vitamins as fresh cabbage. Cabbage kimchi, in fact, has much higher vitamin B levels than unfermented Chinese cabbage.

Along with the recipes for sauerkraut, kimchi, and other forms of brined cabbage, you'll find here a sampling of recipes for vinegar-pickled cabbage.

Although kimchi and Japanese salt-pickled cabbage shouldn't be canned, sauerkraut can be, and so can some cabbage-in-vinegar pickles. The recipes specify when canning is possible. See Chapter 1 for complete instructions on boiling-water processing.

SAUERKRAUT IN HISTORY

Sauerkraut has always been a health food. Because it contains high levels of vitamin C, European ships carried ample supplies to prevent scurvy among sailors before citrus fruits were available. On ship and shore, Europeans also appreciated sauerkraut for its mild laxative properties, especially in winter, when fresh produce was scarce. Some country people here in Oregon still eat a helping of sauerkraut every day, and believe it keeps them healthy.

It's no accident that we use a German name for fermented shredded cabbage; although sauerkraut is popular throughout most of Europe and North America, Germans have long loved it the most. They were fermenting cabbage in the early seventeenth century, and a hundred years later German immigrants were popularizing sauerkraut in America. Even today, 85 percent of Germany's cabbage crop goes into commercial sauerkraut production. So does 20 percent of the U.S. cabbage crop.

Sauerkraut with Juniper Berries

THE BASIC RECIPE for sauerkraut is very simple, since there are only two ingredients, cabbage and salt. Few Americans add anything else. In the past, though, added flavorings were common; juniper berries, caraway, bay, garlic, onions, and wine have all made sauerkraut more interesting, much as ginger, garlic, onions, and hot peppers flavor Korean cabbage kimchi. If you're going to the trouble of making your own kraut, you may well prefer to make it special.

In this recipe I call for juniper berries, whose balmy aroma and bittersweet flavor always remind me of the forest. Juniper berries aren't sold in many stores, but you can gather your own from wild or cultivated common juniper plants or order some from Penzeys (see page 367). Or you can leave them out, of course.

This recipe uses 15 pounds of cabbage, as much as will fit comfortably in a 3-gallon crock. If you want to make more or less sauerkraut, the adjustments are simple. Just use 3 tablespoons salt for each 5 pounds of cabbage. You can fit 5 pounds of cabbage in a 1-gallon jar, 25 pounds in a 5-gallon crock or bucket.

If you use fresh-picked cabbage, it will easily release enough liquid to cover itself. If the cabbage has been stored for a few weeks, though, you may have to add brine to the crock.

15 pounds trimmed fresh white head cabbage

9 tablespoons pickling salt

3 tablespoons juniper berries

1. Working with 5 pounds of cabbage at a time, quarter and core the heads. Shred the cabbage very thin, about the thickness of a quarter. You can use a kraut board, a meat slicer, or a kitchen knife for this purpose. (I don't recommend a food processor, which can easily turn cabbage to mush.) Add 3 tablespoons of the salt and 1 tablespoon of the juniper berries to the first 5 pounds of cabbage, and thoroughly mix the ingredients with your hands. (I do this right in the crock, but if you're going to ferment the cabbage in a gallon jar, do the mixing in a large bowl or nonreactive pot.) Pack the cabbage into the crock, bucket, or jar. When it has softened and released some liquid—as it probably will have done by the time you've shredded the next 5 pounds of cabbage—tamp it down very firmly, using a potato masher or your hands. Shred, mix, and pack the rest of the cabbage in the same way, 5 pounds at a time.

2. When all the cabbage is mixed and packed, weight it to keep it immersed in its brine and thereby protected from air. You can use a food-grade plastic bag (such as one meant for cooking a turkey in), or more than one bag, filled

NOTES ON FERMENTING SAUERKRAUT

Sauerkraut that ferments at cooler temperatures—65 degrees F or lower—has the best flavor and color and highest vitamin C levels. That's why most people make sauerkraut in the fall, using cabbage planted for late harvest. But fermentation is slow at low temperatures; at 60 degrees F, the curing may take 5 to 6 weeks. Sauerkraut fermented at 70 to 75 degrees, however, also has good flavor and is ready in only three weeks or so. Above 90 degrees F, the kraut will ferment in just eight to ten days, but most of the work will be done by homofermentative bacteria, which produce lactic acid but not acetic acid and other substances that contribute to the complex flavor of a really good sauerkraut. If the days are really hot, ferment the kraut in a cellar, an air-conditioned room, or another cool place. I've made good sauerkraut in 85- to 90-degree weather by using a stone crock set on a concrete floor in a dark corner of a shed.

Full-flavored sauerkraut ferments in stages: *Leuconostoc mesenteroides* produces carbon dioxide to create anaerobic conditions for *Lactobacillus plantarum*, which produces a lot of acids and removes a bitter-flavored compound (mannitol) produced by *Leuconostoc*. Other bacteria may contribute to the process, too, depending on temperature, salt concentration, and how long fermentation is allowed to continue. All this happens with remarkably little intervention on the part of the sauerkraut maker.

with brine in case of a leak. (I use three 1-gallon freezer bags, which I carefully place in a 3-gallon crock to seal out all air.) To make the brine, use 1½ tablespoons salt per 1 quart water. Or you can cover the cabbage with a pie plate or dinner plate a little smaller than the container opening, and top the plate with large, clean rocks or 2 or 3 quart jars filled with water. Some people cover the shredded cabbage with whole cabbage leaves before adding the plate; some use a clean piece of muslin or 2 layers of cheesecloth. This way, if the brine gets scummy you can replace the leaves or cloths with fresh ones instead of trying to skim off the scum. Cover the container with a towel or other cloth (I use a pillowcase). Put the container in a cool place.

3. Within 24 hours, the cabbage should be submerged in its own brine. If it isn't, dissolve 1½ tablespoons salt in 1 quart water, and pour enough of this over the cabbage to cover it. Check the sauerkraut once every day or two to see if scum has formed. If you do find scum, remove it, and wash the plate and weights.

4. Start tasting the sauerkraut after 2 weeks. It will be fully fermented in 2 to 4 weeks at 70 to 75 degrees F, or 5 to 6 weeks at 60 degrees F. It will be pale gold with a tart, full flavor. Within 2 days after fermentation is complete, little bubbles will have stopped rising to the surface.

5. When the sauerkraut is ready, you can store it in the refrigerator or another very cool place (at about 38 degrees F), tightly covered.

6. If you're lacking refrigerator space or another cold storage place, then can your kraut. Pack the cold sauerkraut and juices into pint or quart mason jars, leaving ½ inch headspace at the top of each jar. Close the jars with hot two-piece caps. In a boiling-water bath, process pint jars for 20 minutes, quart jars for 25 minutes. (Make sure the water in the canner isn't too hot when you add the jars, or they may break.)

7. Store the cooled jars in a cool, dry, dark place.

Makes 6 quarts

TROUBLESHOOTING GUIDE: SAUERKRAUT

Problem	Possible Causes
White scum on top	Yeast—the plate or brine bag did not exclude all air during fermentation. Skim off the scum daily.
Sliminess	The temperature was too high during fermentation, or the salt content was too low. Dump this batch.
Soft texture	Too little salt was used, the salting was uneven, fermentation temperatures were too high, or the kraut wasn't firmly packed in the crock.
Rot at the top	The plate or brine bag did not exclude all air during fermentation. Discard rotten kraut.
Mold on top	The fermentation temperature was too high, and the kraut wasn't well covered. Remove moldy kraut promptly.
Dark color at top	Oxidation—the salting was uneven, fermentation temperatures were too high, or the kraut was stored for too long or at too high a temperature. Discard the darkened kraut.
Pink color on top	Yeast. Too much salt was used, the salting was uneven, or the kraut wasn't well covered or weighted during fermentation. Skim off pink kraut.

Wine Kraut

WHEN MY HUSBAND took a taste of this kraut from the crock, he thought I had the wrong kind of fermentation going on. But the wine had just added its own complex flavors to that of the fermenting cabbage.

As with the basic kraut recipe, you can multiply or divide the quantities here to suit the amount of cabbage you have on hand. Leave out the caraway if you don't like it. You might instead try adding juniper berries or garlic.

---

15 pounds trimmed fresh white head cabbage

9 tablespoons pickling salt

6 teaspoons caraway seeds

1½ cups dry white wine

---

1. Working with 5 pounds of cabbage at a time, quarter and core the heads. Shred the cabbage very thin, about the thickness of a quarter.

2. Add 3 tablespoons of the salt and 2 teaspoons of the caraway seeds to the first 5 pounds of cabbage, and thoroughly mix the ingredients with your hands. Pack the cabbage into the crock, bucket, or jar. When it has softened and released some liquid—as it probably will have done by the time you've shredded the next 5 pounds of cabbage—tamp it down very firmly. Continue with the next 2 batches.

3. When all the cabbage is mixed and packed, weight it with a food-grade plastic bag, or more than one, filled with brine (to make the brine, use 1½ tablespoons salt per 1 quart water). Or cover the cabbage with a pie plate or dinner plate a little smaller than the container opening, and top the plate with large, clean rocks or 2 or 3 quart jars filled with water. Cover the container with a towel or pillowcase. Put the container in a cool place.

4. After 24 hours, remove the weights, and add the wine. Replace the weights. Check the sauerkraut once every day or two to see if scum has formed. If you do find scum, remove it, and wash the plate and weights.

5. Start tasting the sauerkraut after 2 weeks. The kraut will be fully fermented in 2 to 4 weeks at 70 to 75 degrees F, or 5 to 6 weeks at 60 degrees F. It will be pale gold with a tart, full flavor. Within 2 days after fermentation is complete, little bubbles will have stopped rising to the surface.

6. When the sauerkraut is ready, either store it in the refrigerator or another very cool place (at about 38 degrees F), tightly covered, or can it. Pack the cold sauerkraut and juices into pint or quart mason jars, leaving ½ inch headspace at the top of each jar, and close the jars with hot two-piece caps. In a boiling-water bath, process pint jars for 20 minutes, quart jars for 25 minutes. (Make sure the water in the canner isn't too hot when you add the jars, or they may break.)

7. Store the cooled jars in a cool, dry, dark place.

Makes 6 quarts

• • •

"Cold as kraut," say people in Appalachia, who traditionally stored their sauerkraut on the back porch through the winter.

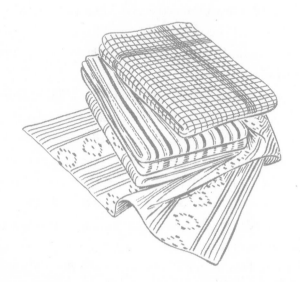

Russian Soured Cabbage

THIS RECIPE, BASED on one in Anne Volokh's book *The Art of Russian Cuisine* (1983), exemplifies the refinement of Russian pickling. The cabbage is fermented only four to five days with a little less salt than usual, in a sort of half-sour version of sauerkraut.

Sweet apple, darkly aromatic caraway, and tart, colorful cranberries all contribute to the beauty of the finished dish. Serve this kraut as a salad or as an accompaniment for pork, poultry, or game.

---

2 tablespoons pickling salt

5 pounds trimmed fresh white head cabbage, 2 outer leaves reserved,
    the rest shredded

2 medium carrots, coarsely grated

1 apple, cored and sliced into 16 wedges

¾ cup cranberries

2 tablespoons caraway seeds

For brine bag: 1½ tablespoons salt dissolved in 1 quart water

---

1. In a large bowl, mix the salt with the shredded cabbage, rubbing the salt into the cabbage with your hands. Gently mix in the carrots, apple, cranberries, and caraway seeds. Pack the mixture into a 1-gallon jar, pressing the cabbage down firmly. Add any liquid that accumulated in the bowl. Lay the reserved cabbage leaves on top.

2. Dissolve 1½ tablespoons salt in a quart of water. Push a freezer bag into the mouth of the jar, and fill it with brine. Seal the bag. Set the jar in a spot out of direct sunlight at a temperature of 65 to 72 degrees F. Two or three times a day during the next 2 or 3 days, push a long chopstick or the handle of a wooden spoon to the bottom of the jar to let gases escape.

3. Let the mixture ferment for 4 to 5 days, until the cabbage is as sour as you like. Remove the brine bag, cap the jar, and refrigerate it. The kraut should be ready to eat in 1 to 2 days. "For braising or for stuffing a goose," says Anne Volokh, "it should mature a little longer, about another week in the refrigerator."

Makes about 3 quarts

• • •

Except on grand occasions, when she entertained lavishly, Catherine the Great of Russia subsisted on sauerkraut, rye bread, black coffee, and rusks.

Turkish Pickled Cabbage

ALTHOUGH THIS PICKLE uses shredded white head cabbage, it is more like a typical kimchi than like sauerkraut, in both method and flavorings. The cabbage is briefly brined to reduce its volume, then fresh brine is added with the flavorings. These flavorings—garlic, ginger, and chile pepper—are very familiar to kimchi fans. The finished pickle is sour, hot, and spicy.

I've left out one distinctly Turkish ingredient, fresh chickpeas, since they are so rarely available in North America. If you happen to have a source for them, add a half cup along with the other flavorings.

2¾ pounds trimmed fresh white head cabbage, shredded

¼ cup pickling salt

2 tablespoons minced garlic

2 tablespoons minced fresh ginger

2 tablespoons hot pepper flakes

1 teaspoon sugar

3 cups water

1. In a large bowl, mix the cabbage with 2 tablespoons of the salt. Let the cabbage stand for 2 to 3 hours.

2. Drain and rinse the cabbage, and drain it again well. Mix it with the garlic, ginger, pepper flakes, and sugar. Pack the mixture into a 2-quart jar. Dissolve the remaining 2 tablespoons salt in the 3 cups water. Pour enough of the brine over the cabbage to cover it. Push a freezer bag into the mouth of the jar, and pour the remaining brine into the bag.

3. The next day and each day following, stir the cabbage briefly, then replace the brine bag. Seal the bag.

In 10 to 14 days, fermentation will have slowed and the pickled cabbage will be ready to eat.

4. Remove the brine bag, cap the jar tightly, and store it in the refrigerator. The cabbage will keep well for months.

Makes about 1 ½ quarts

Cabbage Kimchi

KOREANS ARE EVEN MORE ENTHUSIASTIC about their kimchi than Germans are about their sauerkraut. The favorite kimchi vegetable is Chinese (napa) cabbage. The Koreans ferment it in enormous quantities. They then pack the kimchi into huge earthenware jars, bury the jars in the ground up to the neck, and cover the lids with straw until the kimchi is needed.

Kimchi almost always includes hot pepper, usually dried and either ground or crushed into flakes. Because the ground dried hot pepper sold in Korean markets is generally fairly mild, Koreans can use generous quantities. Some of the Mexican (and New Mexican) ground peppers now sold in supermarkets are comparable. If you can't find ground pepper with a moderate heat level, you might combine sweet paprika and cayenne to suit your taste.

3 tablespoons plus 1 teaspoon pickling salt

6 cups water

2 pounds Chinese cabbage, cut into 2-inch squares

6 scallions, cut into 2-inch lengths, then slivered

1½ tablespoons minced fresh ginger

2 tablespoons Korean ground dried hot pepper (or other mildly hot
  ground red pepper)

1 teaspoon sugar

1. Dissolve the 3 tablespoons salt in the water. Put the cabbage into a large bowl, a crock, or a nonreactive pot, and pour the brine over it. Weight the cabbage down with a plate. Let the cabbage stand for 12 hours.

2. Drain the cabbage, reserving the brine. Mix the cabbage with the remaining ingredients, including the 1 teaspoon salt. Pack the mixture into a 2-quart jar. Pour enough of the reserved brine over the cabbage to cover it. Push a freezer bag into the mouth of the jar, and pour the remaining brine into the bag. Seal the bag. Let the kimchi ferment in a cool place, at a temperature no higher than 68 degrees F, for 3 to 6 days, until the kimchi is as sour as you like.

3. Remove the brine bag, and cap the jar tightly. Store the kimchi in the refrigerator, where it will keep for months.

Makes about 1½ quarts

THE KOREAN NATIONAL PASSION

Although kimchi is now sold in stores, in Korea most is still made at home. Every autumn, Korean women throughout the country rush to market to buy vegetables for pickle making. They use several kinds of vegetables, including daikon and turnips. In fact, Korean pickles come in so many types that a Seoul museum is entirely devoted to the subject; it features 160 different kinds of kimchi.

Koreans eat kimchi at every meal, including breakfast. At least one and preferably three or four kinds of kimchi are served among the *panchan*, or side dishes, at even a simple family dinner. Besides standing as dishes in their own right, kimchis are added to soups, stews, stir-fries, and pancakes. In winter, a Korean adult consumes as much as a half pound of kimchi per day.

Korean scientists have found that fresh cabbage kimchi is actually more nutritious than unfermented Chinese cabbage. When kimchi tastes best—before it becomes overly sour—its levels of vitamins B_1, B_2, B_{12}, and niacin are twice what they were initially, and its vitamin C level equals that of fresh cabbage. Scientists have also found that undesirable bacteria and parasites are destroyed during fermentation.

Cabbage and Radish Kimchi

DAIKON IS OFTEN COMBINED with cabbage in kimchi. The radish slices provide a pleasant crunch.

---

3 tablespoons pickling salt

5 cups water

1 pound Chinese cabbage, cut into 2-inch squares

1 pound daikon, cut in half lengthwise and sliced thin crosswise

1 ½ tablespoons minced fresh ginger

5 scallions, cut into thin rounds

1 ½ tablespoons Korean ground dried hot pepper (or other mildly hot ground red pepper)

1 teaspoon sugar

---

1. Dissolve 2 tablespoons plus 2 teaspoons of the salt in the water. Combine the vegetables in a large bowl, a crock, or a nonreactive pot, and cover them with the brine. Weight the vegetables down with a plate, and let them stand 12 hours.

2. Drain the vegetables, reserving the brine. Combine the vegetables with the remaining ingredients, including the remaining 1 teaspoon salt. Pack the mixture into a 2-quart jar. Pour enough of the reserved brine over the cabbage to cover it. Push a freezer bag into the mouth of the jar, and pour the remaining brine into the bag. Seal the bag. Let the kimchi ferment in a cool place, at a temperature no higher than 68 degrees F, for 3 to 6 days, until the kimchi is as sour as you like.

3. Remove the brine bag, cap the jar tightly, and store the kimchi in the refrigerator, where it will keep for months.

Makes about 1 ½ quarts

...

KIMCHI: KOREAN SAUERKRAUT?

Cabbage kimchi differs from sauerkraut in several ways. First, it is usually made from Chinese cabbage rather than white head cabbage, and it is heavily seasoned with hot pepper, ginger, and onions or garlic or both. Kimchi is also a little saltier than sauerkraut, and it's fermented for a much shorter period, so it doesn't get nearly so sour. Unfortunately, kimchi doesn't tolerate pasteurization well. It must be stored in the refrigerator or another dark, cool place.

Kimchi with Radish Juice and Onion

THIS KIMCHI IS UNUSUAL in a couple of ways. First, it's made not with ground hot pepper but with pepper flakes, which I think provide a prettier appearance. Second, the kimchi is never brined; instead, it's dry-salted initially, then moistened with daikon radish juice before it ferments.

3 tablespoons plus 1½ teaspoons pickling salt

2 pounds Chinese cabbage, cut into 2-inch squares

2 garlic cloves, chopped

One 1-inch piece fresh ginger, chopped

5 small dried chile peppers, chopped

¾ cup daikon juice (see Note)

2 scallions, cut into 2-inch lengths, then slivered

1 medium onion, cut into thin rings

1½ teaspoons sugar

1. In a large bowl, a crock, or a nonreactive pot, mix 3 tablespoons of the salt with the cabbage. Let the cabbage stand for 2 to 3 hours. Drain and rinse it, then drain it well again.

2. In a blender, grind the garlic, ginger, and peppers with the daikon juice. Add this mixture to the cabbage, then add the scallions, onion, sugar, and remaining 1½ teaspoons salt. Mix well. Pack the mixture into a 2-quart jar. Cover the vegetables with a plate slightly smaller than the container opening, and weight the plate with a quart jar filled with water. Or push a freezer bag into the mouth of the jar, fill it with brine made from 7 teaspoons salt per 1 quart of water, and seal it. Let the kimchi ferment in a cool place, at a temperature no higher than 68 degrees F, for 3 to 6 days, until the kimchi is as sour as you like.

3. Remove the brine bag, cap the jar tightly, and store the kimchi in the refrigerator, where it will keep for months.

Note: To make ¾ cup radish juice, grate 10 ounces of daikon fine, then squeeze the pulp to extract the liquid. You needn't strain it.

Makes about 1½ quarts

· · ·

MICROBE KILLERS FROM KIMCHI

The bacteria active in food fermentation produce *bacteriocins*—natural, narrow-spectrum antibiotics whose targets are often germs that cause food poisoning, such as *Listeria monocytogenes* and *Clostridium botulinum*. Now food scientists are scouting out these microbe killers, some of which survive boiling and freezing, and devising ways to use them in commercially prepared foods and their packaging. Having already mined yogurt, cheese, cured meats, and miso for their "biopreservatives," scientists will no doubt soon be extracting bacteriocins from brined cucumbers, kimchi, and sauerkraut.

Kimchi with Anchovies

KOREANS OFTEN FLAVOR and enrich their kimchi with seafood, such as dried shrimp or anchovies or even oysters. This recipe calls for canned anchovies; try to find some packed in a bland oil rather than olive oil. The anchovy flavor will get stronger as the kimchi ages.

Note that this is a quick kimchi, with no brine to mix. Because the fermentation takes so little time, you needn't bother weighting down the cabbage.

---

4 pounds Chinese cabbage, cut crosswise into 2-inch lengths
¼ pound daikon, halved or quartered lengthwise, then cut crosswise
⅛ inch thick
5 garlic cloves, minced
3 scallions, cut into 2-inch lengths and slivered
¼ cup pickling salt
3 tablespoons hot pepper flakes
I small can anchovies, sliced crosswise, with oil

---

1. In a large bowl, a crock, or a nonreactive pot, mix the cabbage and daikon. Add the remaining ingredients, and mix well. Cover the container with a towel, pillowcase, or loose-fitting lid, and let the kimchi ferment at room temperature for 2 days.

2. Pour the oil from the anchovies over the vegetables, add the anchovies, and mix well. Pack the kimchi into a 2-quart jar, and store the jar in the refrigerator. The kimchi will keep for at least 10 days.

Makes about 2 quarts

Kimuchi

Hᴇʀᴇ's ᴀ Jᴀᴘᴀɴᴇꜱᴇ ᴠᴇʀꜱɪᴏɴ of kimchi. I like this pickle for its pretty carrot slivers and the subtle sweetness provided by the apple. Eat kimuchi with rice, or as a snack with sake or beer.

2¼ pounds Chinese cabbage

3 tablespoons plus 1½ teaspoons pickling salt

1 medium carrot, sliced thin diagonally, then slivered

1 small apple, peeled and coarsely grated

3 scallions, cut into very thin rounds

2 teaspoons minced fresh ginger

1 garlic clove, minced

1 tablespoon Korean ground dried hot pepper (or other mildly hot
   ground red pepper)

1 cup water

1. Trim off the base of the cabbage, and remove the wilted outer leaves. Halve the cabbage lengthwise by slicing through only the base, then gently separating the leaves. In the same way, separate each half into 2 or 3 lengthwise wedges, each about 2 inches wide. Sprinkle the cabbage wedges with the 3 tablespoons salt. With your fingers, rub the salt into the cabbage leaves, especially the thick, white parts. Put the cabbage into a bowl, crock, or nonreactive pot, cover the cabbage with a plate, and weight the cabbage with a well-scrubbed rock or a quart jar filled with water. Press the cabbage for 8 to 10 hours.

2. Rinse and drain the cabbage, and gently squeeze each wedge to remove excess liquid. Cut the cabbage into 1-inch squares, and put them into a bowl. Mix in the carrot, apple, scallions, ginger, garlic, hot pepper, and remaining 1½ teaspoons salt. Pack the mixture into a 2-quart jar, and pour in the 1 cup water. Cap the jar loosely, and let the kimuchi ferment in a cool place for 3 to 6 days, until it is as sour as you like.

3. Cap the jar tightly, and store the kimuchi in the refrigerator.

Makes about 1½ quarts

• • •

A BEVY OF BRASSICAS

Asian cabbages come in many varieties, all of which can be pickled. The heading types—Chinese or napa cabbage—are favored for most kimchis, because they soften readily. Nichols, Territorial, and Johnny's all carry seeds of these types; varieties include wong bok, Takii's Spring, Nerva, Blues, Eiki, and China Express (see page 367). Nichols also carries seeds of Michihili, a kind of pe-tsai, or celery cabbage, with long, narrow heads; tah tsai, a beautiful, deep-green plant that spreads its spoon-shaped leaves in ground-hugging rosettes and self-sows like a weed in my garden; minato santo, a light-green, loose-headed cabbage with slightly curly, lettuce-like leaves that are unfortunately very susceptible to attacks by slugs and other pests; and several varieties of mustard and pak choi. The all-time favorite at my house is mei qing choy, a "baby" pak choi that is as delicious briefly soured, Japanese style, as it is gently pan-fried whole until tender.

Japanese Salt-Pickled Cabbage

Today the Japanese usually make pickles of this sort—*shio-zuke*, or salt pickles—in small plastic tubs with inner lids that screw down to press the vegetables inside. But you can use the same improvised equipment—plate and rock or water-filled jars in a crock or other container—that serves for other sorts of brining.

This delicate, lightly soured cabbage pickle is particularly simple to make. You can pickle cucumber halves (seeded, if they're large) in the same way.

---

2 pounds Chinese cabbage
1 ½ tablespoons pickling salt
1 small dried chile pepper
Zest of ½ lemon, in strips (optional)

---

1. Trim off the base of the cabbage, and remove and reserve the wilted outer leaves. Halve the cabbage lengthwise by slicing through only the base, then gently separating the leaves. In the same way, cut and separate each half into 2 or 3 lengthwise wedges, each about 2 inches wide. Lay the wedges on a tray or platter, and place this in a sunny window or in a greenhouse. Let the wedges wilt for 2 to 3 hours.

2. Sprinkle the cabbage wedges with the salt. With your fingers, rub the salt into the leaves, especially the thick, white parts. Lay the wedges in a Japanese pickle press, a crock, or a nonreactive bowl. Crumble the pepper, and sprinkle the seeds and broken pod over the cabbage. Sprinkle the lemon zest over all. Cover the cabbage with the wilted outer cabbage leaves.

3. If you're using a Japanese pickle press, screw the inner lid down hard for 5 to 6 hours. If you don't have one of these devices, cover the cabbage with a plate, then weight the plate heavily. You can use 3 quart jars filled with water, some well-scrubbed heavy rocks, or a plastic bag filled with gravel. Let the cabbage rest under its weights until it releases its liquid; this will take about 8 hours for a 10-pound weight.

4. Loosen the screw on the pickle press, or remove most of the weight on the cabbage. Let the pickle mature in its brine for 12 to 24 hours, until the brine is slightly sour. If you won't be serving all of the pickle immediately, pack it into a 1-quart jar, pour the brine over, and refrigerate the jar.

5. To serve the cabbage, rinse the wedges briefly under cold water, and squeeze out excess moisture. Cut the wedges into 1-inch lengths. Serve the pickle in small dishes, seasoned, if you like, with a few drops of soy sauce.

Makes 1 quart

• • •

THE JAPANESE PICKLE PRESS

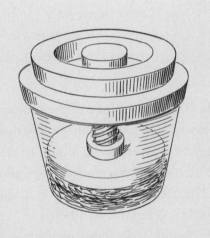

Like everything else in Japanese households, Japanese home pickling is always small in scale. Heavy crocks and rocks are no longer needed for salt-pickling, since a family usually has a special little plastic container that does the same job. Called a *shokutaku tsukémono ki*, this tub has an inner lid that screws down to quickly press the brine out of vegetables. In the United States, you can probably buy such a pickle press at a Japanese market (not just any Asian grocery) for about thirty dollars.

Lemony Pickled Cabbage

CABBAGE AND LEMON, I believe, are as beautifully matched in their flavors as cucumber and dill. Here lemon juice as well as zest gently flavor a simple quick pickle from Japan.

2 pounds Chinese cabbage

1½ tablespoons pickling salt

1 small dried chile pepper

Zest of 1 small lemon, in strips

6 tablespoons rice vinegar

5 teaspoons lemon juice

1½ teaspoons mirin (sweet rice wine)

1½ teaspoons light Japanese soy sauce

1. Trim off the base of the cabbage, and remove and reserve the wilted outer leaves. Halve the cabbage lengthwise by slicing through only the base, then gently separating the leaves. In the same way, cut and separate each half into 2 or 3 lengthwise wedges, each about 2 inches wide. Lay the wedges on a tray or platter, and place this in a sunny window or in a greenhouse. Let the wedges wilt for 2 to 3 hours.

2. Sprinkle the cabbage wedges with the salt. Using your fingers, rub the salt into the leaves, especially the thick, white parts. Lay the wedges in a Japanese pickle press, a crock, or a nonreactive bowl. Crumble the pepper, and sprinkle the seeds and broken pod over the cabbage. Sprinkle the lemon zest over all. Cover the cabbage with the wilted outer cabbage leaves.

3. If you're using a Japanese pickle press, screw the inner lid down hard for 5 to 6 hours. If you don't have one of these devices, cover the cabbage with a plate, then weight the plate heavily. You can use 3 quart jars filled with water, some well-scrubbed heavy rocks, or a plastic bag filled with gravel. Let the cabbage rest under its weights until it releases its liquid, about 8 to 12 hours.

4. Squeeze the cabbage wedges, reserving the brine. Pack the wedges into a 1-quart jar. Combine the brine with the vinegar, lemon juice, mirin, and soy sauce, and pour this liquid over the cabbage wedges. Close the jar, and let the pickle mature at room temperature for 2 to 5 hours.

5. Refrigerate the pickle if you won't be serving it immediately. It will keep in the refrigerator for about 2 weeks.

6. To serve the cabbage, squeeze the excess moisture out of each wedge, and cut the wedge into 1-inch lengths. Serve the pickle in small dishes, seasoned, if you like, with a drop or two of soy sauce.

Makes 1 quart

Pickled Red Cabbage

IN ENGLAND, RED CABBAGE is traditionally pickled with vinegar, as in this recipe. You can substitute white cabbage; just use white wine vinegar in place of red.

Canning the cabbage with a boiling-water bath is, of course, a modern twist on the traditional recipe. If you want to forego this step, let the cabbage dry in the sun for two to three hours before tossing it with the salt. Cover the cabbage well with the flavored vinegar, and cap the jars tightly. Store them in a cool place.

2¼ pounds trimmed red cabbage, shredded

1 tablespoon pickling salt

½ teaspoon whole cloves

½ teaspoon blade mace, preferably, or small pieces of nutmeg

½ teaspoon whole allspice

½ teaspoon black peppercorns

½ teaspoon celery seeds

One 1-inch cinnamon stick
1⅓ cups red wine vinegar
¼ cup brown sugar
4 teaspoons yellow mustard seeds

1. In a large bowl or crock, toss the cabbage with the salt. Cover the container, and let it stand in a cool place for 8 to 12 hours.

2. In a nonreactive saucepan, combine the vinegar, the sugar, and the mustard seeds. Tie the other spices in a spice bag or scrap of cheesecloth, and add them to the saucepan. Bring the contents to a boil, and simmer 5 minutes. Let the liquid cool.

3. Drain the cabbage thoroughly, then pack it into pint mason jars. Pour the cooled liquid over the cabbage. (If you don't have quite enough liquid, divide what you have between the jars, then top them off with vinegar.) Close the jars with hot two-piece caps.

4. Process the jars for 20 minutes in a boiling-water bath.

5. Store the cooled jars in a cool, dry, dark place for at least 3 weeks before eating the cabbage.

Makes 2 pints

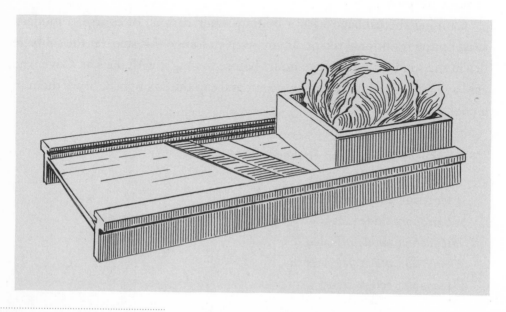

Pickled Cabbage and Peppers

IN THIS RECIPE, white cabbage and sweet peppers are combined in a crisp and colorful vinegar pickle.

2 pounds trimmed fresh white head cabbage, shredded

5 cups green or red (or mixed green and red) bell peppers, cut
   into thin strips

¼ cup pickling salt

1 cup sugar

1½ cups white wine vinegar

½ teaspoon hot pepper flakes

4 teaspoons black mustard seeds

6 garlic cloves, minced

1. In a large bowl or crock, toss the cabbage and peppers with the salt. Cover the container, and let it stand in a cool place 8 to 12 hours.

. . .

REVIVING THE KRAUT BOARD

The traditional tool for shredding cabbage is a kraut board (opposite), also known as a mandoline (pronounced "mandolin"). Today most mandolines sold in stores and catalogs are expensive, plastic versions of their wood-and-metal predecessors. You can still buy the real thing, though, without haunting antique stores. Lehman's Hardware, Cumberland General Store, and Johnny's Selected Seeds all carry a model made in Austria (where it's called a *krauthobel*) of hardwood with stainless-steel blades. Cumberland also carries a smaller, cheaper model. (See page 367.)

2. In a nonreactive saucepan, combine the sugar and vinegar. Bring the mixture to a boil, then let it cool.

3. Rinse the cabbage, and drain it well. Toss it with the pepper flakes, mustard seeds, and garlic. Pack the vegetable mixture loosely into pint mason jars. Pour the vinegar mixture over the vegetables. Close the jars with hot two-piece caps.

4. Process the jars for 20 minutes in a boiling-water bath.

5. Store the cooled jars in a cool, dry, dark place for at least 3 weeks before eating the cabbage.

Makes 4 pints

Cortido

THIS FRESH CABBAGE PICKLE comes from El Salvador. Serve it as a salad, like cole slaw.

1½ pounds trimmed fresh white head cabbage, cored and shredded

1 small red onion, halved and sliced very thin

1 medium carrot, cut thin diagonally, then slivered

2 garlic cloves, minced

¾ teaspoon pickling salt

2 to 3 pinches coarse-ground black pepper

½ cup white wine vinegar

¼ cup pineapple juice

---

1. In a large bowl, toss together the cabbage, onion, carrot, garlic, salt, and pepper. Combine the vinegar and pineapple juice, and pour the liquid over the vegetables. Mix well.

2. Pack the mixture into a jar or plastic tub, cover the container tightly, and refrigerate it for at least 12 hours. During this period, occasionally stir the mixture or shake the container.

The pickled cabbage will keep well, covered and refrigerated, for at least 4 days.

Makes about 6 cups

RICE-BRAN, MISO, AND SOY-SAUCE PICKLES

RICE-BRAN, MISO,
AND SOY-SAUCE PICKLES

WITH THE EXCEPTION of the pickled garlic and ginger, all of the pickles in this chapter are Japanese. Pickles are of paramount importance in the traditional Japanese diet. They are eaten at every meal, and are sometimes the *only* food at a meal besides rice. When other dishes are served, pickles always conclude the meal, along with hot rice and tea.

Japanese pickling methods are impressively varied. Recipes for Japanese dry-salted, pressed pickles appear in Chapter 4 and Chapter 7. Recipes for some Japanese vinegar pickles appear in Chapter 3. In this chapter, I describe three other kinds of Japanese pickles: *nukamiso* pickles, briefly soured in rice-bran mash; miso pickles, flavored in fermented soybean paste; and *shoyu* pickles, made with soy sauce. The Chinese and Koreans also make soy-sauce pickles, and a few of their recipes are included here. But the rice-bran and miso pickles are uniquely Japanese.

Today the Japanese usually pickle foods not to preserve them for long periods, but to enhance their flavor, digestibility, and nutritional value. So these recipes call for small quantities of vegetables and short pickling times, from a few hours to a few days. If you garden year-round or if you regularly visit a good year-round produce market, some of these pickles may turn out to be your favorites.

• • •

INGREDIENTS FOR YOUR NUKAMISO POT

Rice bran, or nuka, looks very much like wheat bran. In Japanese markets and some natural foods stores, nuka is sold in 2-pound packages, just the amount you'll need for pickling. If you can't find rice bran, use wheat bran. Shizuo Tsuji (*Japanese Cooking*, 1980) claims that even oatmeal or cornflakes will work in nukamiso.

Often added to nukamiso is either beer or *koji*, grain (usually rice) inoculated with *Aspergillus* mold. You can find koji at Japanese markets; some natural foods stores carry it, too. Koji must be kept refrigerated.

For a touch of sweetness and to balance the moisture content, dried kombu, or kelp, is always added to the nukamiso pot. You can buy kombu at a Japanese market or natural foods store.

Pickles in Rice-Bran Mash

EVERY JAPANESE HOME once had a barrel of *nukamiso*, or fermenting rice-bran mash, often stored under the floor boards. Each day, the family would fish pickled vegetables out of the mash, rinse them, and eat them at the end of a meal or with tea and rice alone. Fresh vegetables would be buried in the mash to become the next day's pickles.

Mild and delectable, rice-bran pickles are also very healthful. Like other fermented pickles that haven't been pasteurized, they are full of *Lactobacilli* bacteria, which aid in digestion. And because rice bran contains high levels of niacin, vitamin B_1, linoleic acid, and vitamin E, so do rice-bran pickles.

Nukamiso is usually made in spring, summer, or fall, because fermentation gets under way more quickly and reliably in warmer weather. The mash requires a 7- to 10-day conditioning period, during which you must feed it with vegetable scraps.

---

2 pounds nuka *(rice bran)*

¾ cup pickling salt

3 dried chile peppers, seeded and broken

One 1-inch piece fresh ginger

Two 5-inch strips dried kombu *(kelp)*, cut into small pieces

1½ cups koji *(Aspergillus-inoculated rice)*, soaked in lukewarm water
    just to cover for 15 minutes *(optional)*

2 cups water, if you're using koji, or 1 cup water and 1 cup beer

Vegetables for pickling, whole or in large pieces: cucumbers, carrots,
    Chinese cabbage, daikon, radishes, turnips, celery, green pepper

---

1. In a 1-gallon crock or similar container, combine the nuka, salt, peppers, ginger, and kombu. Add the soaked koji and water, or the 1 cup water and 1 cup beer. Using your hands, mix well. Bury 2 or 3 vegetables or vegetable pieces in the mash; use wilted vegetables or unwaxed peels, if possible, since you're going to discard them. The vegetables should not touch one another. Cover the crock, and set it in a place where the temperature stays at about 60 to 70 degrees F.

2. After 24 hours, remove and discard the vegetables. Mix the nukamiso well, and add more wilted vegetables or scraps. Do this every day for 6 days more.

3. After a week, the nukamiso should be getting smelly. The odor should improve after you stir the mash. Start tasting the pickles, if you haven't already. Rinse them first in cold water. When the mash is ready, the pickles will taste pleasingly salty, crunchy, and a little tangy, with an earthy aftertaste. Rinse, drain, and slice the pickles before serving them.

4. Continue to stir the mash every day, even if you have no vegetables in it. You can leave vegetables in longer than a day—even as long as a month, if you like strong-flavored pickles—but don't neglect to stir the nukamiso.

When the nukamiso has absorbed too much water from the vegetables, sink a small bowl or cup into the center of the mash, and let the excess liquid collect there. Remove the cup and liquid the next day.

Since some of the mash will adhere to the pickles when they're taken from the crock, the mash will gradually diminish in volume. To replenish it, add 3 tablespoons salt to ½ pound rice bran, and discard the next day's pickles. If the volume isn't decreasing much, remove and replace half the mash every 30 days.

Makes about 2 quarts

Daikon Pickled in Sweet Miso

BY SIMPLY COVERING VEGETABLES in miso for a day or two, you can make the tasty, nutritious pickles called *miso-zuke*. The easiest way to make them is to submerge the vegetables in a bowl of miso, but this technique uses a lot of miso and necessitates rinsing the vegetables before eating them. The technique I describe here, using cheesecloth, requires less miso and keeps it from clinging to the vegetables.

This recipe uses the light-colored miso that is often labeled "sweet" or "mellow." It has less salt and more carbohydrates than darker misos.

> I pound daikon, cut into 2-by-½-by-½-inch sticks, or small whole white
>   radishes
> ¾ teaspoon salt
> ½ cup white or yellow miso

1. In a bowl, toss the daikon or small radishes with the salt. Let the contents stand for 1 hour or more.
2. Drain the daikon or small radishes. Spread ¼ cup miso over a dinner plate,

then cover the plate with a piece of cheesecloth. Spread the daikon or small radishes in a single layer on top. Cover the vegetables with another piece of cheesecloth, and spread the remaining miso on top. Cover the whole plate with plastic wrap, and refrigerate the plate for 2 to 4 days.

3. Remove the plastic wrap and the top layer of cheesecloth. The pickles are ready to serve. Leftover pickles can be stored in the miso, but their flavor will grow stronger with time.

Although the liquid from the vegetables will dilute the miso, you can reuse it 2 or 3 times.

Makes about 1 pint

. . .

ABOUT MISO

Miso is a thick, protein-rich paste made from fermented soybeans. Like wine and beer, miso comes in many varieties, from sweet and light-colored to salty and dark.

To make miso, *koji*—grain or beans inoculated with *Aspergillus* mold—is mixed with cooked soybeans, salt, and water. The type of koji—rice, barley, or soybean—partly determines the flavor of the finished miso. Along with microorganisms from the environment, koji breaks down the beans and grains into readily digestible amino acids, fatty acids, and simple sugars. Unpasteurized miso is not only easy to digest, but it helps break down other foods in the digestive system, and can be used as a meat tenderizer.

Although much Japanese miso is now quick-fermented in a tempera-ture-controlled process, resulting in inferior flavor, American natural foods stores stock naturally aged (although pasteurized) misos of excel-lent quality. Many natural foods stores carry three or more varieties, any of which can be used for pickling.

Store miso in the refrigerator, where it will keep well for at least a year.

Celery in Red Miso

MEDIUM-SALTY RED MISO is here mellowed with the additions of sake and mirin. As with any miso pickle, you can vary the vegetables. Try daikon, sliced kohlrabi, very small turnips, or larger turnips, quartered or sliced. I particularly like celery in this recipe.

½ cup red miso
2 tablespoons sake (dry rice wine)
1 tablespoon mirin (sweet rice wine)
4 celery stalks, halved lengthwise, then cut into 3-inch lengths

1. In a bowl, mix together the miso, sake, and mirin to make the *miso-doko*. Spread ¼ cup of this pickling paste over a dinner plate, then cover the plate with a piece of cheesecloth. Spread the celery in a single layer on top. Cover the celery with another piece of cheesecloth, and spread the remaining pickling paste on top of that. Cover the whole plate with plastic wrap, and refrigerate it for about 6 hours. (Denser vegetables will need longer pickling.)
2. Remove the plastic wrap and the top layer of cheesecloth. Serve the celery sticks whole or cut into bite-sized pieces. Leftover celery can be stored in the pickling paste, but the pickles will get darker and saltier over time.

You can use the miso-doko in miso soup.

Makes about 1 pint

Turnip or Kohlrabi Pickles in Two Misos

HERE THE MISO-DOKO, or miso pickling paste, is made from medium-salty red and sweet white rice misos, a combination suggested by Jan and John Belleme (*Cooking with Japanese Foods*, 1986). Barley miso and mellow barley miso, say the Bellemes, also combine well in miso-doko.

¼ cup red miso
¼ cup white miso
1 pound turnips or kohlrabi, or some of each, peeled and sliced ½ inch
*   thick*

1. In a small bowl, blend the two kinds of miso. Spread ¼ cup of the mixture over a dinner plate, then cover the plate with a piece of cheesecloth. Spread the vegetables in a single layer on top. Cover the vegetables with another piece of cheesecloth, and spread the remaining miso on top of that. Cover the whole plate with plastic wrap, and refrigerate the plate for 3 days.
2. Remove the plastic wrap and the top layer of cheesecloth. The pickles are ready to eat. Leftover pickles can be stored in the miso, but they will get darker and saltier with time.

Although the liquid from the vegetables will dilute the miso, you can reuse it 2 or 3 times.

Makes about 1 pint

Korean Pickled Garlic

IN THIS RECIPE, the entire garlic bulb is pickled and eaten, so you will need to use spring garlic—bulbs which are nearly full in size, but not yet covered with papery skin. Their tops won't have yellowed or bent over yet.

The easiest way to obtain spring garlic bulbs is to grow your own (or make friends with a garlic farmer). You can start by planting cloves from the grocery store, although special varieties are available from seed companies. Set the cloves flat end down, 4 inches apart. Just a 3-by-3-foot patch will yield about 18 pounds of garlic bulbs in as few as 90 days. The bulbs will probably grow bigger if you plant them in autumn, but in most areas garlic does well enough when planted in early spring.

Serve this pickle as a side dish for a Korean or Japanese meal.

---

2 spring garlic bulbs

½ cup soy sauce

½ cup rice vinegar

2 tablespoons sugar

½ teaspoon pickling salt

---

1. Put the garlic into a small jar or bowl. Stir together the remaining ingredients, and pour them over the garlic. Cover the container, and let it stand for 3 days.

2. Pack the garlic into a 1-cup jar (a rounded half-pint mason jar works well). Pour the liquid into a small, nonreactive saucepan, and bring the liquid to a boil. Reduce the heat, and simmer the liquid, uncovered, until it is reduced by half. Let it cool.

3. Pour the liquid over the garlic, and cap the jar. Let the jar stand in a cool place for 4 weeks or more. Before serving, slice the garlic bulbs crosswise into 3 rounds per bulb.

The pickle should keep for 1 year or longer in a cool, dry, dark place.

Makes 1 half-pint

...

A QUICK WAY TO PEEL GARLIC

No matter what kind of garlic pickle you're making, the only really time-consuming part of the job is peeling the garlic cloves. But this task can be quick, easy, and fun if you use an E-Z-Rol Garlic Peeler. You put a clove of garlic into this rubber tube, roll the tube on a hard surface, and the garlic clove pops out of its skin. Designed by Ben Omessi, the tube can be washed in a dishwasher. You can buy an E-Z-Rol Garlic Peeler from a cookware store for about eight dollars.

Mrs. Kim's Pickled Garlic

A Korean-Californian who has run a Greek restaurant and a hotdog stand as well as Asian restaurants, Mrs. Kim pickles garlic using mature bulbs. Her son Michael sent me this recipe, along with a big jar of his mother's pickled garlic.

3 to 4 garlic bulbs with small to medium cloves
½ to ⅔ cup brown rice vinegar (see Note)
2 to 3 tablespoons brown sugar
2 to 3 tablespoons soy sauce

1. Separate and peel the garlic cloves. Put them into a jar, and cover them with the vinegar. Cap the jar, and let it stand at room temperature for 1 week.
2. Pour half the vinegar out of the jar (you can use it for dressing salads or making quick pickles). Add the brown sugar and soy sauce, cap the jar, and

shake it to mix the ingredients and dissolve the sugar. Store the jar in the refrigerator.

The garlic will be ready to eat after 1 week. Refrigerated, it will keep for at least 1 year.

Note: Brown rice vinegar is available in Korean markets and natural foods stores.

Makes ½ to ⅔ cup

Ginger Pickled in Soy Sauce

WHEN FRESH YOUNG GINGER comes on the market—with skin so thin it tends to rub off—be sure to pickle some. These young roots, usually available in December, are much less fibrous than older ones.

I think of this Chinese pickle as a seasoning rather than a condiment. I use it in Chinese- and Japanese-style dishes when I have no fresh ginger in the house.

2 ounces young, thin-skinned fresh ginger, sliced paper-thin
½ teaspoon sugar
¼ teaspoon pickling salt
About 5 tablespoons light soy sauce

1. In a bowl, toss the ginger with the sugar and salt. Let the mixture stand for 1 hour.

2. Put the ginger into a small jar. Pour over the ginger enough soy sauce to cover it, and cap the jar. Let the jar stand at room temperature. The ginger will be ready to use in 24 hours.

Store the jar in the refrigerator, where the ginger will keep for 1 year or longer.

Makes about ½ cup

Daikon Pickled in Soy Sauce

HERE IS THE PUREST sort of *shoyu* (soy sauce) pickle, in which the soy sauce alone seasons the vegetable. I think you'll agree that no other flavoring is needed.

1 pound daikon
½ cup light Japanese soy sauce

1. Cut the daikon into ¼-inch-thick rounds (or half-rounds or quarter-rounds, depending on the thickness of the radish). Pack the daikon pieces into a jar, and pour the soy sauce over them. Cap the jar, and refrigerate it. After several hours, the soy sauce should almost cover the daikon. Keep the jar in the refrigerator for at least 24 hours, shaking it occasionally.
2. If you don't eat the pickle immediately, store it in the refrigerator for up to 1 week.

Makes about 1 pint

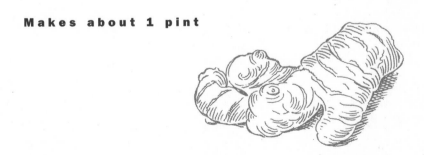

Cucumber Pickled in Soy Sauce with Kombu

KOMBU (OR KONBU) is kelp, sold dried and packaged in natural foods stores and many Asian markets. The seaweed adds a subtle sweetness to this quick Japanese pickle. For variety, add a carrot, cut into matchstick strips.

I pound Asian or pickling cucumbers, about ¾ inch in diameter
I teaspoon pickling salt
One 2-inch piece dried kombu, cut with scissors into very thin strips
I fresh chile pepper, such as jalapeño, cut into thin rings
½ cup light Japanese soy sauce

1. Gently wash the cucumbers, and remove their blossom ends. Halve them lengthwise, then cut them crosswise into ½-inch-thick pieces. In a bowl, toss the cucumbers with the salt. Let them stand at room temperature for about 1 hour.

2. Rinse the cucumbers, and drain them well. Mix them with the remaining ingredients. Let the mixture stand at room temperature for 6 to 10 hours, stirring occasionally.

If the pickles aren't to be eaten right away, store them in the refrigerator, where they should keep for about 1 week.

You can reuse the pickling liquid 2 or 3 times if you keep it refrigerated.

Makes about 1 pint

COMMERCIAL JAPANESE PICKLES

In Japan, pickling isn't just a homemaker's art—it's also a big business. Since some pickling processes are carefully guarded secrets or just very complicated and time-consuming, they are the province of pickling specialists. If you visit a large Japanese grocery, you'll see dozens of kinds of pickles, or even hundreds, packed in jars, or, more often, in vacuum-sealed plastic bags. Check the labels before buying any; many will be adulterated with dyes or other chemicals. But you'll also find some traditional Japanese pickles that you won't be able to make at home. Here are a few examples:

Umeboshi. These are salt-pickled *ume*, a fruit related to the apricot but in English called a plum. Picked underripe, the fruits are brined with leaves of red shiso (or perilla, or beefsteak plant, an annual herb whose seeds are sold by Nichols, Johnny's, and Shepherd's; see page 367). The fruits are then sun-dried, and later brined again. *Umeboshi* are used medicinally to treat all kinds of stomach disorders and to fortify the liver and kidneys. Added to rice gruel, umeboshi is the Japanese mother's cure-all.

Takuan. Developed by vegetarian monks during Japan's feudal period, *takuan* is daikon partially dried in the shade, then fermented in rice bran. Real takuan is usually a pale yellow color; bright yellow takuan is probably dyed with chemicals.

Nara-zuke. "The pickles of Nara" (a cultural center near Kyoto) are matured for several years in a malty yeast paste. The favorite vegetables for this pickle are *shiro uri*, a zucchini-like vegetable, and small, round eggplants. Before eating *nara-zuke* pickles, rinse off any excess pickling paste, and pat the pickles dry.

Cucumber and Eggplant Pickled in Soy Sauce

HERE'S A PICKLE you can start making just three hours before you serve it.

---

2 small Japanese eggplants (or any small, slender eggplants)
Two 4-inch pickling cucumbers
One 2-inch piece dried kombu (kelp)
¾ cup Japanese soy sauce
1 tablespoon sake (dry rice wine)

---

1. Wash the eggplants, and halve them lengthwise. Slash the halves diagonally from the skin side, making many close cuts. Put the eggplants into a small bowl, cover them with cold water, and let them soak for 30 minutes. Meanwhile, gently wash the cucumbers, and remove the blossom ends. Slash the cucumbers diagonally, making many close cuts.

2. Drain the eggplants, then cut both the eggplants and the cucumbers into ¾-inch pieces. In a jar, combine the vegetables, kombu, soy sauce, and sake. Cover the jar, and shake it gently. Let the jar stand at room temperature for 2 hours, giving it a shake or two during this period.

If you don't eat all the pickle immediately, store it in the refrigerator for up to 1 week.

Makes about 1 pint

Pickled Cucumbers with Sesame Oil

WITH ITS STRONG FLAVORS of sesame, ginger, and hot pepper, this Japanese pickle shows a Chinese influence.

1 pound Asian or pickling cucumbers, about ¾ inch in diameter

1 teaspoon pickling salt

1 scallion, cut into 1-inch lengths, then slivered

One 1-inch piece fresh ginger, slivered

1 to 2 fresh chile peppers, such as jalapeño, seeded and slivered

3 tablespoons rice vinegar

5 tablespoons soy sauce

1 tablespoon sesame oil

1. Gently wash the cucumbers, and remove the blossom ends. Halve the cucumbers lengthwise, then cut them into 1-inch-long pieces. In a bowl, toss the cut cucumbers with the salt. Let them stand 1 hour.

2. Drain the cucumbers, and return them to the bowl. Mix them with the scallion, ginger, and peppers. In a small bowl, stir together the rice vinegar, soy sauce, and sesame oil, and pour this mixture over the cucumbers. Cover the bowl with plastic wrap. Let the pickle stand at room temperature for 2 to 3 hours, or in the refrigerator for 24 hours, turning the cucumbers occasionally.

The pickle will keep in the refrigerator, well covered, for about 1 week.

Makes about 1 pint

Kombu and Carrot Pickle

THE PLENTIFUL PICKLING liquid here makes a tasty seasoning for rice.

Four 6-inch strips dried kombu (kelp), soaked in water 10 minutes
2 large carrots, cut thin diagonally, then slivered
½ cup rice vinegar
½ cup soy sauce
½ cup mirin (sweet rice wine)
¼ cup sake (dry rice wine)

1. Slice the soaked kombu strips in half lengthwise, then cut them crosswise into thin strips. Combine the kombu and carrot strips in a bowl.

2. In a nonreactive saucepan, bring the vinegar, soy sauce, mirin, and sake to a boil. Boil the liquid for 1 minute, then immediately pour it over the carrot and kombu, and cover the bowl with a towel. Let the pickle stand at room temperature for about 4 hours before serving it.

Refrigerated, the pickle will keep for about 1 week.

Makes about 2½ cups

Chapter 6

SWEET PICKLES

SWEET PICKLES

MORE LIKE SWEET PRESERVES than like sour fresh or brined pickles, the pickles in this chapter are traditionally eaten with meats. Any of them can make a delightful accompaniment to a holiday roast. Try them also with grilled meats, and, if you're not a big meat eater, with rice and other grain dishes. You might like these pickles on their own, too. My children love pickled plums, pears, apricots, and watermelon rind for dessert, and I snack on pickled oranges.

Because of the high sugar content as well as the vinegar, these pickles are very well preserved. In most cases, though, I still recommend using a boiling-water bath, which helps to ensure a good seal. Where a boiling-water bath might harm the pickle's texture, the open-kettle method will do. With this method, remember, you must use sterile (boiled) jars and very hot (but not boiled) lids, and the pickle must be very hot when placed in the jars. Jars that aren't vacuum-sealed should be stored in the refrigerator. (Check for a vacuum seal on cooled jars by pressing down on the center of each lid. It should not pop up.)

Sweet Gherkin Pickles

IN THIS CLASSIC RECIPE, the salt, sugar, and vinegar are added in several steps to keep the cucumbers from shriveling. You can use American-style pickling cucumbers, European gherkins (cornichons), or West Indian gherkins; just be sure your cucumbers are very small. Leave a bit of stem attached to each one, and wash the cucumbers very gently. Lightly rub off the prickles if you're using cornichons; leave the prickles in place if you're using American-style cucumbers. Scrape off the blossom ends. Since little cucumbers deteriorate quickly, begin processing them within a half day after picking.

7 pounds 1- to 2-inch-long pickling cucumbers

½ cup pickling salt

18 quarts boiling water (you'll use 6 quarts at a time)

6 cups distilled white vinegar

8 cups sugar

1 teaspoon ground turmeric

2 teaspoons celery seeds

2 teaspoons mixed pickling spice

Two 4-inch cinnamon sticks

½ teaspoon fennel seeds

1. Gently wash the cucumbers, and remove the blossom ends. Put the cucumbers into a large bowl or crock, and cover them with 6 quarts boiling water. Let them stand for 6 to 8 hours.

2. Drain the water from the cucumbers. Dissolve ¼ cup of the salt in 6 quarts boiling water, and pour this over the cucumbers. Let them stand 6 to 12 hours, then repeat this step.

3. Drain the water from the cucumbers, and stab each once with a table fork. In a nonreactive pot, bring to a boil 3 cups of the vinegar, 3 cups of the sugar, and the spices, stirring to dissolve the sugar. Pour the syrup over the cucumbers. Let them stand 6 to 8 hours.

4. Strain the syrup into the pot. Add 2 cups sugar and 2 cups vinegar, and bring the syrup to a boil. Pour it over the cucumbers. Let them stand 6 to 8 hours.

5. Strain the syrup into the pot again. Add 2 cups sugar and 1 cup vinegar. Bring the syrup to a boil, and pour it over the cucumbers. Let them stand 6 to 8 hours.

6. One last time, strain the syrup into the pot. Pack the pickles into sterile pint or half-pint mason jars. Add 1 cup sugar to the syrup, and bring it to a boil. Cover the pickles with the boiling syrup, dividing the spices evenly among the jars and leaving ½ inch headspace. Close the jars with hot two-piece caps. To ensure a good seal, process the jars for 5 minutes in a boiling-water bath.

7. Store the cooled jars in a cool, dry, dark place for at least 3 weeks before eating the pickles.

Makes 6 to 7 pints

• • •

"Bad dinners go hand in hand with total depravity, while a properly fed man is already half saved."

—Buckeye Cookery and Practical Housekeeping *(1877)*

Sweet Slices
from Brined Cucumbers

THIS RECIPE TURNS fermented cucumbers into sweet, tart, spicy slices. If you prefer, cut the fermented cucumbers into sticks or chunks instead of thin slices.

2 cups water

2 cups distilled white vinegar

3 pounds fermented cucumbers (see Chapter 2), rinsed, drained,
    and sliced ¼ inch thick

2 cups sugar

I lemon, sliced thin

One I-inch piece fresh ginger, chopped

2 teaspoons whole cloves

Two 4-inch cinnamon sticks

1. Combine the water and 1 cup of the vinegar. Pour this liquid over the cucumbers. Let the cucumbers soak for 2 hours.

Stir in the remaining 1 cup vinegar. Let the cucumbers soak 2 hours more.

2. Put the cucumbers and their liquid into a nonreactive pot. Add the sugar, the lemon, and the ginger and dry spices tied in a spice bag or scrap of cheesecloth. Bring the ingredients to a boil, stirring to dissolve the sugar, then reduce the heat. Simmer the cucumbers until they are translucent, about 5 minutes.

3. Transfer the cucumbers and their liquid to a shallow nonreactive container. Let them stand overnight to plump.

4. Strain the liquid into a saucepan. Pack the cucumbers—and, if you wish, the lemon slices—into pint mason jars. Bring the liquid to a boil, and pour it over the cucumbers, leaving ½ inch headspace. Close the jars with hot two-piece caps. To ensure a good seal, process the jars for 15 minutes in a boiling-water bath.

5. Store the cooled jars in a cool, dry, dark place for at least 3 weeks before eating the pickles.

Makes about 5 pints

Sweet Whole Pickles from Brined Cucumbers

HERE'S ANOTHER WAY to make excellent sweet pickles from cucumbers you've already brined. Traditionally "salt-stock" cucumbers are used—those fermented in a 10 percent brine—but pickles from a 5 percent brine work just as well and require no soaking in fresh water.

3 pounds fermented cucumbers (see Chapter 2), about 3 inches long

4 cups cider vinegar or distilled white vinegar

3 cups sugar

One 1-inch piece fresh ginger, sliced thin

2 cinnamon sticks, broken

1 tablespoon whole cloves

1 whole nutmeg, coarsely chopped

1. Rinse and drain the cucumbers, and stick each one twice with a table fork. In a nonreactive pot, combine the vinegar and sugar. Add the ginger and dry spices, tied in a spice bag or scrap of cheesecloth. Bring the liquid to a boil. Add the cucumbers, and bring the contents to a boil again. Boil the cucumbers for 3 minutes. Remove the pot from the heat, and cover the pot. Let the cucumbers stand in their liquid.

2. The next day, drain off the liquid, bring it to a boil, and pour it back over the cucumbers. Do this again the following day.

3. On the fourth day, drain the liquid into a saucepan, and bring it to a boil. Remove the spice bag, and pack the cucumbers into pint or quart mason jars. Pour the hot liquid over the cucumbers, leaving ½ inch headspace. Close the jars with hot two-piece caps. To ensure a good seal, process the jars for 15 minutes in a boiling-water bath.

4. Store the cooled jars in a cool, dry, dark place.

Makes 2 quarts

Quick Sweet Cucumber Slices

SWEET-PICKLE FANS will really appreciate this simple recipe.

2¾ pounds 3- to 4-inch pickling cucumbers
2 tablespoons pickling salt
2¼ cups sugar
3½ cups cider vinegar
½ teaspoon fennel seeds
½ teaspoon coriander seeds
1½ teaspoons whole allspice
1 tablespoon yellow mustard seeds

1. Gently wash the cucumbers. Slice them crosswise into ³⁄₁₆-inch-thick rounds, discarding a thin slice from the ends of each cucumber. In a bowl, toss the sliced cucumbers with the salt. Spread the cubes from an ice tray over the cucumbers. Let them stand 3 to 4 hours.

2. Drain the cucumbers, discarding any ice cubes that haven't melted. In a nonreactive pot, bring to a boil the sugar, vinegar, and spices, stirring to dissolve the sugar. Add the cucumbers. Over medium heat, bring the contents back to a boil, stirring occasionally so the cucumbers heat evenly. Pack them into sterile pint or half-pint mason jars, leaving ½ inch headspace. Close the jars with hot two-piece caps. To ensure a good seal, process the jars for 5 minutes in a boiling-water bath.

3. Store the cooled jars in a cool, dry, dark place for at least 3 weeks before eating the pickles.

Makes 3 ½ pints

. . .

"**A** cucumber should be well sliced, and dressed with pepper and vinegar, and then thrown out, as good for nothing."

—*Samuel Johnson*

Gingery Watermelon Pickles

WHEN ASKED ABOUT their favorite pickled foods, many older Americans will quickly mention watermelon pickles, though they may admit they haven't tasted any since they were children. During the Depression, they may piously add, nothing was wasted. This just shows that their mothers stretched the truth a bit, as they measured out substantial quantities of precious sugar and spices to put up something of almost no nutritional value. But watermelon pickles had *spiritual* value, as you will understand if you present such an old person with a jar of these sweet, tart pickles.

More properly called watermelon *rind* pickles, these pickles are made not of the fruit's sweet pink flesh but of the bland white rind beneath. To make them, you slice the watermelon into manageable pieces, then cut away all of the pink flesh as well as the hard, green skin. The rind remaining will probably be only ¼ to ½ inch thick, though I suspect that older watermelon varieties had thicker rinds. I cut my rind into 1-inch squares, but you might prefer ½-by-1-inch pieces or long strips. You might even cut the rind into fancy shapes, as the Victorians sometimes did.

½ cup pickling salt

2 quarts water

3 quarts prepared watermelon rind (see above)

FOR THE SYRUP:

1 large lemon, sliced thin

Two 3-inch cinnamon sticks, broken

1 teaspoon cardamom seeds

1 teaspoon whole cloves

1 teaspoon allspice berries

One 1½-inch piece fresh ginger, sliced thin

2 cups water

2 cups distilled white vinegar or white wine vinegar

4 cups sugar

1. In a large bowl, dissolve the salt in the 2 quarts water. Add the prepared watermelon rind. Let the rind soak in the brine for 6 to 12 hours.

2. Drain and rinse the rind, and drain it again. In a large nonreactive pot, cover the rind with cold water, bring the water to a boil, and simmer the rind 5 minutes. Drain the rind well, and return it to the bowl.

3. Tie the lemon, dry spices, and ginger in cheesecloth, and put them into the pot along with the 2 cups water, vinegar, and sugar. Bring the mixture to a boil, stirring, then reduce the heat. Simmer the syrup for 5 minutes. Remove the pot from the heat, and add the drained watermelon rind. Let the rind rest in the syrup for 12 to 24 hours.

4. Bring the rind and syrup to a boil. Reduce the heat, and simmer the rind

5 to 10 minutes, until it is translucent.

Remove the pot from the heat, and remove the spices tied in cheesecloth. Pack the hot rind and liquid into pint mason jars, leaving ¼ inch headspace. Close the jars with hot two-piece caps. To ensure a good seal, process the jars for 10 minutes in a boiling-water bath.

5. Store the cooled jars in a cool, dry, dark place.

Makes 6 pints

Minty Watermelon Pickles

THESE PICKLES ARE the way Southerners like them—extra-crisp, from a soak in limewater. The mint sprigs provide a delightfully unusual flavor.

To prepare the rind, cut away all the pink flesh and green skin, then cut the rind into 1-inch squares or other small pieces.

2 tablespoons pickling lime (see page 17)

7 cups water

10 cups prepared watermelon rind

FOR THE SYRUP:

I lemon, sliced thin

Two 3-inch cinnamon sticks, broken

I teaspoon cardamom seeds

I teaspoon whole cloves

I teaspoon allspice berries

One I ½-inch piece fresh ginger, sliced thin

3 cups water

3 cups distilled white vinegar or white wine vinegar

3 cups sugar

4 mint sprigs

1. In a bowl or crock, stir the lime into the 7 cups water. Add the watermelon rind, and let it soak 8 to 12 hours.

2. Drain the rind, and rinse it well. Cover it with fresh water, and soak it for 1 to 2 hours. Repeat this step twice to remove all traces of the lime. Drain the rind well.

3. To make the syrup, tie the lemon, dry spices, and ginger in cheesecloth, and place this in a nonreactive pot with the water, vinegar, and sugar. Bring the ingredients to a boil, stirring to dissolve the sugar. Reduce the heat, and simmer the syrup 5 minutes. Pour it over the watermelon rind. Let the rind rest in the syrup, with the spices, for 12 to 24 hours.

4. Put the rind and the syrup into a nonreactive pot, and bring them to a simmer. Simmer them until the rind is translucent, about 1½ hours. Remove the spices. Pack the hot rind and syrup into pint mason jars, adding a mint sprig to each and leaving ¼ inch headspace. Close the jars with hot two-piece caps. To ensure a good seal, process the jars for 10 minutes in a boiling-water bath.

5. Store the cooled jars in a cool, dry, dark place.

Makes 4 pints

Dark Watermelon Pickles

MY FRIEND JOCELYN WAGNER shared this once secret recipe after its originator had passed on. From the way the recipe was written, I gathered that it's actually older than Jocelyn's friend, who must have been born around 1900. I've substituted jars for the crock and volume measurements for weights, and reduced all the quantities, but Jocelyn said the pickle turned out just as she remembered it from childhood. It's a very sweet pickle, almost a confection.

To prepare the watermelon rind, cut away all the pink flesh and green skin, then cut the rind into pieces ½ by ¾ inch.

7 cups prepared watermelon rind

6 cups cold water

1 quart cider vinegar or distilled white vinegar

5 cups firmly packed dark brown sugar

Two 3-inch cinnamon sticks, broken

1 tablespoon whole cloves

1. Put the watermelon rind into a pot, and cover it with the cold water. Bring the water to a boil, and boil the rind until it is translucent.

2. In another, nonreactive, pot, bring to a boil the vinegar and sugar, stirring to dissolve the sugar. Tie the spices in a spice bag or scrap of cheesecloth, and add them to the syrup. Drain the rind, and add it to the syrup, too. Bring the contents to a simmer. Simmer them for about 1½ hours, until the syrup is dark and thick.

3. Remove the spice bag. Ladle the rind and syrup into pint or half-pint mason jars, leaving ¼ inch headspace, and close the jars with hot two-piece caps. To ensure a good seal, process the jars for 10 minutes in a boiling-water bath.

4. Store the cooled jars in a cool, dry, dark place.

Makes about 5½ pints

Sweet Pickled Pumpkin or Squash

LIKE DARK WATERMELON PICKLES (page 227), these pickles are almost a confection. My recipe is based on one from Germany.

> 1¾ pounds skinned and seeded pumpkin or winter squash
> 2 cups white wine vinegar or distilled white vinegar
> 2 cups water
> 3 cups sugar
> Shredded zest of 1 small orange
> 8 whole cloves
> ¼ teaspoon allspice berries
> ¼ teaspoon black peppercorns
> Two 3-inch cinnamon sticks, broken
> One 2-inch piece fresh ginger, sliced thin

1. Cut the pumpkin or squash into ¾- to 1-inch cubes, scraping away all stringy inner flesh. Put the cubes into a nonreactive bowl. Combine the vinegar and water, and pour the liquid over the cubes. Turn the cubes in the liquid a few times, then drain it off into a saucepan. Bring the liquid to a boil. Pour it over the pumpkin or squash, cover the bowl with a cloth, and let the bowl stand 8 to 12 hours.

2. Drain off the liquid into a nonreactive pot, and add the sugar and orange zest. Add the dry spices and ginger, tied in a spice bag or scrap of cheesecloth. Bring the contents to a boil, stirring to dissolve the sugar, and reduce the heat. Simmer the syrup for 5 minutes.

3. Add the pumpkin or squash cubes to the syrup. Simmer them until they become translucent around the edges, about 1 hour. Remove the pot from the heat, cover it with a cloth, and let it stand for 8 to 12 hours.

4. Remove the spice bag from the syrup. With a slotted spoon, pack the pumpkin or squash cubes into pint or half-pint mason jars. Bring the syrup quickly to a boil and boil it for 3 minutes. Pour it over the pumpkin or squash cubes, leaving ¼ inch headspace. Close the jars with hot two-piece caps. To ensure a good seal, process the jars for 10 minutes in a boiling-water bath.

5. Store the cooled jars in a cool, dry, dark place.

Makes 3 pints

Spiced Orange Slices

THE FIRST ORANGE PICKLES I tasted were made by E. Waldo Ward, a company that's been pickling oranges in California since 1891. The tall orange slices were beautifully packed, upright in their narrow 10-ounce jar, and they tasted as good as they looked—chewy, sweet, tart, and just slightly bitter. Having paid $5.50 (in 1996) for this pretty package, however, I had to try making my own pickled oranges—which, it turns out, isn't difficult at all.

Pickle some oranges for holiday gifts, and your friends and relatives will insist that you do it every year.

8 large or 10 medium seedless oranges
4 cups sugar
1 cup distilled white vinegar or white wine vinegar
½ cup water
10 whole cloves
Two 3-inch cinnamon sticks, broken

1. Cut a thin slice from either end of each orange, so that you can see the flesh and membranes. With a sharp knife, cut out the orange sections along the membranes, from one end of the orange to the other, through both flesh and peel. Put the orange sections into a nonreactive pot, and cover them with water. Bring the water to a boil. Reduce the heat, and simmer the oranges for 45 minutes to 1 hour, covered, until they are tender.

2. In another nonreactive pot, combine the sugar, vinegar, ½ cup water, and spices tied in a spice bag or scrap of cheesecloth. Bring the contents to a boil, stirring to dissolve the sugar. Add the orange slices, bring the ingredients to a boil again, then reduce the heat. Simmer the oranges for about 1 hour, until they are well glazed.

Remove the spice bag. Pack the oranges into half-pint or 12-ounce mason jars, arranging them vertically or diagonally, peels out if your patience allows, and leaving ¼ inch headspace. Cover the oranges with the hot syrup, and close the jars with hot two-piece caps. To ensure a good seal, process the jars for 10 minutes in a boiling-water bath.

3. Store the cooled jars in a cool, dry, dark place.

Makes 3 pints

Pickled Crab Apples

IN LATE DECEMBER, I fought the birds for the last of my neighbor's crab apples so I could make this pickle. Although I should have gotten around to this job two months earlier, the pickles were delicious. The slight bitterness of crab apples is a welcome counterpoint to the sweet and sour pickle flavors, especially for people who generally pass up sweets. These pickles make a fine accompaniment to roasted or grilled meats.

Keep in mind that many crab apple varieties are planted strictly for their value as ornamental trees. If the fruit is to make a good pickle, it must also taste good fresh off the tree.

One 2-inch cinnamon stick, broken
1 teaspoon allspice berries
½ teaspoon whole cloves
1 ¼ cups sugar
¾ cup water
1 cup cider vinegar
1 ½ pounds crab apples, stems on

1. Tie the spices in a spice bag or a scrap of cheesecloth, and put them into a nonreactive saucepan with the sugar, water, and vinegar. Bring the syrup to a boil, stirring to dissolve the sugar, then remove the pot from the heat. Let the syrup cool.

2. With a large needle, pierce each crab apple through to keep it from bursting when heated (some apples may crack anyway). Put the crab apples into the pan of cooled syrup, and bring the syrup slowly to a simmer. Simmer the crab apples until they are tender and translucent, about 15 minutes.

Remove the pot from the heat. Let it rest, covered, for 12 to 18 hours.

3. With a slotted spoon, remove the crab apples from the syrup. Pack them into hot sterile pint mason jars, leaving ¼ inch headspace. Remove the spice bag from the syrup. Bring the syrup to a boil, and pour it over the fruit. Seal the jars with hot two-piece caps.

4. Store the jars in a cool, dry, dark place.

Makes 2 pints

Pickled Pears

ON COLD WINTER NIGHTS, pickled pears are a delightful treat, either with dinner or on their own. If your pears are small, leave them whole, with the stem attached. If they are a large variety, cut them in half and core them. To keep the pears from darkening as you peel them, you can drop them into a solution of 1 teaspoon powdered ascorbic acid per gallon of water. (Ascorbic acid powder may be hard to find, but some stores, including Trader Joe's, do carry it. If you can't find any, you might crush some vitamin C tablets—you need 3,000 milligrams per gallon of water—or you can use a commercial mix of ascorbic and citric acids, which most supermarkets stock in their canning-supplies sections.)

Four 3-inch cinnamon sticks

2 tablespoons whole cloves

One 1-inch piece fresh ginger, sliced thin

3 cups water

2 cups distilled white vinegar or white wine vinegar

4 cups sugar

6 pounds pears, peeled and, if you like, halved and cored

1. Tie the dry spices and ginger in a spice bag or scrap of cheesecloth. In a large, nonreactive pot, combine the water, vinegar, and sugar, and add the spice bag. Bring the syrup to a boil, stirring to dissolve the sugar, then reduce the heat. Simmer the syrup for 5 minutes. Add a single layer of pears, and cook them gently until they are just tender—5 to 15 minutes, depending on the variety.

2. Transfer the pears to quart or pint mason jars, and cook the rest in the same way. When all of the pears are cooked, pour the hot pickling liquid over them, leaving ¼ inch headspace. Close the jars with hot two-piece caps. To ensure a good seal, process the jars for 15 minutes in a boiling-water bath.

3. Store the cooled jars in a cool, dry, dark place.

Makes 3 quarts

PEARS FOR PICKLING

Seckel pears are the traditional pickling variety; because they're small, you can pickle them whole, and because they're very firm, they won't fall apart in the process. Few people today, however, even know what Seckel pears are, since they're seldom sold in markets. If you can't get Seckel pears, don't worry—any sort of pear will do. When I had a very productive Bartlett pear tree, I pickled one or two dozen quarts of Bartletts every year. Bartletts are big, soft, and wet, but provided you use them before they turn to mush, and you cut each one in half to fit into the jar, they make fine pear pickles. Big, firm, spicy Comice pears are my favorite for fresh eating, but I always saved some fruit from my little Comice tree for pickling, too. Some people pickle Asian pears—they are the round, yellow to russet fruits sometimes called apple-pears. Today I have baby trees of all these varieties in my home orchard. Next year or the year after, when the trees start producing, you can bet I will pickle every kind.

Pickled Quince

I THANK MY FRIEND Shawn White for bringing me a big box of quinces just in time to add this recipe to the book. My own quince tree isn't producing yet, and for some reason nobody else I know grows this delicious fruit. At the turn of the century, though, most rural American families had quince trees; they prized the fruit for baking, jelly and marmalade (the word *marmalade* comes from the Portuguese word for quince, *marmelo*), as well as pickles. Quince trees are small and handsome, and you can grow them wherever you grow apples and pears, to which quinces are closely related.

The fruits of most quince varieties are seldom eaten raw, since they are very firm. They are also very tart, which is why this recipe calls for so much sugar. I used pineapple quince, a common American variety that smells strongly like its namesake. Pineapple quince is very prone to browning, so put the pieces into acidified water as you cut them. (Use a solution of 1 teaspoon powdered ascorbic acid per gallon of water. If you can't find ascorbic acid powder, you might crush some vitamin C tablets—you need 3,000 milligrams per gallon of water—or you can use a commercial mix of ascorbic and citric acids, which most supermarkets carry.)

One 3-inch cinnamon stick, broken
1 teaspoon whole cloves
2 teaspoons allspice berries
4 thin slices fresh ginger
1 cup distilled white vinegar
4 cups sugar
1 cup water
7 pounds quinces, peeled, cored, and cut into twelfths or eighths

1. In a large nonreactive saucepan, combine the dry spices and ginger, tied in a spice bag or scrap of cheesecloth; the vinegar; the sugar; and the water. Bring the contents to a boil, stirring to dissolve the sugar. Reduce the heat, and cover the saucepan. Simmer the syrup 10 minutes.
2. While the syrup simmers, put the quince slices into a nonreactive pot, and pour enough cold water over them to cover them. Over high heat, bring the quinces to a boil. Reduce the heat, and simmer the slices 5 to 10 minutes, just until they are tender.
3. Drain the quince slices, and divide them among pint or quart mason jars. Cover the fruit with the hot syrup. Close the jars with hot two-piece caps. To ensure a good seal, process the jars for 10 minutes in a boiling-water bath.
4. Store the cooled jars in a cool, dry, dark place.

Makes 7 pints

Pickled Peaches

I PREFER THIS TRADITIONAL peach pickle recipe, which uses the so-called open-kettle method, to the Extension Service method for pickling peaches, which requires a 20-minute boiling-water bath. Since ripe peaches would turn to mush with this much boiling, the Extension recipe calls for underripe peaches. But underripe peaches are extremely difficult to peel, and not very tasty. (You can easily peel ripe peaches by first dipping them in boiling water, then cooling them in cold water.)

To ensure a good seal with the open kettle method—in which you forego a boiling-water bath—make sure that your jars, lids, and peaches are all quite hot.

To keep the peaches from darkening as you peel them, you can drop them into a solution of 1 teaspoon powdered ascorbic acid per gallon of water. (If you can't find ascorbic acid powder, you might crush some vitamin C tablets—you need 3,000 milligrams per gallon water—or you can use a commercial mix of ascorbic and citric acids, which is available in most supermarkets.)

Pickled peaches aren't just a relish; they also make a delicious dessert.

One 3-inch cinnamon stick, broken
1 teaspoon blade mace, preferably, or nutmeg
One 1-inch piece fresh ginger, sliced thin
1 teaspoon allspice berries
½ teaspoon whole cloves

3 cups sugar
2½ cups water
3½ cups white wine vinegar or distilled white vinegar
4 pounds small ripe (but firm) peaches, peeled

---

1. In a nonreactive pot, combine the dry spices and ginger, tied in a spice bag or scrap of cheesecloth, with the sugar, water, and vinegar. Bring the mixture to a boil, stirring to dissolve the sugar. Reduce the heat, and simmer the mixture for about 10 minutes. Add the peaches, and gently simmer them for a few minutes, until they are heated through and just tender.

2. Remove the peaches from the liquid with a slotted spoon, and pack them into sterile pint or quart mason jars. Boil the syrup until it thickens a bit, about 8 minutes.

3. Pour the hot syrup over the peaches, dividing the spices equally among the jars and leaving ¼ inch headspace. Seal the jars with hot two-piece caps.

4. Store the cooled jars in a cool, dry, dark place for at least 1 month before eating the peaches.

Makes 3 quarts

. . .

"**A**mong pickles, sweet or spiced ones are my favorites, although mamma, no doubt, would object to them as occupying neutral ground between pickles and preserves, as being too undecided, not positive enough, in character to suit her."

—*Emma P. Ewing,* Cooking and Castle-Building *(1880)*

Pickled Apricots

SINCE I COULDN'T find an apricot pickle recipe anywhere, I was compelled by my pickle mania to invent one. There is no better way to preserve apricots than as apricot jam, but this pickle comes close. Serve it as you would pickled peaches.

2 cups white wine vinegar

2 cups white wine

2 cups sugar

Shredded zest of 1 orange

3 tablespoons shredded crystallized ginger

4 pounds apricots, halved, and pitted

1. In a nonreactive pot, bring to a boil all of the ingredients except the apricots, stirring to dissolve the sugar. Add the apricots, and cook them briefly, until they are heated through and barely tender.

2. Divide the apricots and their liquid among hot sterile pint mason jars, leaving ¼ inch headspace. Seal the jars with hot two-piece caps.

3. Store the cooled jars in a cool, dry, dark place for at least 1 month before eating the apricots.

Makes 4 pints

Russian Pickled Cherries

E NCOURAGED BY C ZAR Peter the Great after his tour of Europe in 1697 to 1698, the Russians adopted the Dutch custom of pickling fruits and serving them with meats. This recipe was the favorite among half a dozen like it that I tried on a panel of taste-testing relatives. Feel free to leave out the kirsch (clear cherry brandy) if you haven't any on hand.

These cherries are neither cooked nor water-bathed. Heating them, unfortunately, would ruin their texture.

2 cups sweet cherries, stemmed

1 cup cider vinegar

½ cup sugar

⅓ cup water

Seeds from 1 cardamom pod

Fragment of a cinnamon stick

Pinch of ground mace

1 allspice berry

2 teaspoons kirsch (optional)

1. Put the cherries into a bowl or jar, and cover them with the vinegar. Cover the bowl with a towel or cap the jar, and let the cherries stand overnight.

2. Drain the vinegar into a nonreactive saucepan. Add the sugar, water, and spices. Bring the liquid to a boil, then reduce the heat. Simmer the liquid for 15 minutes. Remove the saucepan from the heat, and let the liquid cool.

3. Stir the kirsch, if you have some, into the liquid in the saucepan. Pour the liquid over the cherries, cover them, and let them stand for 3 days.

4. Drain the liquid into a saucepan again, and bring the liquid to a boil. Let it cool.

5. Put the cherries into a sterile pint jar. Pour the cooled pickling liquid over them, filling the jar to the brim, and cover the jar tightly with a nonreactive cap, preferably one that is all plastic.

Store the jar in a cool, dry, dark place for at least 1 month before eating the cherries. They will keep well for about 1 year.

Makes 1 pint

Extra Sweet Pickled Cherries

THIS SIMPLE AMERICAN cousin of the preceding Russian recipe makes a sweeter, pit-free cherry pickle. It's especially good with cold and smoked meats.

I pound sweet or sour cherries, stemmed and pitted
1½ cups white wine or distilled white vinegar
I cup sugar

1. Put the cherries into a bowl or jar, and cover them with the vinegar. Cover the bowl or jar, and let the cherries stand for 3 days.
2. Drain off the vinegar (see the Note below). Layer the cherries in a sterile pint jar with the sugar. Cap the jar tightly, put it in a cool place, and shake it every day until the sugar has completely dissolved.
3. Let the jar stand in a cool, dark place for at least 1 month before eating the cherries.

Makes 1 pint

Note: You can use this mild cherry-flavored vinegar in salads and other dishes. Just strain the vinegar, sweeten it with a little sugar, if you like, and simmer the vinegar for a few minutes before funneling it into a sterile bottle.

Pickled Whole Blueberries

IN CHAPTER 9 I offer two blueberry relish recipes, but this mildly sweet pickle is different in that the blueberries keep their shape. I've served them instead of cranberries for Thanksgiving dinner; you might also try them with ham or baked beans. The same recipe works wonderfully with blackberries.

Two 2-inch cinnamon sticks, broken
1 teaspoon whole cloves
1 teaspoon allspice berries
1½ cups red wine vinegar
2 quarts firm blueberries
2 cups sugar

1. Tie the spices in a spice bag or scrap of cheesecloth. In a large nonreactive pot, bring the vinegar and spices slowly to a simmer. Cover the pot, and simmer the mixture 5 minutes.

Add the blueberries to the pot. Cook them over medium-low heat just until they are heated through, shaking the pot instead of stirring to avoid breaking the berries. This should take about 8 minutes. Remove the pot from the heat, cover it, and let it stand for 8 to 12 hours.

2. Pour the blueberries and their liquid into a colander set over a bowl. Remove the spice bag. Carefully transfer the drained berries to sterile pint mason jars.

3. Return the liquid to the pot, and add the sugar. Bring the mixture to a boil, stirring to dissolve the sugar. Boil the syrup briskly for about 4 minutes to thicken the syrup a bit. Cover the berries with hot syrup, leaving ¼ inch headspace. Seal the jars with hot two-piece caps.

4. Store the cooled jars in a cool, dry, dark place.

Makes 3 pints

Pickled Dark Grapes

HERE IS ANOTHER RECIPE that transforms the fruits of summer into a sweet, spicy winter condiment. Use vinifera table grapes, such as Red Flame, rather than an American slip-skin variety.

½ cup red wine vinegar or distilled white vinegar

1½ cups sugar

¼ teaspoon ground mace

¼ teaspoon ground ginger

¼ teaspoon ground cinnamon

¼ teaspoon whole cardamom seeds

2 pounds seedless grapes, washed, well drained, and halved lengthwise

1. In a saucepan, bring the vinegar, sugar, and spices to a boil, stirring to dissolve the sugar. Add the grapes. Cook them over medium-low heat until the liquid comes to a simmer and the grapes are heated through. Ladle the grapes and their liquid into hot sterile pint or half-pint mason jars, leaving ¼ inch headspace. Seal the jars with hot two-piece caps.

2. Store the cooled jars in a cool, dry, dark place for at least 1 month before eating the grapes.

Makes 2 pints

Pickled Green Grapes

THIS PICKLE IS a light-colored variation on the foregoing one.

One 1-inch piece fresh ginger, sliced thin

½ teaspoon whole cloves

½ teaspoon blade mace, preferably, or small pieces of nutmeg

One 2-inch cinnamon stick, broken

½ cup white wine vinegar

1 cup sugar

2 pounds Thompson seedless grapes, washed, well drained, and halved
lengthwise

---

1. Tie the ginger and dry spices in a spice bag or scrap of cheesecloth, and put this into a nonreactive pot with the vinegar and sugar. Bring the ingredients to a boil, stirring to dissolve the sugar, then reduce the heat. Simmer the liquid, covered, for 10 minutes.

Add the grapes. Cook them until the liquid begins to simmer again and the grapes are heated through.

2. Ladle the grapes and their liquid into hot sterile pint or half-pint mason jars, and seal the jars with hot two-piece caps.

3. Store the cooled jars in a cool, dry, dark place for at least 1 month before eating the grapes.

Makes 2 pints

Pickled Italian Plums

ITALIAN PLUMS, ALSO called French plums or European plums, are the sweet, oval fruits that become prunes when they're dried. When I had two Italian plum trees, I pickled many quarts every year. Since the fruit is low in acid, pickling greatly enhances its flavor. My family loves these pickles both as a condiment and as a winter dessert.

Since very ripe plums are liable to get mushy when you heat them, use fruits that are still firm.

6½ pounds Italian plums, stemmed

5½ cups cider vinegar

4 cups sugar

Two 3-inch cinnamon sticks

6 small dried chile peppers

12 whole cloves

36 allspice berries

1 tablespoon cardamom seeds

24 thin slices fresh ginger

1. Prick each plum 3 times with a large needle to prevent bursting. In a large nonreactive pot, bring the vinegar and sugar to a boil, stirring to dissolve the sugar. Add the plums, and reduce the heat to low. Let the plums cook gently until they are heated through.

While the plums heat, put one third of a cinnamon stick, 1 chile pepper, 2 cloves, 6 allspice berries, ½ teaspoon cardamom seeds, and 4 slices of ginger, into each of 6 hot sterile quart mason jars. Ladle the hot plums into the jars. Cover them with the hot syrup, leaving about ½ inch headspace, and seal the jars with hot two-piece caps.

2. Store the cooled jars in a cool, dry, dark place for at least 1 month before eating the plums.

Makes 6 quarts

Pickled Plums with Red Wine

THIS PLUM PICKLE, with a thick syrup mellowed by the addition of red wine, makes a very special winter treat. Though more trouble to make than basic pickled plums, it is worth the extra effort.

6 pounds firm Italian plums, stemmed
1 teaspoon whole cloves
Two 3-inch cinnamon sticks, broken
4 thin slices fresh ginger
4⅔ cups sugar
3 cups red wine vinegar
3 cups red wine

1. To prevent bursting, prick each plum 3 times with a large needle. Tie the dry spices and ginger in a spice bag or scrap of cheesecloth, and put the spices into a nonreactive pot with the sugar, vinegar, and wine. Bring the contents to a boil, stirring to dissolve the sugar. Reduce the heat, and simmer the mixture 5 minutes. Remove the pot from the heat, and let the syrup cool.
2. Put the plums into a bowl. Pour the cooled syrup over them, and let them rest 8 to 12 hours.
3. Drain off the syrup into a nonreactive pot, add the spice bag, and bring the syrup to a boil. Remove the pot from the heat, and let the syrup cool. Pour the cooled syrup over the plums. Again, let the plums rest in the syrup for 8 to 12 hours.

Put the plums, syrup, and spice bag into a large, nonreactive pot. Cook the plums over low heat, stirring gently, until their skins begin to crack. Use a slotted spoon to transfer them to hot sterile quart mason jars. Boil the syrup until it is thickened, then pour it over the plums, leaving ½ inch headspace. Seal the jars with hot two-piece caps.
4. Store the cooled jars in a cool, dry, dark place.

Makes about 4 quarts

Pickled Cantaloupe Chunks

THIS RECIPE IS a good use for cantaloupes or muskmelons that crack before they're ripe, as many do in this wet Willamette Valley. The flesh should be orange and sweet, but still as crisp as a cucumber. If the melon has cracked, use it immediately; don't wait for spoilage to set in.

2 cups cider vinegar

1 cup water

Two 3-inch cinnamon sticks

1 tablespoon whole cloves

3 cups sugar

9 cups underripe cantaloupe or muskmelon cubes, each about ¾-inch

1. In a nonreactive saucepan, combine the vinegar and water. Add the spices, tied in a spice bag or scrap of cheesecloth. Bring the contents to a boil. Put the cantaloupe or muskmelon cubes into a bowl, and pour the vinegar mixture over them. Push the spice bag down between the melon cubes. Let the bowl stand 2 to 8 hours, turning the melon cubes occasionally.

2. Drain the liquid into a nonreactive pot, add the spice bag, and bring the mixture to a boil. Add the sugar, and stir until it dissolves. Add the melon cubes. Simmer them, uncovered, until they are translucent around the edges, about 1 hour.

3. Remove the spice bag. With a slotted spoon, divide the melon cubes among pint mason jars. Pour the hot syrup over the melon cubes, leaving ½ inch headspace. Close the jars with hot two-piece caps. To ensure a good seal, process the jars for 10 minutes in a boiling-water bath.

4. Store the cooled jars in a cool, dry, dark place.

Makes 3 pints

Limed Cantaloupe Pickles

WITH THIS RECIPE you can use fully ripe—but not yet mushy—cantaloupe or muskmelon; a soak in limewater will keep the pieces firm. Don't take any shortcuts with the rinsing procedure, though; it's essential for ensuring that the pickle is sufficiently acidic.

I call for melon balls here just for the sake of variety, but you can cut the flesh into chunks, or even into long strips, if you prefer.

---

3 tablespoons pickling lime (see page 17)

3 cups water

5 cups cantaloupe or muskmelon balls

1½ cups cider vinegar

1 cup water

2 cups sugar

2 teaspoons whole cloves

One 3-inch cinnamon stick, broken

2 teaspoons slivered fresh ginger

---

1. In a large bowl, stir the lime into the water. Add the melon balls, and let them stand 4 to 5 hours.

2. Drain the melon balls, rinse them well, and then cover them with fresh water. Let them stand for 1 hour, then drain them again. Give the melon two more hour-long soaks in fresh water. Drain the melon well.

3. In a nonreactive pot, combine the vinegar, the water, the sugar, and the dry spices and ginger tied in a spice bag or scrap of cheesecloth. Bring the mixture to a boil, stirring to dissolve the sugar, and add the melon balls. Bring the syrup to a boil again, reduce the heat, and cover the pot. Simmer the melon about 1 hour, until the balls are translucent around the edges.

4. With a slotted spoon, divide the melon balls between two pint mason jars. Boil the syrup until it thickens a little, and remove the spice bag. Pour the hot syrup over the melon balls, leaving ½ inch headspace. Close the jars with hot two-piece caps. To ensure a good seal, process the jars for 10 minutes in a boiling-water bath.

5. Store the cooled jars in a cool, dry, dark place.

Makes 2 pints

Pickled Figs

ONE OF THE TASTIEST FOODS at my grandmother's funeral banquet was a dish of pickled figs. They evoked memories of the big Black Mission fig tree that spread over the yard of the house where my mother grew up, a tree that gratified the family's sweet tooth through the Depression. (Since I was very young when the tree was cut down, I don't know if I remember it myself, or if I've only absorbed my mother's memories of it.) Learning that my grandmother had pickled the figs herself, two years or more before her death, brought all the good times back again.

1 gallon (about 5¼ pounds) ripe but firm figs

5 cups sugar

2 quarts water

3 cups cider vinegar

Two 3-inch cinnamon sticks

1 tablespoon whole cloves

1 tablespoon whole allspice

1. Put the figs into a bowl, and cover them with boiling water. Let them stand until they are cold, then drain them.

2. In a nonreactive pot, heat and stir 3 cups of the sugar and the 2 quarts water until the sugar has dissolved. Add the figs, bring the mixture to a boil, and reduce the heat. Simmer the figs 30 minutes.

3. Add the remaining sugar, the vinegar, and the spices tied in a spice bag or scrap of cheesecloth. Simmer the figs until they are translucent, about 20 minutes.

Remove the pot from the heat, and cover it. Let it stand 12 to 24 hours.

4. Return the pot to the stove, and bring the contents to a simmer. Pack the hot figs and liquid into pint or quart mason jars, leaving ½ inch headspace. Close the jars with hot two-piece caps. To ensure a good seal, process the jars for 15 minutes in a boiling-water bath.

5. Store the cooled jars in a cool, dry, dark place.

Makes about 8 pints

QUICK
PICKLES

QUICK PICKLES

THE PICKLES IN this chapter may seem a miscellany, but they have one thing in common: You can make them in less than two days. With some recipes, in fact, your produce can go from garden or market to table in only a few hours. Many of the pickles here are like other fresh pickles, except that the spices are cracked and heated with the vinegar, so the flavors diffuse quickly. Although lacking oil, some almost qualify as salads, and may be served in place of salads.

Although some of these pickles will keep for long periods, most are intended to be eaten soon after they're made. All should be stored in the refrigerator if they're not eaten right away.

Pickled Baby Carrots with Dill

ALTHOUGH SHE TAKES two or three foot-long carrots in each bag lunch, my nine-year-old daughter, Rebecca, pulls the carrots from her garden when they are only about 4 inches long. I don't mind, though—these sweet little carrots are perfect for pickling. For variety, you might use tarragon or cilantro in place of the dill.

1 pound (1 quart) 4-inch carrots, scrubbed and trimmed
¼ cup minced dill fronds, or 2 whole dill sprigs
3 large garlic cloves, coarsely chopped
1 to 2 red jalapeño peppers, seeded and sliced
½ teaspoon black peppercorns, crushed
1½ teaspoons pickling salt
1 cup white wine vinegar
1 cup water
¼ cup sugar

1. Blanch the carrots for 2 minutes in boiling water, then immerse them in cold water until they have cooled.

2. Pack the carrots and dill into a 1-quart jar. In a saucepan, bring the remaining ingredients to a boil. Pour the liquid over the carrots. Cap the jar, and let it cool to room temperature.

Refrigerate the jar for 2 days or longer before eating the carrots. Refrigerated, they will keep for at least 2 months.

Makes 1 quart

Vietnamese Pickled Carrot and Radish

SERVED WITH NOODLE dishes in Vietnam, this pickle also makes a nice snack or addition to green salads. I make it with a medium-size carrot and a piece of daikon about triple the carrot's size.

½ pound combined carrot and daikon, sliced thin diagonally, then
    slivered
½ teaspoon pickling salt
4 teaspoons sugar
3 tablespoons rice vinegar

1. In a bowl, toss the carrot and daikon slivers with the salt. Let the vegetables stand about 10 minutes, then drain them well.

2. Dissolve the sugar in the vinegar, and pour this mixture over the vegetables. Let them stand about 1 hour.

3. If you don't eat the vegetables right away, store them in the refrigerator. Tightly covered, they will keep well for about 1 week. Drain them before serving them.

Makes 1 pint

Thai Pickled Carrots

THIS IS AN ALL-CARROT version of the preceding recipe, enlivened with a little hot pepper.

½ pound carrots, sliced thin diagonally, then slivered
2 teaspoons pickling salt
1 cup rice vinegar
2 tablespoons brown sugar
1 to 2 small chile peppers, such as jalapeño, serrano, or Thai, seeded,
    if you like, and minced

1. In a bowl, toss the carrots with the salt. Let the carrots stand for 1 hour.
    Meanwhile, bring the remaining ingredients to a boil in a saucepan, stirring to dissolve the salt and sugar. Let the liquid cool.
2. Drain the carrots. Return them to the bowl, pour the pickling liquid over them, and toss them. Let them stand at room temperature for about 1 hour.
3. If you don't eat the carrots right away, store them tightly covered in the refrigerator. They will keep for at least a week, but are best eaten sooner. Drain them just before serving.

Makes 1 pint

Quick-Pickled Baby Corn

FARMERS USE FIELD CORN for this pickle, when their hunger for fresh corn can't wait until the sweet corn matures in the garden. (More often, though, they just climb off their tractors and eat the young ears whole while standing in the field.) This is a quick version of the pickled baby corn recipe on page 116, with a little tarragon added for its licorice-like flavor.

1 pint husked baby corn ears, each about 3 inches long

½ cup water

½ cup white wine vinegar

1 garlic clove, chopped

2 whole allspice berries, crushed

2 whole cloves

½ bay leaf

1 teaspoon pickling salt

½ teaspoon sugar

1 tarragon sprig

1. Pack the corn into a pint jar. In a nonreactive saucepan, bring the remaining ingredients to a boil, stirring to dissolve the salt and sugar. Reduce the heat, and simmer the liquid for 1 minute.

2. Pour the hot liquid over the corn. With a chopstick or plastic knife, push the tarragon sprig down along the side of the jar. Cap the jar tightly, and let it cool.

3. When the jar is cool, refrigerate it. Let it stand in the refrigerator for a day before eating the corn. Refrigerated, the corn will keep well for about 3 weeks.

Makes 1 pint

Sichuan Cucumber Pickle with Hot Bean Paste

HERE'S A DELIGHTFUL, mildly hot pickle to eat with Chinese food. You can serve it the same day you pick the cucumbers.

Hot bean paste is a thick, brown paste made from fermented soybeans, flour, salt, and crushed hot peppers. Sichuan peppercorns aren't really peppercorns at all, but seeds of the prickly ash tree; they are small and black with very aromatic red-brown husks. Both of these special Sichuan flavorings are sold in Asian markets. Check a Chinese cookbook for other ways to use them.

If you want your pickle hotter, add a little chili oil (sesame or peanut oil infused with dried chile peppers).

1 pound (about 2) Asian, "burpless," or salad cucumbers, cut into
*   2-inch lengths*
1 tablespoon pickling salt
2 garlic cloves, sliced thin
1½ teaspoons hot bean paste
1 teaspoon sugar
1½ teaspoons rice vinegar
1½ teaspoons sesame oil
½ teaspoon Sichuan peppercorns, crushed

1. Toss the cucumber pieces with the salt. Let them stand for 2 to 3 hours.
2. Rinse the cucumber pieces, and drain them thoroughly. Mix together the remaining ingredients, then toss them with the cucumbers in a bowl. Let the cucumbers marinate for 3 to 5 hours at room temperature.

Cover the bowl, and chill the cucumbers for at least 1 hour before serving them.

Makes about 1 pint

Thai Pickled Cucumbers

THIS QUICK PICKLE is traditionally eaten with satay, but you could serve it with any dishes that might be complemented by a sweet salad. For the best flavor, roast raw peanuts yourself, in a dry skillet or in the oven. Although the pickle is meant to be eaten as soon as it's mixed, you can prepare the pickling liquid ahead of time.

¼ cup rice vinegar

¼ cup water

¼ cup sugar

½ teaspoon pickling salt

1 pound pickling or Asian cucumbers, peeled

1 teaspoon minced red chile pepper, such as jalapeño, serrano, or Thai

3 tablespoons chopped shallots

1 tablespoon minced dry-roasted peanuts

Cilantro leaves

1. In a nonreactive saucepan, bring to a boil the vinegar, water, sugar, and salt, stirring to dissolve the sugar and salt. Let the liquid cool to room temperature.

2. Make shallow lengthwise incisions in the cucumbers, if you like, so that the slices will be prettier. If the cucumbers are bigger than 1 inch in diameter, halve them lengthwise. Then slice the cucumbers crosswise ³⁄₁₆ inch thick.

When you're ready to serve, mix the cucumbers, pepper, and shallots in a serving bowl (or bowls). Pour the cooled liquid over, and sprinkle the peanuts and cilantro on top.

Makes about 1 quart

Quick Japanese Pickled Daikon

LIGHTLY SALTED AND PRESSED daikon makes a pleasant appetizer or side dish. You can buy *shichimi* in Japanese markets.

¾ pound daikon, peeled

2 teaspoons pickling salt

2 teaspoons soy sauce

2 teaspoons rice vinegar

¼ teaspoon sugar

Toasted sesame seeds or shichimi-togarashi (seven-spice seasoning)

---

1. Cut the daikon into ¼-inch-thick rounds, half-rounds, or quarter-rounds, depending on the thickness of the root. In a wide bowl, toss the daikon with the salt. Lay a plate on top of the daikon, top it with a large, clean rock or a quart jar filled with water, and press the daikon 4 to 8 hours.

2. Drain the daikon well, then toss it with the soy sauce, vinegar, and sugar. If you won't be eating the daikon right away, refrigerate it for no longer than a few days.

Serve the daikon in small dishes, sprinkled with toasted sesame seeds or shichimi.

Makes about 1 pint

Quick-Pickled Eggplant with Basil

TO MAKE THIS TREAT in winter from imported Mexican eggplants, you can use pesto from your freezer in place of the fresh basil.

I love this pickle with tabbouleh (a Middle Eastern salad of bulghur with parsley and mint).

---

1 quart water

1 tablespoon plus 1 teaspoon pickling salt

2 medium to large eggplants (about 3¼ pounds total), cut into
   ¾-inch cubes

¼ cup white wine vinegar

1 tablespoon minced fresh basil

¼ teaspoon fresh-ground black pepper

2 garlic cloves, crushed

¼ cup olive oil

---

1. In a nonreactive saucepan, bring the water and 1 tablespoon of the salt to a boil. Add half of the eggplant cubes, and simmer them about 5 minutes, until they are tender. Put them into a colander, and cook the remaining eggplant cubes in the same way. Add them to the colander, rinse the eggplant, and drain it.

2. In a bowl, mix the cooked eggplant cubes with the vinegar, basil, pepper, garlic, and remaining 1 teaspoon salt. Cover the bowl, and refrigerate it for 8 hours or more. The eggplant will keep well for about 1 week in the refrigerator.

3. Just before serving, stir in the olive oil.

Makes about 1 quart

Pickled Fennel with Orange

THE FENNEL THAT'S USED as a vegetable, especially in Italy, is properly called *finocchio* or Florence fennel, although many supermarkets label it as anise or sweet anise. (Anise is another umbelliferous plant, one grown only for its seeds.) Finnochio is very much like common fennel, except that the finnochio plant swells into a fat bulb at the base of the stems. The bulb is the part you need for this pickle.

In the garden, finocchio is easy to grow, but do give it rich ground. Harvest the bulbs when they are about two inches wide. You can also use the tender stems as you would celery, and the seeds for spice or tea.

Slices of orange-scented pickled fennel make a tossed salad really special.

---

2 fennel bulbs (about ¾ pound), sliced thin
1 teaspoon pickling salt
Zest of ½ orange, in strips
1 or 2 small fennel fronds (optional)
6 tablespoons white wine vinegar
6 tablespoons orange juice
1 tablespoon sugar
4 black peppercorns, cracked

---

1. In a bowl, toss the fennel slices with the salt. Let them stand 1 hour.
2. Drain the fennel slices, and toss them with the orange zest. Pack them into a pint jar, placing a fennel frond or two against the side of the jar, if you like.
3. In a saucepan, heat the vinegar, orange juice, sugar, and peppercorns to a simmer, stirring to dissolve the sugar. Pour the hot liquid over the fennel. Cap the jar, and let it cool to room temperature.
4. Store the pickle in the refrigerator. It will be ready to eat in a day or two, and will keep for at least several weeks.

Makes 1 pint

...

FLAVORED VINEGARS

Perhaps the easiest way to make quick pickles is to keep some flavored vinegar on hand. The spicy and herbal flavors diffused through the vinegar can quickly permeate the vegetables. All you need to do is add water and salt to taste, then refrigerate the pickle for a day or so.

Flavored vinegars are easy to make. Put some herbs, spices, garlic, citrus zest, or a combination of these into a jar, and fill the jar with cold vinegar, preferably a good wine or cider vinegar. Close the jar with a non-reactive cap, such as an all-plastic mason jar cap, and let the jar stand for about two weeks. Then strain the vinegar into a bottle, and seal it with a cork or plastic cap. The vinegar will be ready to use whenever you please.

If you heat the vinegar before adding the aromatics, you can skip the aging step. When the vinegar has cooled, strain and bottle it.

Here are a few ideas to get you started:

Lemon-mint vinegar: Bruise 1 cup mint leaves in a mortar. Put them into a quart jar with the zest of 1 lemon, in strips. Fill the jar with white wine vinegar and cap the jar. After 2 weeks, strain the vinegar into a bottle.

Tarragon-allspice-pepper vinegar: Put into a quart jar 1 tablespoon each allspice and black peppercorns and a large handful of tarragon sprigs. Fill the jar with white wine vinegar and cap the jar. Strain and bottle the vinegar after 2 weeks.

Red wine vinegar with garlic, bay, and savory: Put into a quart jar 4 garlic cloves, halved; 2 bay leaves; and a large handful of summer savory sprigs. Fill the jar with red wine vinegar, and cap the jar. Strain and bottle the vinegar after 2 weeks.

Other good flavor combinations you might try include dill, garlic, and pepper; thyme, lemon zest, and pepper; and allspice, cloves, cinnamon, mace, and ginger.

Quick-Pickled Jícama

I LOVE FRESH JÍCAMA dressed with nothing but salt and lime juice, but this quick pickle is nice for a change. The thick skin of a jícama peels off easily with a knife.

I pound jícama, peeled
2 teaspoons pickling salt
I cup rice vinegar
I cup water
I teaspoon coriander seeds, cracked
I jalapeño pepper, seeded and sliced thin
4 thin slices fresh ginger
3 tablespoons sugar

1. Slice the jícama into pieces about 1 by 2 by ³⁄₁₆ inch. In a bowl, toss the jícama slices with the salt. Let the jícama stand for 1 hour.

2. Drain the jícama, and pack it into a 1-quart jar. In a nonreactive saucepan, bring the remaining ingredients to a boil, stirring to dissolve the sugar. Pour the hot liquid over the jícama. Cap the jar, and let it cool to room temperature.

Store the jícama in the refrigerator for at least a day before eating it. Refrigerated, it will keep for several weeks, at least.

Makes 1 quart

Quick Kohlrabi Pickle

KOHLRABI IS A CABBAGE that puts most of its energy into a swollen stem instead of into leaves. Although commercial farmers in the United States apparently haven't discovered this vegetable yet, many home gardeners love it. With a mild, sweet cabbage flavor, it's delicious either raw or cooked. Kohlrabi is just the thing to grow if you like the crisp texture of turnips and radishes but not their strong flavors.

Looking like pale green or purple balls with a few leaves attached, kohlrabies are generally best picked when no more than 2 inches in diameter. Some varieties, however, can get quite large without getting woody; I just hauled a 13-pounder out of the garden. (This one is a Czechoslovakian variety called Kohlrabi Gigante, seeds of which are available from Nichols; see page 367.)

Peel kohlrabies with a sturdy knife. Big ones can be hard to handle, so halve or quarter them before trying to slice them further.

1½ pounds kohlrabi, peeled and cut into pieces about 1 by 2 by ¼ inch

1½ teaspoons pickling salt

1 cup rice vinegar

1 cup water

3 large garlic cloves, coarsely chopped

Zest of 1 lemon, in strips

2 tablespoons sugar

½ teaspoon black peppercorns, crushed

4 thin slices fresh ginger

¼ teaspoon hot pepper flakes

---

1. In a bowl, toss the kohlrabi with the salt. Let the kohlrabi stand about 1 hour.

2. Drain the kohlrabi, and pack it into a quart jar. Bring the remaining ingredients to a boil, and immediately pour them over the kohlrabi. Cover the jar, and let it cool to room temperature.

Store the pickle in the refrigerator. It will be ready to eat in a day or two, and will keep about 3 weeks.

Makes 1 quart

Green Olives with Lemon and Thyme

IT'S VERY HARD to find fresh olives to cure if you don't live in a commercial olive-growing region (in northern California or near the Mediterranean Sea) or happen to have an olive tree in your garden. But you can add the flavors of your choice to plain cured olives, which are available at Italian delis, Middle Eastern groceries, and some natural foods stores. This recipe makes Lebanese-style olives.

1 pound (about 1 pint) cracked green olives, drained
Grated zest of 1 small lemon
1 tablespoon thyme leaves
1 tablespoon olive oil

1. Mix all the ingredients, pack them into a pint jar, and cover the jar. Let it stand at room temperature for 6 to 24 hours before eating the olives.
2. For longer storage, refrigerate the olives, but bring them back to room temperature before eating them.

Makes 1 pint

Black Olives with Orange, Bay, and Garlic

THIS RECIPE CALLS for brined black olives, but I also like to use it with dry-cured olives—the dark, wrinkly, salty kind.

1 pound (about 1 pint) brined black olives (such as Kalamata or
*   Niçoise), drained*
2 tablespoons orange zest
4 bay leaves, crumbled
2 garlic cloves, minced
1½ teaspoons olive oil

1. Mix all the ingredients in a bowl, pack them into a pint jar, and cover the jar. Let it stand at room temperature for 6 to 24 hours before eating the olives.

2. For longer storage, refrigerate the olives, but bring them back to room temperature before eating them.

Makes 1 pint

. . .

"**P**ickle jars are . . . a colorful feature of Middle Eastern streets. Squatting on the pavements of busy streets, vendors sell homemade pickled turnips swimming in a pink solution, or eggplants looking fiercely black and shiny in the enormous jars. Passersby dip their hands in the liquor, searching for the tastiest and largest pieces, and savor them with Arab bread provided by the vendor, soaking it in the pink salt and vinegar solution or seasoned oil. . . . And when the pickles are finished, the vendor sometimes sells the precious, flavorsome liquor as a sauce for rice."

—*Claudia Roden, A Book of Middle Eastern Food (1980).*

Basic Pickled Onion Rings

THIS IS A SIMPLE but appealing relish for Mexican dishes, chili, and many other foods. If your onion is sweet, you can skip the blanching step.

1 medium white or red onion, sliced into thin rings
¼ cup distilled white vinegar
¼ cup water
½ teaspoon pickling salt

1. Put the onion into a bowl, and cover it with boiling water. Let the onion stand for 1 minute, then drain it.

2. Combine the vinegar and water, and stir in the salt. Pour the liquid over the onion. Let the onion stand for at least an hour before serving it.

If you won't be eating the onion right away, cover it and store it in the refrigerator. It will keep for at least 1 week.

Makes about 1 cup

Spiced Pickled Onion Rings

THIS FANCY VERSION of the preceding pickle is a universal table condiment on the Yucatán Peninsula. Sometimes the onions are chopped rather than sliced into rings.

If your onion is sweet, you can skip the blanching step, as in the preceding recipe.

---

1 large (¾ to 1 pound) red onion, sliced into thin rings

¼ cup white wine vinegar

½ cup water

½ teaspoon pickling salt

2 garlic cloves, minced

3 allspice berries, crushed

10 black peppercorns, crushed

1 teaspoon dried oregano

---

1. Put the onion rings into a bowl, and cover them with boiling water. Let them stand 1 minute, then drain them.

2. In a nonreactive saucepan, bring the remaining ingredients to a boil. Pour the hot liquid and spices over the onion rings. Let them stand for 2 hours or more.

If you won't be serving the pickle right away, store it in the refrigerator. It will keep for at least 1 week.

Makes 1 ½ to 2 cups

Shallots or Onions Pickled with Mint

THIS DELIGHTFULLY DIFFERENT pickle comes from Iran.

¾ pound shallots or small boiling onions, unpeeled
8 garlic cloves
40 mint leaves
¾ teaspoon pickling salt
1 cup white wine vinegar

1. Put the shallots or onions into a bowl, and pour boiling water over them. Let them stand for 3 minutes, then cut off the base of each one, and slip off the skin. If you're using onions or large shallots, cut a deep cross in the bottom of each one. Pack the onions or shallots into a pint jar.

2. In a blender, purée the garlic and mint with the salt and ¼ cup of the vinegar. Combine this mixture with the remaining vinegar, and pour the liquid over the onions. Cap the jar tightly, and let it stand at room temperature for 24 hours.

If you don't eat the shallots or onions at once, store them tightly covered in the refrigerator. They will keep well for at least 1 week.

Makes 1 pint

···

ABOUT SHALLOTS

I started growing shallots after my mother-in-law planted some she'd bought at a grocery store, and shared her abundant harvest with me. I planted her shallots along with some I'd bought through a seed catalog, and I've had plenty of shallots to share with friends ever since.

Sweeter and milder than garlic and onions, shallots aren't just for pickling, but can smooth and enhance soups, stews, and sauces. Shallots are expensive to buy, but they are easy to grow in any good garden soil. You can plant shallots in fall or spring, and they keep well from harvest to spring planting when stored in a cool, dry place. You can buy shallot sets from many mail-order catalogs and some garden centers. Territorial, Johnny's, and PineTree sell shallot seeds (see page 367).

Pink Pickled Shallots

THESE MILD, SWEET shallot slices, colored by red wine vinegar, are delicious in salads.

¾ cup red wine vinegar
½ cup water
¼ cup sugar
½ teaspoon pickling salt
1 bay leaf, torn in half
2 tarragon sprigs

2 thyme sprigs

¾ pound shallots, peeled and sliced thin lengthwise (about 2 cups)

1. In a nonreactive saucepan, bring to a boil the vinegar, water, sugar, salt, bay leaf, and herb sprigs. Add the shallots, reduce the heat to medium, and simmer the shallots for 2 minutes.

2. Pack the shallots, herbs, and liquid into a pint jar. Cap the jar. When it has cooled to room temperature, store it in the refrigerator.

The shallots will be ready to eat in a day or two, and will keep in the refrigerator for 3 weeks or more.

Makes 1 pint

Quick Green Tomato Pickle

THIS IS AN OLD Mennonite recipe. Last year, the pickle kept well in my refrigerator through the winter and on into spring. I think it got better with age.

2½ pounds green tomatoes, sliced ³⁄₁₆ inch thick (about 2 quarts tomato slices)

1½ pounds (about 5 medium) white or yellow onions

1½ teaspoons mustard seeds

2 tablespoons pickling salt

½ cup sugar

2 cups cider vinegar

1. In a large bowl or crock, combine the tomatoes, onions, and mustard seeds. Add the salt, and mix gently. Let the mixture stand for 8 to 12 hours.

2. Combine the sugar and vinegar, and stir until the sugar has dissolved. Drain the vegetables well, and pack them into a 2-quart jar. Pour the sugar-vinegar solution over the vegetables. Cap the jar tightly. Let the pickle stand for 24 hours or more before serving it.

Store the pickle in a cool, dark place, preferably the refrigerator.

Makes 2 quarts

Quick-Pickled Baby Turnips

IF YOU HAVE AVOIDED TURNIPS because of their sharp, bitter taste, try to find some of the sweeter, milder, Japanese varieties, which occasionally are available in produce markets or at farmers' markets. If you have a garden, Presto, Hakurei, and Market Express are quick-growing mild white turnips that are harvested at only 1 to 2 inches in diameter. They make wonderful quick pickles. (Presto seeds are available from Nichols, Hakurei from Johnny's, and Market Express from Shepherd's; see page 367.)

> *I pound small turnips (I to 2 inches in diameter), trimmed at top and*
>   *bottom and peeled*
> *2 teaspoons pickling salt*
> *I ½ cups water*
> *I fresh red jalapeño pepper, seeded and minced, or I tablespoon*
>   *minced pimiento*
> *3 tablespoons sugar*
> *I ½ cups rice vinegar or white wine vinegar*

1. Score each turnip several times at top and bottom. Put the turnips into a bowl. Dissolve the salt in the water, and pour the brine over the turnips. Let them stand for 30 minutes to 1 hour.

2. Drain the turnips well, then return them to the bowl with the minced pepper, and toss well. Combine the sugar and vinegar, and stir until the sugar dissolves. Pour the liquid over the turnips. Cover the bowl with plastic wrap, and refrigerate the turnips for two days, after which they will be ready to eat. Well covered and refrigerated, they will keep for several months.

Makes about 1 pint

Quick Mango Pickle
with Shredded Ginger

THIS PICKLE IS traditionally made with green mangoes of the sort that aren't sweet at all, but I use the mangoes sold in supermarkets, and really like their sweetness in this pickle. Try it with *raita* (yogurt salad) and Indian bread.

---

2 underripe mangoes, peeled and cut into ½-inch cubes
⅓ cup grated fresh ginger
1 tablespoon pickling salt
1 teaspoon cayenne
3 tablespoons mustard oil or other vegetable oil
1½ teaspoons black mustard seeds

---

1. In a bowl, combine the mango cubes with the ginger, salt, and cayenne.

2. In a small skillet, heat the oil until it is very hot, and add the mustard seeds. Heat them until they stop sputtering and turn gray (use a splatter screen, if you have one). Pour the oil and seeds over the mangoes, and mix well. Let the pickle stand for 30 minutes before eating it.

Makes 1 quart

Pickled Pineapple

THIS IS A *SAMBAL*, or relish, from Sri Lanka. Serve it as you might any chutney.

I tablespoon dry mustard
I teaspoon minced fresh ginger
I large garlic clove, minced
¼ cup cider vinegar
I teaspoon sugar
2 pinches pickling salt
¼ teaspoon hot pepper flakes
½ slightly underripe pineapple, peeled and cut into ½- to ¾-inch cubes

1. In a small bowl, blend the mustard, ginger, garlic, and 2 tablespoons of vinegar into a paste. In a larger bowl, blend the sugar, salt, and pepper flakes with the remaining vinegar.
2. Stir the first mixture into the second, then gently mix in the pineapple. Cover the container, and chill the sambal for 1 hour.

Refrigerated and tightly covered, the sambal will keep for several days.

Makes about 1 pint

Dolores's Pickled Prunes

WHEN MY PARENTS had a commercial prune orchard in Sonoma County, California, my mother pickled prunes for every big family party. This is her recipe.

2½ cups (about 1 pound) unpitted prunes
¾ cup firmly packed brown sugar
1 cup cider vinegar
1 tablespoon mixed pickling spice

1. Put the prunes into a large nonreactive saucepan, and cover them with water. Bring the contents to a boil, then reduce the heat. Simmer the prunes for 15 to 20 minutes.

2. Empty the saucepan into a sieve set over a bowl. Return 1 cup of the cooking liquid to the saucepan (if there isn't enough liquid, add enough water to make 1 cup). Add the sugar, vinegar, and mixed pickling spice to the saucepan. Bring the mixture to a boil, stirring to dissolve the sugar, and reduce the heat. Simmer the mixture for 10 minutes.

3. Add the prunes to the saucepan. Simmer them for 5 minutes.

4. Put the prunes and their liquid into a 1-quart jar, and cap the jar tightly. When the jar has cooled, store it in the refrigerator. After a day or two, the prunes will be ready to eat. They will keep well for several weeks, at least.

Makes 1 quart

Chapter 8

FREEZER
PICKLES

FREEZER PICKLES

IF YOU LIKE sweet pickles and want to make them in the quickest, cleanest, coolest way possible, here are the recipes to try. Putting pickles into the freezer for long-term storage will save you from dealing with steaming kettles, canning jars, and two-piece lids that refuse to seal. And you'll have delicious, summer-flavored side dishes to accompany heavier foods through the winter.

Some people say that these modern-day pickles aren't true pickles at all, since, although they are packed in vinegar, their main preserving agent is the freezer. For some reason, cucumber and other vegetable slices packed in vinegar and sugar before freezing don't turn to mush, but stay rather crisp. This is a very effective way to preserve not just vegetables but also herbal flavors that weaken or die in canning and drying. For this reason, I've enlivened the recipes here with fresh dill, cilantro, and mint. Once you taste your homemade freezer pickles, you won't worry whether they're *real* pickles or not.

You can pack freezer pickles in rigid plastic containers, freezer bags, or wide-mouth canning jars. Because food expands when it freezes, allow about ½ inch headspace.

These pickles are best chilled, so serve them right from the refrigerator after thawing them.

Freezer Dill Slices

FRESH RED PEPPER adds attractive color to these sweet pickle chips.

2½ pounds pickling cucumbers

3 tablespoons pickling salt

4 garlic cloves, minced

⅓ cup minced dillweed

1 teaspoon dill seeds

1 cup chopped red bell pepper

1½ cups sugar

1½ cups cider vinegar

1. Gently wash the cucumbers, and slice them thin, discarding a slice from both ends of each cucumber. You should have about 8 cups. In a large bowl, toss the cucumber slices with the salt. Let the cucumbers stand for 2 to 3 hours, then drain them.

2. In another bowl, stir together the remaining ingredients. Pour the mixture over the cucumbers, and stir well. Refrigerate the mixture for 8 to 10 hours.

3. Pack the cucumber slices and syrup in freezer bags or rigid containers, and freeze the containers.

Thaw the pickle for about 8 hours in the refrigerator before serving it.

Makes 4 pints

Lime-Mint Freezer Pickle

THIS IS MY FAVORITE freezer pickle. Even a year after it goes into the freezer, the mint tastes fresh-picked.

2½ pounds pickling cucumbers
3 tablespoons pickling salt
½ cup sliced onion
1 small red bell pepper, chopped
Grated zest of 1 lime
2 garlic cloves, minced
¼ cup minced mint leaves
1½ cups sugar
1½ cups distilled white vinegar

---

1. Gently wash the cucumbers, and slice them thin, discarding a slice from both ends of each cucumber. You should have about 8 cups. In a large bowl, toss the cucumber slices with the salt. Let the cucumbers stand for 2 to 3 hours, then drain them.

2. In another bowl, stir together the remaining ingredients. Pour the mixture over the cucumbers, and stir well. Refrigerate the mixture for 8 to 10 hours.

3. Pack the cucumbers and syrup in freezer bags or rigid containers, and freeze the containers.

Thaw the pickle for about 8 hours in the refrigerator before serving it.

Makes 4 pints

• • •

According to Pickle Packers International, a trade and research association founded in 1893, the perfect pickle should exhibit seven "warts" per square inch for American tastes.

Freezer Pickle with Carrots

GOT A GLUT of zucchini? For this recipe, you can substitute sliced young zucchini for the cucumbers, if you like.

2 ½ pounds pickling cucumbers
3 tablespoons pickling salt
2 medium carrots, grated (about 1 cup, firmly packed)
1 ½ cups sugar
1 ½ cups cider vinegar
1 tablespoon chopped dillweed

1. Gently wash the cucumbers, and slice them thin, discarding a slice from both ends of each cucumber. You should have about 8 cups. In a large bowl, toss the cucumber slices with the salt. Let the cucumbers stand for 2 to 3 hours, then drain them.

2. Mix the remaining ingredients in another bowl. Pour the syrup over the cucumbers, and mix well. Refrigerate the mixture for 8 to 10 hours.

3. Pack the cucumber mixture in freezer bags or rigid containers, and freeze the containers.

Thaw the pickle in the refrigerator for 8 to 10 hours before serving it.

Makes 4 pints

Freezer Pickle with Mango

FRESH MANGO, COMPLEMENTED by ginger, adds bright, tropical color and flavor to this freezer pickle.

2 pounds pickling cucumbers

1 barely ripe mango, cut into ¾-inch cubes

1 cup sliced onions

3 tablespoons pickling salt

1 teaspoon hot pepper flakes

1 tablespoon minced fresh ginger

1 teaspoon ground allspice

1½ cups sugar

1½ cups cider vinegar

1. Gently wash the cucumbers, and slice them thin, discarding a slice from both ends of each cucumber. You should have about 7 cups. In a large bowl, toss the cucumbers, mango, and onions with the salt. Let them stand for 2 to 3 hours, then drain them.

2. In another bowl, stir together the remaining ingredients. Pour the mixture over the cucumbers, mango, and onions, and stir well. Refrigerate the mixture for 8 to 10 hours.

3. Pack the cucumber mixture and syrup in freezer bags or rigid containers, and freeze the containers.

Thaw the pickle in the refrigerator for about 8 hours before serving it.

Makes 4 pints

Cilantro Freezer Pickle

THE ONLY WAY I know to preserve the fresh bite of cilantro is by freezing the herb, as in this recipe.

2 pounds pickling cucumbers

2 cups sliced sweet onions

3 tablespoons pickling salt

1 small red bell pepper, chopped

1 teaspoon ground cumin

¼ cup chopped cilantro

1½ cups sugar

1½ cups cider vinegar

1. Gently wash the cucumbers, and slice them thin, discarding a slice from both ends of each cucumber. You should have about 7 cups. In a large bowl, toss the cucumber and onion slices with the salt. Let the vegetables stand for 2 to 3 hours, then drain them.

2. In another bowl, stir together the remaining ingredients. Pour the mixture over the vegetables, and stir well. Refrigerate the mixture for 8 to 10 hours.

3. Pack the vegetables and syrup in freezer bags or rigid containers, and freeze the containers.

Thaw the pickle for about 8 hours in the refrigerator before serving it.

Makes 4 pints

Freezer Pickled Cabbage

CABBAGE AS WELL as cucumber makes a delicious freezer pickle, especially in a colorful shredded mix with carrot and green pepper.

2 pounds shredded green cabbage

I cup shredded green bell pepper

I cup shredded onion

I cup shredded carrot

I tablespoon pickling salt

2 cups sugar

I ½ cups cider vinegar

1. In a bowl, toss the shredded vegetables with the salt. Let the mixture stand 2 to 3 hours.

2. Drain the vegetables, pressing out excess liquid. Combine the sugar and vinegar, stirring to dissolve the sugar. Pour the syrup over the drained vegetables, and mix well.

3. Pack the vegetables and syrup in freezer bags or rigid containers, and freeze the containers.

Thaw the pickle for about 8 hours in the refrigerator before serving it.

Makes about 2 quarts

CHUTNEYS, SALSAS, AND OTHER RELISHES

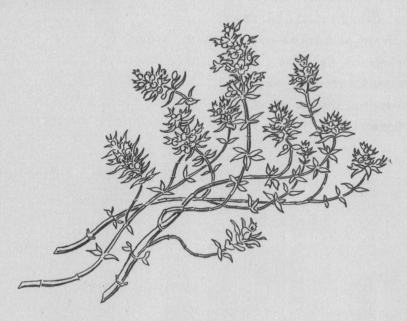

CHUTNEYS, SALSAS, AND OTHER RELISHES

CHOWCHOW, CHUTNEY, KETCHUP, hot sauce, pickle relish—these are all names for minced, ground, or puréed vegetables or fruits preserved in vinegar or otherwise acidified. Always tart, often sweet or piquant, and sometimes sweet, sour, and hot all at once, these are pickles to be eaten in the same mouthful as other foods. Most of these relishes have traditional associations—tomato ketchup with hamburgers, chutney with rice, salsa with tortillas, chili sauce with baked beans, and so on. But once your raw produce is transfigured into jars of heavenly flavors on your refrigerator shelf, you may find chutney glorifying your cheese sandwich, hot ketchup exalting your vegetable soup, and blueberry relish consecrating your bowl of vanilla ice cream. Put up your relishes in small jars so you can have several kinds open at once, and so you can share with your friends, who will be ever grateful for the blessing.

Red and Green Relish

ALTHOUGH MUCH LIKE standard pickle relish, this condiment has a cleaner, fresher taste, due to the smaller proportion of sugar and the omission of spices. Garlic, horseradish, and jalapeños give this relish a little zing.

For a colorful pickle, use a mixture of red and green peppers.

2 pounds pickling cucumbers, chopped (about 6 cups)
¾ pound sweet peppers, chopped (about 3 cups)
3 jalapeño peppers, chopped
6 tablespoons pickling salt
⅔ cup sugar
3 cups cider vinegar
2 tablespoons chopped garlic
2 tablespoons grated horseradish

1. In a nonreactive bowl, toss the chopped cucumbers and peppers with the salt. Empty the cubes from 3 ice trays on top of the vegetables, and let them stand for about 4 hours.

2. Drain the vegetables in a colander, and return them to the bowl. Top them with fresh ice from 3 trays. Let the vegetables stand for 1 to 2 hours.

3. Drain the vegetables thoroughly, discarding any remaining ice. In a nonreactive pot, bring the sugar and vinegar to a boil, stirring to dissolve the sugar. Immediately add the cucumbers and peppers, and the garlic and horseradish. Stir well, and bring the mixture to a boil. Ladle the hot relish into pint or half-pint mason jars, leaving ½ inch headspace. Close the jars with hot two-piece caps. To ensure a good seal, process the jars for 10 minutes in a boiling-water bath.

4. Store the cooled jars in a cool, dry, dark place for at least 3 weeks before eating the relish.

Makes 4 to 4½ pints

Piccalilli

I IMAGINE THE NAME of this traditional relish being born in the whimsy of a tired but satisfied pickler, as she surveyed her crocks of sauerkraut and brined cucumbers, her shelves of ketchups and preserves, and decided what to do with the last of the cabbage and those green tomatoes and peppers that must be saved from the coming frost. She would chop them all together, sweeten and spice them, and give the mélange a name that reflected not the individual ingredients, which likely would differ a bit next year, but the carefree preparation and the diminutive size of the pieces.

Vary the vegetables—you might include snap beans, for instance—and their relative proportions at your convenience; just be sure they add up to about 13½ cups. For a colorful relish, try to include some red pepper. And definitely include green tomatoes.

5½ cups (about 1¾ pounds) coarsely chopped green tomatoes

5 cups (about 1 pound) coarsely chopped green head cabbage

2 cups coarsely chopped bell peppers (from about 2 large peppers)

1 cup coarsely chopped onion

¼ cup pickling salt

2¼ cups cider vinegar

¾ cup brown sugar

1 tablespoon yellow mustard seeds

1 tablespoon grated horseradish

1 tablespoon minced garlic

2 teaspoons hot pepper flakes

2 teaspoons minced fresh ginger

---

1. In a bowl, toss the vegetables with the salt. Let them stand for 3 to 4 hours.

Drain and rinse the vegetables, and drain them again.

2. In a large nonreactive pot, bring the remaining ingredients to a boil, stirring to dissolve the sugar. Reduce the heat, and simmer the liquid for 10 minutes.

3. Add the vegetables. Bring the mixture to a boil, then immediately pack it into pint mason jars, leaving ¼ inch headspace. Close the jars with hot two-piece caps. To ensure a good seal, process the jars for 10 minutes in a boiling-water bath.

4. Store the cooled jars in a cool, dry, dark place for at least 3 weeks before eating the relish.

Makes 3½ to 4 pints

...

ABOUT CHOWCHOW

The term *chowchow* may derive from a Chinese word (*chiao*, meaning "meat dumpling" or *chao*, meaning "stir-fried"), but the pidgin English *chowchow* was used in India as well as China during the era of Western imperialism. Generally, *chowchow* meant any mixture or medley; specifically, it meant a pickle of mixed vegetables, flavored with mustard and usually chopped. Then as now, the terms *chowchow* and *piccalilli* were used somewhat interchangeably in England and the United States. In both relishes, the type and size of vegetable pieces could vary; for instance, you might use snap beans, whole gherkins, or whole tiny onions instead of some of the ingredients listed here, or you might chop everything fine so you couldn't tell one vegetable from another in the finished pickle. But whereas piccalilli always included green tomatoes, chowchow often didn't, and whereas chowchow usually included both ground and whole mustard seeds, piccalilli might exclude mustard altogether.

Chowchow

L IKE PICCALILLI, CHOWCHOW is essentially a Victorian pickle, born under Chinese and Indian influence in the age of Western imperialism.

Chowchow, piccalilli, and similar relishes have tended to get sweeter over the years. My chowchow is much less sweet than most, so feel free to add more sugar if you like.

I quart small cabbage pieces (from about I small head)
3 cups small cauliflower pieces (from about I small head)
3 cups small bell pepper pieces, some or all of them red
2 cups small cucumber pieces or coarsely chopped green tomatoes
2 cups small onion pieces
3 tablespoons pickling salt
2¾ cups cider vinegar
½ cup brown sugar
2 teaspoons yellow mustard seeds
2 teaspoons dry mustard
I teaspoon ground turmeric
I teaspoon celery seeds
I teaspoon ground ginger
2 teaspoons hot pepper flakes
¼ teaspoon ground coriander

1. In a bowl, toss the vegetables with the salt. Let them stand for 3 to 4 hours, then drain and rinse them. Drain them again.
2. Bring the remaining ingredients to a boil in a large nonreactive pot. Reduce the heat, and let the mixture simmer for 5 minutes.

Add the vegetables to the pot. Bring the mixture back to a boil, stirring occasionally. Reduce the heat, and let the mixture simmer 10 minutes.
3. Using a slotted spoon, pack the vegetables into pint mason jars, leaving ¼

inch headspace. Cover the vegetables with the pickling liquid, and close the jars with hot two-piece caps. To ensure a good seal, process the jars for 10 minutes in a boiling-water bath.

4. Store the cooled jars in a cool, dry, dark place for at least 3 weeks before eating the relish.

Makes 4 pints

Cherry Relish

I WENT SEARCHING for recipes like this one after my friend Melody Bycroft reminisced about her aunt's cherry relish, a much-anticipated treat at each year's Thanksgiving table. Sadly, the aunt's recipe was lost with her passing.

The few cherry relish recipes I found included pecans. Since I don't like hard lumps in my relish, this recipe is nutless. If you'd prefer a nutty relish, add 1½ cups chopped pecans at the end of the process described here, and cook the relish 3 minutes more.

Even with a good tool, pitting cherries is time-consuming, so I've kept the quantities small here. Save this beautiful red relish to serve as a very special treat—at the Thanksgiving table, perhaps.

One 3-inch cinnamon stick
½ teaspoon whole cloves
¼ teaspoon cardamom seeds
3½ cups stemmed and pitted cherries, preferably sour
½ cup sugar
1 cup golden raisins
¼ cup honey
1½ cups cider vinegar

1. Tie the spices in a spice bag or scrap of cheesecloth. In a heavy non-reactive saucepan, simmer all of the ingredients for about 1 hour, stirring occasionally, until the syrup has thickened.

2. Ladle the relish into 1 pint or 2 half-pint mason jars. Close the jars with hot two-piece caps. To ensure a good seal, process the jars for 10 minutes in a boiling-water bath.

3. Store the cooled jars in a cool, dry, dark place.

Makes 1 pint

PICKING AND PITTING

Sour cherries are traditional in cherry relish, but I use various kinds of cherries from our planted and volunteer trees. If you can't get sour cherries, use sweet ones instead.

Pitting cherries can be a lot of trouble, depending on the tool you use. I recommend a plunger-type plastic pitter, which costs about twenty dollars; it's much quicker than any hand-held pitter.

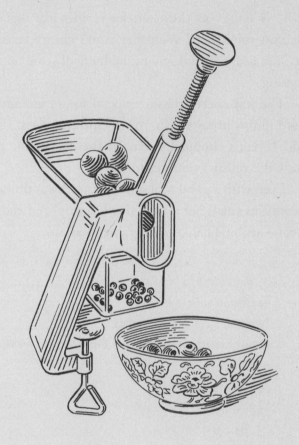

Corn Relish

AN OLD-FASHIONED STAND-IN for salad, corn relish is especially good chilled. Mix a little with cooked rice for an easy, flavorful side dish.

I developed this recipe after examining the corn relishes at the Oregon State Fair. The prizewinner omitted the usual turmeric and powdered mustard, which render pickling liquid a muddy yellow. This recipe follows her example.

8 cups fresh corn kernels (from about 18 ears)
2 cups diced green bell pepper
2 cups diced red bell pepper
2 cups chopped onions
¼ cup chopped garlic
1 tablespoon pickling salt
2 tablespoons yellow mustard seeds
1 quart cider vinegar
1 cup water
⅔ cup brown sugar

1. In a nonreactive pot, bring all of the ingredients to a boil. Reduce the heat, and simmer the mixture 20 minutes.
2. Pack the relish into pint or half-pint mason jars, leaving ½ inch headspace, and close the jars with hot two-piece caps. Process the jars for 15 minutes in a boiling-water bath.
3. Store the cooled jars in a cool, dry, dark place.

Makes about 6 pints

Corn Relish with Tomatoes

THIS UNUSUAL CORN RELISH is enlivened with the sweet-tart flavor of tomatoes. Halve the tomatoes crosswise, and gently squeeze out the seeds and excess liquid before dicing the flesh.

4 cups fresh corn kernels (from about 9 ears)

3 cups seeded and diced red tomatoes

1½ cups diced green bell pepper

¾ cup diced red bell pepper

1 cup chopped onion

½ cup sugar

2 cups cider vinegar

1 tablespoon pickling salt

2 teaspoons yellow mustard seeds

1. Combine all the ingredients in a nonreactive pot. Bring them to a boil, then reduce the heat. Simmer the mixture for 20 minutes.

2. Ladle the relish into pint or half-pint mason jars, leaving ½ inch headspace. Close the jars with hot two-piece caps. Process the jars for 15 minutes in a boiling-water bath.

3. Store the cooled jars in a cool, dry, dark place.

Makes about 4½ pints

Eggplant-Tomato Relish

THIS RECIPE WAS inspired by similar ones from England and France. Try this relish in sandwiches.

---

1 pound eggplant, peeled and cut into ¾-inch cubes

2 teaspoons pickling salt

6 tablespoons olive oil

1 large onion, chopped

1 large green or red bell pepper, chopped

3 garlic cloves, minced

3 cups peeled and coarsely chopped tomatoes

1 cup chopped parsley

¾ cup cider vinegar

1 bay leaf

1 teaspoon yellow mustard seeds

1 tablespoon pine nuts

1 tablespoon drained capers

A few grindings of black pepper

---

1. In a bowl, toss the eggplant with the salt. Put the salted eggplant into a colander, and let it drain for 1 to 2 hours. Rinse the eggplant, and drain it well.

2. Heat the olive oil in a large nonreactive pot. Add the eggplant, and sauté it over medium heat for about 5 minutes. Add the onion and pepper, and sauté about 10 minutes. Add the remaining ingredients. Over medium heat, bring the mixture to a simmer. Simmer it uncovered, stirring often, for about 1 hour.

3. Remove the bay leaf. Ladle the mixture into pint or half-pint mason jars, leaving ¼ inch headspace. Close the jars with hot two-piece caps. To ensure a good seal, process the jars for 15 minutes in a boiling-water bath.

4. Store the cooled jars in a cool, dry, dark place.

Makes 2 pints

Peach and Pepper Relish

THIS RECIPE, FROM Mona Carlisle of Vancouver, British Columbia, is a favorite in my husband's family. Like its cousin, pepper jelly, Peach and Pepper Relish is usually served as an appetizer or party food with cream cheese and crackers. I've found that this relish is also a very good addition to stir-fry dishes, since it provides sweetness, tartness, and a little heat all at once.

6 sweet red peppers, such as bell or pimiento, minced
6 red chile peppers, such as jalapeño, minced
6 peaches or nectarines, chopped
3 lemons, halved
6 cups sugar
2 cups cider vinegar

1. Put the peppers into a nonreactive bowl, and cover them with boiling water. Let them stand until they are cool.

2. Drain the peppers, and put them into a nonreactive pot with the chopped peaches or nectarines. Squeeze the lemons, and add both the juice and peels to the pot. Boil the mixture for 15 minutes.

3. Remove the lemon peels from the pot, and add the sugar and vinegar. Bring the mixture to a boil again. Let it boil, stirring constantly, until it forms a 2-inch thread, or reaches 230 degrees F on a candy thermometer.

4. Remove the pot from the heat, and immediately ladle the relish into half-pint mason jars. Close the jars with hot two-piece caps. To ensure a good seal, process the jars for 10 minutes in a boiling-water bath.

5. Store the cooled jars in a cool, dry, dark place.

Makes about 6 half-pints

Pepper-Onion Relish

I USE THIS RELISH in the kitchen rather than at the table; it's a great addition to pan-fried onions, vegetable stews, and other dishes. Traditional pepper-onion relishes are made with equal quantities of red and green sweet peppers, but I use a mixture of peppers that are all red and mostly hot. This isn't because I'm a fiery foods fiend—since the heat of the peppers is dampened through processing, my finished relish is actually quite mellow.

1 teaspoon allspice berries

1 teaspoon whole cloves

1 teaspoon whole black peppercorns

5 cups seeded and minced red peppers (bell, chile, or a combination)

3 cups minced onions

4 cups cider vinegar

⅔ cup sugar

1 tablespoon pickling salt

1. Tie the spices in a spice bag or scrap of cheesecloth. Combine all of the ingredients in a nonreactive pot. Bring the mixture to a simmer, and simmer it until it is thick, about 30 minutes.

2. Ladle the relish into sterile pint or half-pint mason jars, leaving ¼ inch headspace. Close the jars with hot 2-piece caps, and process the jars for 5 minutes in a boiling-water bath.

3. Store the cooled jars in a cool, dry, dark place.

Makes about 4½ pints

Zucchini Relish

IN THIS SWEET pickle relish of fairly recent origin, zucchini takes the place of cucumbers. Zucchini relishes are very popular among gardeners who never fail to grow too much of this squash, or to let some fruits get monstrously huge, as they seem to do overnight. (My solution is to forego planting any zucchini; the neighbors supply me with all I can use.) My zucchini relish is quite sweet, though not nearly as sweet as most, and enhanced with ginger and cinnamon in addition to the usual celery and mustard seeds. Instead of chopping the vegetables, I grind them with an old-fashioned food grinder.

4 cups (about 1¾ pounds) coarsely ground or chopped zucchini
1½ cups (about ½ pound) coarsely ground or chopped onions
1½ cups coarsely ground or chopped red, or mixed red and green,
*   bell peppers (from about 2 large or 3 to 4 small peppers)*
1½ tablespoons pickling salt
¾ cup sugar
1¾ cups cider vinegar
1 teaspoon celery seeds
1 teaspoon yellow mustard seeds
7 thin slices fresh ginger
Seven 1-inch cinnamon sticks

1. In a bowl, mix the zucchini, onions, peppers, and salt. Cover the vegetables with cold water. Let them stand 2 hours.

Drain and rinse the vegetables, and drain them again.

2. In a nonreactive pot, bring to a boil the sugar, vinegar, and celery and mustard seeds, stirring to dissolve the sugar. Add the vegetables, and bring them to a boil. Reduce the heat. Simmer the vegetables 10 minutes.

3. While the vegetables simmer, divide the ginger and cinnamon among pint or half-pint mason jars, allotting one piece of each for each half-pint. Ladle the hot relish into the jars, allowing ¼ inch headspace. Close the jars with hot two-piece caps. To ensure a good seal, process the jars for 10 minutes in a boiling-water bath.

4. Store the cooled jars in a cool, dry, dark place for at least 3 weeks before eating the relish.

Makes about 3 ½ pints

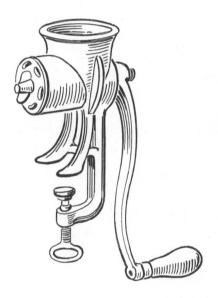

Tomato Preserves

THIS GLOSSY CONDIMENT of tomatoes and lemons is quite tart enough to serve as a pickle without the addition of vinegar. Try Tomato Preserves with roasted or grilled meats, or with crackers and cream cheese. You might even let them stand in for jam on your morning toast.

2½ pounds red tomatoes

4 cups sugar

I tablespoon mixed pickling spices

3 thin slices fresh ginger

2 medium lemons, sliced

1. Scald the tomatoes for about 2 minutes, then plunge them into cold water. Core, peel, and quarter them. In a bowl, gently mix the sugar with the tomatoes. Let the mixture stand 6 to 12 hours.

2. Drain the liquid from the tomatoes into a heavy nonreactive pot. Tie the pickling spices and ginger in a spice bag or a scrap of cheesecloth. Bring the tomato liquid to a boil, and boil it, stirring, until the syrup forms a thread or reaches 230 degrees F on a candy thermometer. Add the tomatoes, lemons, and spices. Reduce the heat to low, and cook the mixture until the tomatoes are dark red and translucent.

3. Skim off any foam, and ladle the preserves into pint or half-pint mason jars, leaving ¼ inch headspace. Close the jars with hot two-piece caps. Process the jars for 20 minutes in a boiling-water bath.

4. Store the cooled jars in a cool, dry, dark place.

Makes about 2 pints

Spiced Blueberries

HERE'S A THICK, sweet relish that's a perfect accompaniment for holiday roasts. Like fruit ketchups, fruit relishes such as this were once quite common in American cellars and pantries.

3 cups sugar

1½ cups water

4 pounds (about 9 cups) blueberries

Zest of 2 lemons, in strips

Two 3-inch cinnamon sticks, broken

1½ teaspoons allspice berries

½ teaspoon whole cloves

1½ cups cider vinegar

1. In a large nonreactive pot, bring the sugar and water to a boil, stirring to dissolve the sugar. Boil the syrup 1 minute. Add the blueberries, and boil them gently for about 5 minutes, until the berries are soft and shriveled.

2. Pour the berries into a sieve over a bowl, and drain off the syrup. Return the syrup to the pot, and put the berries into the bowl. Tie the lemon zest and spices in a spice bag or scrap of cheesecloth, and add them to the pot with the vinegar. Bring the mixture to a boil. Boil it over medium-high heat until the syrup jells, or reaches 220 degrees F on a thermometer. This should take about 30 minutes.

3. Remove the spice bag from the syrup, and add the berries. Bring the mixture to a boil, and boil the relish gently until the syrup again jells, or reaches 220 degrees F on the thermometer. This will take only a few minutes.

Ladle the hot relish into pint or half-pint mason jars, leaving ¼ inch headspace. Close the jars with hot two-piece lids. To ensure a good seal, process the jars for 15 minutes in a boiling-water bath.

5. Store the cooled jars in a cool, dry, dark place.

Makes 1½ pints

Blueberries Pickled in Molasses

I FOUND SEVERAL variants of this recipe in old American cookbooks. The basic method is this: Blueberries are covered with molasses, then left to ferment at room temperature to produce a pleasantly tart relish. I like the cloves and lemon zest in this version.

¼ teaspoon ground cloves
Grated zest of 1 small lemon
1¾ cups blueberries
About 1 cup molasses

1. Gently mix the cloves and lemon zest with the blueberries, and put the mixture into a sterile pint jar. Pour in the molasses, leaving about ½ inch headspace so the contents don't bubble out of the jar. Cover the jar with muslin or 2 layers of cheesecloth, and secure the cloth with a rubber band. Let the blueberries ferment at room temperature for several days.

2. When the berries have soured to your taste, cover the jar, and store it in the refrigerator.

Makes 1 pint

• • •

"Next to eating such quantities of cake and pastry, I think Americans are most absurd in their free use of pickles and condiments."

—*Emma P. Ewing,* Cooking and Castle-Building *(1880)*

Chinese-Style Plum Sauce

THIS CHUTNEY-LIKE RELISH is vastly superior to the gooey, over-sweetened version served in most Chinese-American restaurants. Use plum sauce with pork, poultry, and spring rolls, and in any way that you might use chutney.

2 pounds peaches or nectarines, pitted and coarsely cut

3 pounds plums, pitted and coarsely cut

4 cups cider vinegar

1½ cups sugar

1½ cups firmly packed brown sugar

4 medium red or yellow bell peppers, roasted, peeled, and coarsely
  chopped (see page 139)

3 or more small red chile peppers, chopped

⅓ cup minced fresh ginger

6 large garlic cloves, minced

1 medium red onion, coarsely chopped

½ cup Chinese rice wine

4 teaspoons pickling salt

¼ cup yellow mustard seeds, lightly toasted in a dry pan

1 cinnamon stick

1. In a large nonreactive pot, combine the peaches or nectarines and the plums with 3 cups vinegar. Simmer the mixture until the fruit is very soft, about 25 minutes.

2. In another nonreactive pot, bring the remaining vinegar and the sugars to a boil, stirring to dissolve the sugars. Add the fruit mixture and the remaining ingredients. Simmer about 45 minutes, stirring occasionally.

3. Remove the cinnamon stick, then press the plum sauce through the coarse disk of a food mill (this allows the mustard seeds to come through). Return the puréed sauce to the pot, and simmer until the sauce is quite hot and thickened to your taste, 5 to 15 minutes.

4. Ladle the plum sauce into pint or half-pint mason jars, leaving ¼ inch headspace. Close the jars with hot two-piece caps. To ensure a good seal, process the jars for 10 minutes in a boiling-water bath.

5. Store the cooled jars in a cool, dry, dark place.

Makes 4 to 5 pints

Banana Chutney

AFTER TASTING SOME commercial banana chutney from Jamaica, I had to duplicate it.

---

1 pound onions, coarsely chopped

8 chile peppers such as serrano or jalapeño, coarsely chopped

1 cup raisins

¼ cup coarsely chopped fresh ginger

2 cups firmly packed brown sugar

2 cups cider vinegar

4 teaspoons ground allspice

2 teaspoons pickling salt

3 pounds (about 8 to 10) green-tipped bananas

---

1. Put the onions, peppers, raisins, and ginger through a food grinder, or mince them very fine. Combine them in a large nonreactive pot with the remaining ingredients. Simmer the chutney, stirring often, about 1 hour, until it is thick and glossy.

2. Pack the chutney into pint or half-pint mason jars, leaving ¼ inch headspace. Close the jars with hot two-piece caps. To ensure a good seal, process the jars for 10 minutes in a boiling-water bath.

3. Store the cooled jars in a cool, dry, dark place.

Makes 6½ pints

Mango Chutney

MANGO CHUTNEY is the ancestor of all our Anglo-Indian fruit chutneys. Now that mangoes are cheaper than peaches, in season, why not return to the roots of the relish? This chutney is wonderfully hot, sweet, and gingery.

3 large ripe but firm mangoes (about 3 pounds total), peeled and cut into chunks
2 cups cider vinegar
2 cups firmly packed brown sugar
1 tablespoon minced fresh ginger
2 teaspoons hot pepper flakes
½ teaspoon pickling salt
½ cup golden raisins

1. In a bowl, stir together all the ingredients but the raisins. Cover the bowl with plastic wrap, and let the mixture stand 12 hours.

2. Transfer the contents of the bowl to a nonreactive pot. Add the raisins, and cook the chutney over low heat, stirring often, until it is thick, about 1½ hours.

3. Spoon the chutney into pint or half-pint mason jars, leaving ¼ inch headspace. Close the jars with hot two-piece caps. To ensure a good seal, process the jars for 10 minutes in a boiling-water bath.

4. Store the cooled jars in a cool, dry, dark place.

Makes about 2 pints

Mango and Apple Chutney

THIS CHUTNEY COOKS faster than most, because of the inclusion of the apples, and the mango keeps its pretty orange color.

1 large ripe but firm mango, peeled and cut into chunks
½ teaspoon pickling salt
⅓ cup sugar
⅓ cup cider vinegar
4 garlic cloves, chopped
2 large tart apples, such as Gravenstein or Granny Smith, cored, peeled, and chopped
⅓ cup golden raisins
1 red chile pepper such as jalapeño, seeded or not, and chopped
2 teaspoons grated fresh ginger
½ teaspoon black mustard seeds

1. In a bowl, toss the mango with the salt. Cover the bowl, and let it stand for 8 to 12 hours.

2. Drain off any excess liquid from the mango. In a nonreactive pot, heat the sugar and vinegar, stirring to dissolve the sugar. Add the mangoes and other ingredients. Cook the chutney over low heat, stirring frequently, about 30 minutes, until the chutney is thick.

3. Spoon the hot chutney into pint or half-pint mason jars, leaving ¼ inch headspace. Close the jars with hot two-piece caps. To ensure a good seal, process the jars for 10 minutes in a boiling-water bath.

4. Store the cooled jars in a cool, dry, dark place.

Makes 2 pints

Ann Kaiser's Peach Chutney

I DECIDED TO LEAVE my own peach chutney out of this book after I tasted my mother-in-law's. Dark, sweet, and hot (mostly from the ample ginger), it's really the best.

Ripe peaches and nectarines are easy to peel if you first blanch them in boiling water, then immediately cool them in cold water.

I use Korean or Mexican ground dried red pepper in place of the chili powder.

½ cup coarsely chopped onion

½ pound (1 cup plus 6 tablespoons) golden raisins

1 garlic clove

4 pounds (about 10 to 14) peaches or nectarines, peeled and coarsely chopped

⅔ cup minced fresh ginger

2 cups cider vinegar

1½ pounds (3 cups plus 6 tablespoons, firmly packed) brown sugar

2 tablespoons chili powder

2 tablespoons yellow mustard seeds

1 tablespoon pickling salt

1. Put the onion, raisins, and garlic through a food grinder, or mince them very fine. Put them into a large nonreactive pot with the remaining ingredients. Boil the mixture, stirring often, for about 1 hour, until it is thick and a rich brown color.

2. Pack the chutney into pint or half-pint mason jars, leaving ¼ inch headspace. Close the jars with hot two-piece caps. To ensure a good seal, process the jars for 10 minutes in a boiling-water bath.

3. Store the cooled jars in a cool, dry, dark place.

Makes 3½ pints

Plum Chutney

In MY HUSBAND'S FAMILY, this gingery chutney always brings back warm memories of Katcha Haberkorn, an old friend who shared the recipe about thirty years ago.

¾ cup cider vinegar

1 cup sugar

1 cup firmly packed brown sugar

1½ teaspoons hot pepper flakes

½ cup slivered crystallized ginger

2 teaspoons pickling salt

2 teaspoons yellow mustard seeds

2 large garlic cloves, sliced thin

¼ cup coarsely chopped onion

1 cup golden raisins

3½ cups halved and pitted Italian plums

1. In a heavy nonreactive pot, bring the vinegar and sugars to a boil, stirring to dissolve the sugar. Add all of the remaining ingredients except the plums, and mix well. Stir in the plums. Simmer the mixture, stirring gently and frequently toward the end of the cooking, until the chutney thickens, about 50 minutes.

2. Ladle the hot chutney into pint or half-pint mason jars, leaving ¼ inch headspace. Close the jars with hot two-piece caps. To ensure a good seal, process the jars for 10 minutes in a boiling-water bath.

3. Store the cooled jars in a cool, dry, dark place.

Makes 2 pints

Rhubarb Chutney

HERE'S A CHUTNEY for those lucky enough to have an abundance of rhubarb.

2 cups cider vinegar

1½ cups firmly packed brown sugar

1¾ pounds rhubarb, sliced ½ inch thick

3 cups chopped onions

2 tablespoons minced fresh ginger

1 teaspoon hot pepper flakes

Grated zest of 1 orange

One 4-inch cinnamon stick

1 cup golden raisins

½ teaspoon pickling salt

1. In a nonreactive pot over medium heat, heat the vinegar and sugar, stirring until the sugar dissolves. Add the remaining ingredients. Simmer about 35 minutes, stirring occasionally.

2. Remove the cinnamon stick. Pack the chutney into pint or half-pint mason jars, and close the jars with hot two-piece caps. To ensure a good seal, process the jars for 10 minutes in a boiling-water bath.

3. Store the cooled jars in a cool, dry, dark place.

Makes 3½ pints

Sweet Tomato Chutney

I THINK OF THIS thick, glossy, sweet chutney as an elegant, exotic version of tomato ketchup. You might serve this relish with fried fish or cold poultry.

4 pounds red tomatoes, peeled and chopped, or 7 cups tomato purée

1½ cups sugar

1½ cups white wine or distilled white vinegar

1 tablespoon pickling salt

Juice and grated zest of 1 large or 2 small limes

¼ cup chopped garlic (about 1 head)

2 tablespoons chopped fresh ginger

½ teaspoon hot pepper flakes

½ teaspoon fennel seeds

½ teaspoon cumin seeds

½ teaspoon fenugreek seeds

½ cup dark raisins

1. In a heavy nonreactive pot, combine all of the ingredients. Bring them to a boil, and reduce the heat. Simmer 1½ to 2 hours, stirring often, until the chutney is thick.

2. Ladle the chutney into pint or half-pint mason jars, leaving ¼ inch headspace, and close the jars with hot two-piece caps. To ensure a good seal, process the jars for 10 minutes in a boiling-water bath.

3. Store the cooled jars in a cool, dry, dark place.

Makes 1½ to 2 pints

Hyderabadi Tomato Chutney

THIS CHUTNEY IS arguably not a pickle at all, since it contains no vinegar or citrus juice and should probably be frozen for long-term storage. But it is my very favorite chutney, so I couldn't leave it out of the book. If you like very hot, garlicky foods, you will love this.

12 garlic cloves, peeled

7 cups peeled and chopped tomatoes or tomato purée

2 teaspoons grated fresh ginger

½ teaspoon cayenne

½ cup vegetable oil

2 teaspoons cumin seeds

1 teaspoon black mustard seeds

½ teaspoon fenugreek seeds

4 small dried chile peppers

1 teaspoon pickling salt

1. Mash 4 of the garlic cloves, and combine them in a bowl with the tomatoes, ginger, and cayenne.

2. Heat the oil in a large nonreactive skillet over medium heat. Add the 8 remaining garlic cloves. Fry them, turning them once or twice, until they are golden brown. Add the cumin, mustard, and fenugreek to the skillet, and let the seeds sizzle for 2 seconds. Add the dried peppers whole, and stir once; they will swell and darken. Add the tomato mixture carefully; it will splatter a bit at first. Cook the chutney, stirring almost constantly, for 15 to 20 minutes, until it is quite thick. Stir in the salt. Spoon the chutney into small jars or plastic storage containers, and cover them.

The chutney will keep well in the refrigerator for a week. For long-term storage, freeze the containers.

Makes 1 pint

Tomato Ketchup

THIS KETCHUP TASTES the way tomato ketchup should, rich and natural with no bitter or metallic off flavors. You'll never crave store-bought ketchup again once you've tasted your own homemade version.

1 gallon tomato purée
1½ cups chopped onions
½ cup chopped red chile peppers
2 garlic cloves, minced
2 cups cider vinegar
1 tablespoon pickling salt
1 bay leaf, crumbled
2 tablespoons coriander seeds
1 tablespoon yellow mustard seeds
1 tablespoon black peppercorns
1 tablespoon allspice berries
One 3-inch cinnamon stick, broken
¼ cup white sugar
½ cup firmly packed brown sugar

1. In a large nonreactive pot, combine the tomato purée, onions, hot peppers, garlic, vinegar, and salt. Bring the mixture to a boil.

2. Add to the pot the spices, tied in a spice bag or scrap of cheesecloth, and the sugars. Cook the mixture over medium-high heat, stirring often, until it thickens.

3. Squeeze the spice bag to extract all its flavors, and remove it. Purée the mixture in a food mill, using a fine disk, or press the mixture through a fine sieve.

4. Return the mixture to the pot. Bring the mixture to a boil again, and continue to boil it, stirring constantly, until it mounds slightly in a spoon.

5. Ladle the ketchup into pint or half-pint mason jars, leaving ¼ inch head-space. Close the jars with hot two-piece caps, and process the jars for 15 minutes in a boiling-water bath.

Store the cooled jars in a cool, dry, dark place for at least 1 month before using the ketchup.

Makes 4 pints

Mary Randolph's Sugar-Free Tomato Ketchup

ALTHOUGH TODAY'S TOMATO ketchups are very sweet condiments, early versions were sweetened very little or not at all. This simple recipe, from Mary Randolph's book, *The Virginia Housewife* (1824), is a wonderful example. You might want to vary the seasonings; I'm tempted to add garlic next time, and if you can't find mace you can use scraps of nutmeg instead. But I think you'll find this ketchup plenty sweet for most purposes without added sugar, and plenty tart without vinegar. (My ketchup tested at a pH of 3.9, much lower than that of most tomatoes, since the long boiling concentrates the acids).

Mrs. Randolph wisely advised making this pickle "in August, in dry weather." She meant that you shouldn't wait until cool, damp weather invites mold and late blight to the tomato patch. A boiling-water bath should keep disease organisms from growing, but tomatoes that are starting to spoil, and even those just overripe, could lower the acidity of the ketchup, making it less flavorful and possibly even allowing botulinum bacteria to grow. If you're in doubt about your tomatoes, add ½ cup vinegar to the tomato purée.

1 peck (2 gallons) tomatoes, stemmed and washed

2 tablespoons pickling salt

1 cup minced onions

1½ teaspoons blade (unground) mace

1 tablespoon black peppercorns

1. Put the tomatoes into a large nonreactive pot, squeezing each one firmly as you drop it in. Sprinkle the salt over the tomatoes, then bring them to a boil. Stirring occasionally, boil the tomatoes, uncovered, for 1 hour.

2. Put the tomatoes through a tomato strainer or food mill (Mrs. Randolph advised straining them "through a colander, and then through a sieve"). Return the purée to the pot, and add the onions, mace, and pepper. Bring the mixture to a boil, and boil it, stirring often, until it is quite thick, as thick as commercial tomato ketchup.

3. Ladle the ketchup into pint or half-pint mason jars, leaving ¼ inch headspace. Close the jars with hot two-piece caps, and process the jars for 15 minutes in a boiling-water bath.

4. Store the cooled jars in a cool, dry, dark place.

Makes 2½ pints

Hot Orange Ketchup

THIS UNSWEETENED KETCHUP gets its color from yellow or orange tomatoes and yellow Cascabella peppers. Cascabellas (which are not to be confused with cascabel peppers, a round variety from Mexico) were developed in California and named for their beautiful skins. These small, waxy, conical chile peppers start out yellow and turn orange before ripening red. In this recipe, you can substitute any hot yellow peppers, such as caricillo, Floral Gem, or Hungarian Wax. If you don't like heat, use yellow bell peppers, but, for their festive look in the garden, plant some Cascabellas anyway.

You'll need about 5 pounds yellow or orange tomatoes for this recipe.

6½ cups yellow or orange tomato purée (see page 334)

6 ounces (about 1 pint) yellow Cascabella peppers, seeded and chopped

½ pound white or yellow onions, chopped

10 garlic cloves, chopped

1 small lemon

1 cup white wine vinegar

2 teaspoons pickling salt

2 teaspoons mustard seeds

2 teaspoons coriander seeds

1 teaspoon whole cloves

One 2-inch cinnamon stick, broken up

3 thin slices fresh ginger

1. In a large nonreactive saucepan, bring the tomato purée, peppers, onions, and garlic to a boil. Reduce the heat, and simmer the mixture until the peppers and onions are tender, about 20 minutes. Meanwhile, remove the zest of the lemon in strips, and squeeze out the juice.

2. Purée the hot mixture in batches in a blender, and return the purée to the saucepan. Add the lemon juice, vinegar, and salt. Tie the lemon zest, dry spices, and fresh ginger in a spice bag or scrap of cheesecloth, and add this to the pan, too. Simmer the ketchup, stirring it occasionally, for about 1½ hours, until it is as thick as you like.

3. Ladle the ketchup into pint or half-pint mason jars, leaving ¼ inch headspace, and close the jars with hot two-piece caps. Process the jars for 15 minutes in a boiling-water bath. Store the jars in a cool, dry, dark place. Or funnel the ketchup into sterile bottles, seal the bottles with nonreactive caps or corks, and store the ketchup in the refrigerator.

Makes about 2 pints

...

THE OTHER KETCHUPS

Not all ketchup is made from tomatoes. Until about 1850, in fact, an American recipe that called for a spoonful of ketchup most likely meant mushroom, walnut, or oyster. These ketchups were themselves inspired by Asian pickled fish brines; called *ké-tsiap* in Amoy Chinese and *kēchap* in Malay, fish ketchups were like the *nuoc mam, nam pla,* or *tuk trey* still so important in the cuisines of Southeast Asia. (Ancient Rome had its own version; known as *liquamen,* it was brewed commercially and used ubiquitously in Roman cuisine.)

Early English and American ketchups were more like their Asian predecessors than like today's tomato ketchup. Nineteenth-century mushroom ketchup was usually preserved with salt, not vinegar; oyster and lobster ketchups were preserved with sherry. These ketchups were used primarily in cooking, much as we use soy sauce and Vietnamese fish sauce today.

When sugar became common and cheap, Americans started making ketchups from various fruits. Even a cookbook published in 1965 gives recipes for ketchups made from a dozen kinds of fruits other than tomatoes.

Currant or Gooseberry Ketchup

MOST AMERICANS HAVE never tasted a gooseberry or a currant. This wasn't always so; until the 1920s, gooseberry and currant bushes were common garden plants, and recipes like this one were popular. But then many states outlawed the cultivation of plants in the genus *Ribes*, on the grounds that they can serve as alternate hosts for white pine blister rust, a disease that infects five-needled pine trees. Recently, however, someone has noticed that wild *Ribes* species grow all over the place, and that these woodland shrubs are a greater threat to commercial foresters than plants on the farm or in the garden. So state legislators have made currant and gooseberry growing legal again, and high-priced little packages of the fruits are appearing in chic markets. The sensible thing to do, though, is to plant your own; a young bare-root bush costs about as much as a pint of fruit from the store.

For a colorful ketchup, use red or black currants or red gooseberries. Since my bushes are just starting to produce fruit, I combined black and red currants in developing this recipe.

2 pounds currants or gooseberries, stemmed

3 cups sugar

1 ¼ cups cider vinegar

1 tablespoon ground cinnamon

1 teaspoon ground mace

1 teaspoon ground allspice

1 teaspoon ground ginger

1. In a nonreactive pot, bring the fruit, sugar, and vinegar to a boil. Reduce the heat, and simmer the mixture until the fruit is soft.

2. Purée the mixture in a food mill, or press it through a sieve. Return the mixture to the pan, add the spices, and cook the ketchup until it is thick.

3. Ladle the ketchup into pint or half-pint mason jars, leaving ¼ inch head-space. Close the jars with hot two-piece caps. To ensure a good seal, process the jars for 10 minutes in a boiling-water bath.

4. Store the cooled jars in a cool, dry, dark place.

Makes 2 pints

Cranberry Ketchup

THIS FRUIT KETCHUP is a smooth, spicy alternative to conventional cranberry sauce. Try Cranberry Ketchup with pork and beef as well as with turkey. It's especially good in sandwiches.

One 3-inch cinnamon stick, broken into pieces
3 thin slices fresh ginger
1½ pounds (2 bags) cranberries
1¼ cups cider vinegar
1¼ cups water
1 teaspoon ground cloves
1 teaspoon ground allspice
½ teaspoon ground nutmeg
Grated zest of 1 large orange
1½ cups firmly packed brown sugar

1. Tie the cinnamon pieces and ginger in a spice bag or scrap of cheesecloth. Put this into a nonreactive saucepan with all of the ingredients but the sugar, and bring the mixture to a simmer. Simmer until the cranberries are soft, about 20 minutes.

2. Remove the spice bag, and purée the mixture in a food mill or press it through a sieve. Return the purée to the saucepan. Add the sugar, and simmer the ketchup until it is glossy and thick, about 15 minutes.

3. Ladle the ketchup into pint or half-pint mason jars, leaving ¼ inch headspace. Close the jars with hot two-piece caps. To ensure a good seal, process the jars for 10 minutes in a boiling-water bath.

Store the cooled jars in a cool, dry, dark place.

Makes 1 ½ pints

ABOUT WALNUT KETCHUP

Most American and English cookbooks published in the mid-nineteenth century included recipes for walnut pickles and ketchup. Like other early ketchups, walnut ketchup was usually thin, unsweetened, and used in cooking rather than at the table. This version, basically that of Mary Randolph (*The Virginia Housewife*, 1824), is really just a flavored vinegar. Next year I'll try Mrs. Beeton's recipe (*Mrs. Beeton's Book of Household Management*, 1861), which includes anchovies and port wine. Mrs. Beeton used her walnut ketchup as a steak sauce, with pounded horseradish, shallots, and spices added.

Walnut Ketchup

To make walnut ketchup, you must have access to an English walnut tree. Also called Persian walnut, after their native land, these trees bear nuts with elongated shells; they are the sort packaged by Blue Diamond and sold in supermarkets. Don't try using nuts from the black walnut, a native American tree that is valued more for its wood than its nuts, which are round and very hard to crack.

Before you decide to forego making this ketchup because you have no English walnut tree in your yard, look around. I gathered all the green walnuts I needed from a roadside tree.

Gather your nuts between late June and mid-July, when they are full size or close to it, but before the shells have developed. You should be able to easily run a needle through the nuts. At this stage the nuts won't be lying on the ground, of course, but will be firmly attached to the tree. So bring along a child or two to climb the tree and toss the nuts down to you.

2 pounds green English walnuts

6 tablespoons pickling salt

3 cups white wine vinegar

6 garlic cloves

1 teaspoon ground cloves

1 teaspoon ground mace

1. Pierce each nut about 6 times with a large needle, and put the nuts into a 2-quart jar. Dissolve 2 tablespoons of the salt in 1 quart boiling water, and pour the water over the nuts. Cap the jar, and leave it at room temperature for 3 days.

2. Drain off the water. Dissolve another 2 tablespoons salt in 1 quart boiling water, and pour this over the nuts. Repeat the process 3 days later.

3. Nine days after first putting the nuts in the jar, drain them, and leave them in a colander in the sun for 2 to 3 days to blacken. Bring them in at night and in wet weather. Turn them occasionally.

4. In a blender, grind the nuts with the vinegar (or pound them in a large marble mortar, as Mary Randolph advises). Return the nuts to the 2-quart jar, and close it tightly with a nonreactive cap. Leave the jar at room temperature for 1 week, shaking it or stirring the contents daily.

5. Strain the walnut-vinegar mixture through a jelly bag, squeezing the bag to extract all the liquid. In a blender or mortar, grind the garlic and spices with a little of the walnut liquid. Combine the purée with the remaining liquid in a nonreactive saucepan, and simmer the mixture 15 minutes.

6. Pour the hot liquid into sterile bottles, and seal them with nonreactive caps or with corks. Store the bottles in a cool, dry, dark place.

Makes 3 to 3½ cups

Prepared Horseradish

Fresh prepared horseradish is immensely more flavorful than the adulterated commercial stuff, and the preparation is quick and easy.

If you don't like grating horseradish, you can instead use a blender or food processor; just cut the peeled root into small pieces, put them into the machine with the vinegar, and grind the horseradish briefly so the pieces remain coarse. But keep your face away from the blender jar or processor bowl; fresh horseradish is very pungent stuff, and it burns the eyes as no onion can.

Whether you grate your horseradish or use a blender or food processor, you might add a little sugar to smooth the flavor, and ascorbic acid to prevent browning.

Preparing horseradish this way makes it easy to use in pickling and cooking, but there are better ways to preserve the root for long periods (keep it frozen in the garden, if your climate is very cold, or peel the root, wrap it, and store it in the freezer). Since prepared horseradish gradually loses its flavor and pungency as the weeks go by, you shouldn't plan to keep it for more than a month or so.

1 cup peeled and grated horseradish
½ cup white wine vinegar or distilled white vinegar
½ teaspoon pickling salt
Pinch of sugar (optional)
Pinch of ascorbic acid (optional)

Mix the ingredients, and pack the mixture into a small jar. Cap the jar tightly, and store it in the refrigerator.

Makes ½ pint

Pique

THE SIMPLEST HOT SAUCE of all—and one that is immensely popular in the West Indies—is vinegar in which hot peppers have been steeped. In Puerto Rico a rum bottle full of *pique* sits on every restaurant table, displaying long, thin peppers in assorted colors.

12 medium-size long or conical chile peppers, such as cayenne,
*   de árbol, or jalapeño*
4 garlic cloves, halved lengthwise
12 black peppercorns
⅛ teaspoon pickling salt
About 1 cup cider vinegar

1. Put the peppers, garlic, peppercorns, and salt into a bottle with a capacity of about 12 ounces. A rum bottle is most authentic, but I use a small vinegar bottle. (If no one has thrown out the inner plastic cap that keeps the contents from pouring out too fast, I use that as well.) Using a funnel, pour enough vinegar over the other ingredients to cover them well. Close the bottle with a nonreactive cap or a cork, and give the bottle a shake to dissolve the salt.

2. Let the bottle sit undisturbed for 1 to 2 days so the vinegar can absorb the other flavors. The longer the sauce sits, the hotter it will get. Store the bottle in the refrigerator or another cool place. Until the pepper flavor gets weak, you can top up the bottle with fresh vinegar as needed.

Makes about 1½ cups

Chili Sauce with Chiles

THIS IS A TRADITIONAL CHILI sauce with a little hot pepper added for interest.

One 3-inch cinnamon stick, broken
1 tablespoon yellow mustard seeds
2 teaspoons celery seeds
2 teaspoons chopped fresh ginger
1 teaspoon allspice berries
¼ teaspoon whole cloves
10 pounds tomatoes, coarsely chopped
4 large onions, minced (about 4 cups)
4 red bell peppers, chopped (about 2½ cups)
4 red jalapeño peppers, minced
½ cup firmly packed brown sugar
2 tablespoons pickling salt
2 cups cider vinegar

1. Tie the dry spices and ginger in a spice bag or in a scrap of cheesecloth. Combine all of the ingredients in a heavy nonreactive pot. Bring the mixture to a boil, then reduce the heat, and simmer the chili sauce until it is thick, about 3 hours.

2. Ladle the chili sauce into pint or half-pint mason jars, leaving ¼ inch headspace. Close the jars with hot two-piece caps. To ensure a good seal, process the jars for 15 minutes in a boiling-water bath.

3. Store the cooled jars in a cool, dry, dark place.

Makes about 6 pints

WHAT'S CHILI SAUCE, ANYWAY?

The first time I made chili sauce I was mystified at the result, and ended up running the whole batch through the blender to turn it into ketchup, a pickle I understood. My husband's Eastern-born relations had to explain what chili sauce was about; my mother-in-law likes it with meat loaf and burgers, my husband's aunt eats it with roast beef and baked beans. Simply a chunky version of tomato ketchup, chili sauce has a texture that many people prefer.

But where is the chile in chili sauce? I wondered. None of the old recipes I've found call for hot peppers, though *The Picayune Creole Cook Book* (1901) considers them an optional addition. I suspect chili sauce originated as Mexican chile salsa. Just as *chile con carne*, or chili, became tempered with beans, tomatoes, and other ingredients as it traveled eastward, so that now hot peppers are often left out entirely, chili sauce long ago became Yankeefied.

Aunt Mary Goodsell's Chili Sauce

THIS OLD NEW ENGLAND recipe was handed down from Mary Jane Summers Goodsell, born in 1851 in Newtown, Connecticut; she was the aunt of my husband's grandfather. Family lore has it that Aunt Mary won first prize for this sauce year after year at the Danbury fair. My husband's aunt, Eleanor Thompson, recalls smelling the wonderful, cinnamony aroma of this simple chili sauce upon coming home from school on a fall afternoon to find her mother, Blanche Waterhouse, making an annual batch.

24 large red tomatoes (about 10 pounds), coarsely chopped

6 green bell peppers, coarsely chopped

4 large onions, coarsely chopped

½ cup sugar

2 tablespoons pickling salt

2 tablespoons ground cinnamon

3 cups white wine, cider, or distilled white vinegar

1. In a large nonreactive pot, bring all of the ingredients to a boil, then reduce the heat. Simmer the chili sauce, stirring occasionally, until it is thick, about 3 hours.

2. Ladle the chili sauce into pint or half-pint mason jars, leaving ¼ inch headspace. Close the jars with hot 2-piece caps. To ensure a good seal, process the jars for 15 minutes in a boiling-water bath.

3. Store the cooled jars in a cool, dry, dark place.

Makes 3 pints

Classic Barbecue Sauce

Ever since my husband and I finished college and bought our first hibachi, I've been making quick versions of this sauce while the charcoal burned down. It's nice, however, to have some barbecue sauce ready to go on the pantry shelf, allowing more time to prepare the rest of dinner.

Slather this sauce on your meat shortly before taking it off the grill, or heat the sauce and serve it at the table.

11 cups tomato purée

2 celery stalks, chopped

2 medium onions, chopped

1 medium red bell pepper, chopped

1½ cups chopped red chile peppers

4 garlic cloves, minced

1 teaspoon black peppercorns

1 tablespoon cumin seeds

1 tablespoon dry mustard

1 cup molasses

1 tablespoon pickling salt

1¾ cups red wine vinegar

1. In a large nonreactive pot, bring to a boil the tomato purée, celery, onion, bell and chile peppers, and garlic. Reduce the heat, and simmer the vegetables until they are soft and the mixture is reduced by about one-third.

2. Tie the peppercorns in a spice bag or a scrap of cheesecloth, and toast the cumin seeds in a dry pan until they are fragrant.

3. Purée the mixture through a food mill, and return it to the pot. Add the remaining ingredients. Cook the sauce until it is about as thick as ketchup, about 1½ hours. As the mixture thickens, stir often to prevent sticking.

4. Remove the spice bag. Ladle the sauce into pint or half-pint mason jars, leaving ¼ inch headspace. Close the jars with hot two-piece caps. To ensure a good seal, process the jars for 20 minutes in a boiling-water bath.

5. Store the cooled jars in a cool, dry, dark place.

Makes about 3½ pints

Razorback Hot Sauce

THIS IS A SWEET, Southern-style hot sauce. Serve it at a pig roast or with fried clams.

> 8 cups tomato purée (see page 334)
> 2 cups seeded and minced red chile peppers
> 1 quart distilled white vinegar
> 2 tablespoons mixed pickling spices
> 1 cup sugar
> 2 teaspoons salt

1. In a heavy nonreactive pot, bring to a boil the tomato purée, red peppers, and 2 cups of the vinegar. Reduce the heat, and simmer the mixture, stirring often, until it is reduced by half.

2. Purée the mixture in a food mill or blender, and return it to the pot. Tie the spices in a spice bag or a scrap of cheesecloth, and add them to the pot with the remaining vinegar, the sugar, and the salt. Simmer, stirring often, until the sauce is as thick as you like.

3. Ladle the sauce into pint or half-pint mason jars, leaving ¼ inch headspace. Close the jars with hot two-piece caps, process the jars in a boiling-water bath for 15 minutes, and store the cooled jars in a cool, dry, dark place. Or funnel the sauce into sterile bottles, cap or cork the bottles, and store them in the refrigerator.

Makes about 2 pints

HOW TO PURÉE TOMATOES

The best tool for puréeing tomatoes is a tomato strainer, either the all-metal Squeezo model or the mostly plastic Victorio. Either one will, with the turn of a crank, thoroughly wring out the tomato skins, then automatically expel them with the seeds, while the pulp pours into a bowl.

The second best tool for this purpose is a Mouli or Foley food mill, which also separates the tomato pulp from the skins and seeds. You may have to struggle to keep the mill balanced over your bowl, though, and milling raw tomatoes may prove too difficult unless you chop them well. If you do decide to buy a food mill, look for one that's stainless steel rather than tin-plated; the tin-plated ones tend to rust out quickly.

If you put raw tomatoes through your strainer or food mill, you'll produce a very thin purée, comparable to commercially canned tomato juice. With the following method, though, you can get a thick purée even from regular (non-plum) tomatoes:

Drop the tomatoes one by one into a large kettle, giving each a squeeze as you do so to release some of the seeds and liquid. Boil the tomatoes for about 10 minutes, until they soften. Then pour the contents of the kettle into a strainer set over a large bowl. Let the tomatoes drain a bit, then pour them into another bowl. From there you can ladle them into the tomato strainer or food mill.

Don't throw out the juice you drained off; instead, can it separately. Come winter, it can make a wonderfully sweet, light soup or beverage. Strained through cheesecloth, it becomes a heavenly consommé.

In case your tomatoes are abnormally low in acid, add 1 tablespoon of lemon juice or ¼ teaspoon citric acid to each quart of juice or purée. Reheat tomato purée and juice to a boil before ladling them into jars.

Process the jars in a boiling-water bath as follows: 35 minutes for pints of juice or purée, 40 minutes for quarts of juice, and 45 minutes for quarts of purée.

A tomato strainer (above) and a food mill (below)

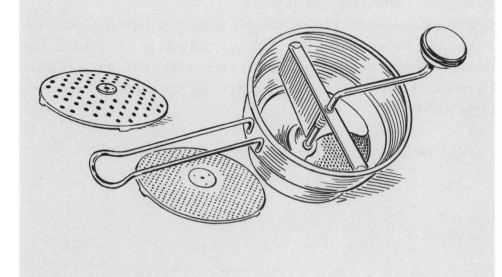

Tomato-Pepper Sauce

THE TOMATOES PROVIDE the only sweetening needed in this mildly hot sauce.

4½ pounds tomatoes, coarsely chopped, or 3½ cups tomato purée
     (see page 334)
2 cups seeded and minced or ground red chile peppers
3½ cups distilled white vinegar or cider vinegar
6 garlic cloves, mashed
2 teaspoons pickling salt

1. In a nonreactive saucepan, bring to a boil the chopped tomatoes or tomato purée, peppers, and 1½ cups of the vinegar. Boil the mixture until it is reduced by half.

2. Purée the mixture in a food mill or blender. Return the purée to the saucepan. Add the garlic, salt, and remaining 2 cups vinegar. Boil the mixture, stirring often, until it's as thick as you like.

3. Ladle the sauce into pint or half-pint mason jars, leaving ¼ inch headspace. Close the jars with hot two-piece caps, and process the jars for 15 minutes in a boiling-water bath. Store the cooled jars in a cool, dry, dark place. Or pour the sauce into sterile bottles, cap or cork the bottles, and store them in the refrigerator.

Makes about 2 pints

Tomato Salsa

THIS IS A PRESERVED VERSION of *salsa cruda*, the popular Mexican table sauce. Because this salsa is briefly cooked, it doesn't taste quite like the fresh version, but I think you'll much prefer it to any salsa you can buy in a store. For a fresher taste, stir in some chopped cilantro just before serving.

Plum tomatoes such as Romas work best in this recipe; other varieties tend to make for a runny salsa. To remove some of the excess liquid and seeds from salad-type tomatoes, squeeze them gently before chopping them. If your salsa still turns out runny, just drain off the excess liquid before serving.

Jalapeños are probably the favorite salsa pepper, but choose your chiles to suit your taste. Most people prefer a mixture of sweet and hot peppers.

---

5 pounds tomatoes, preferably plum, cored and chopped (about 12 cups)

2 pounds chile peppers, or a combination of chile and bell peppers, chopped (about 8 cups)

1 pound onions, chopped (about 2½ cups)

1 cup lime juice or white wine vinegar

1 tablespoon pickling salt

---

1. In a large nonreactive pot, bring all of the ingredients to a simmer. Simmer them for 10 minutes.

2. Ladle the salsa into pint mason jars, leaving ½ inch headspace. Close the jars with hot two-piece caps. Process the jars in a boiling-water bath for 15 minutes.

3. Store the cooled jars in a cool, dry, dark place. Once a jar is opened, the salsa will keep well in the refrigerator for at least 1 week.

Makes about 7 pints

Salsa Verde

WHEN RIPE, TOMATILLOS are yellow and quite sweet; I dry them, cut them, and use them as I might use raisins. If you grow your own tomatillos, though, pick them green for this salsa. That's the way Mexicans like them, and the way you'll find them in the market.

Like tomato salsa, this is delicious with chopped fresh cilantro stirred in just before serving. Salsa Verde is great with tacos, chips, and other tortilla dishes.

2½ pounds tomatillos, husks removed
½ pound (about 8) roasted, peeled, and seeded Anaheim peppers,
*   chopped (see page 139)*
2 cups chopped onions
4 garlic cloves, chopped
¾ cup lime juice
2½ teaspoons pickling salt

1. Wash and chop the tomatillos. You should have 7 cups. Combine the chopped tomatillos with the remaining ingredients in a nonreactive pot. Bring the mixture to a boil over medium heat, then reduce the heat. Simmer the mixture 15 minutes.

2. In batches, grind the mixture briefly in a blender or food processor. Ladle the salsa into pint or half-pint mason jars, leaving ½ inch headspace. Close the jars with hot two-piece caps. Process the jars for 15 minutes in a boiling-water bath.

3. Store the cooled jars in a cool, dry, dark place. Once a jar is opened, the salsa will keep well in the refrigerator for at least 2 weeks.

Makes about 3 pints

PICKLED MEAT, FISH, AND EGGS

PICKLED MEAT, FISH, AND EGGS

D<small>RY-SALTING</small>, <small>BRINING</small>, <small>SPICING</small>, pickling in vinegar—these are all ways that people around the world have found to extend the storage life of meat, fish, and eggs, by a little or by a lot. The recipes in this chapter use various combinations of these techniques, but each recipe is guaranteed to transform plain fresh food into something new and delectable.

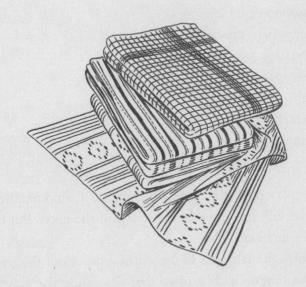

Pickled Beef Tongue

GERMAN JEWISH IMMIGRANTS brought this recipe to the United States from Europe 150 years ago. The same recipe can be used with a 4-pound beef brisket.

Saltpeter (potassium nitrate) helps preserve the color and flavor of cured meat, and also inhibits the growth of *Clostridium botulinum*, the bacteria that cause botulism. You can buy saltpeter from a pharmacist.

Sliced pickled tongue is delicious hot or cold, with prepared horseradish (see page 326) or grainy mustard.

One 4-pound beef tongue
3 tablespoons pickling salt
1 tablespoon brown sugar
1 teaspoon crushed black pepper
2 teaspoons ground ginger
½ teaspoon ground cloves
2 bay leaves, crumbled
¼ teaspoon ground mace
¼ teaspoon cayenne
3 garlic cloves, minced
1½ teaspoons saltpeter
½ cup warm water

1. Cut any excess fat from the tongue. Combine the salt, sugar, spices, and garlic, and rub the mixture well into the meat. Put the meat into a nonreactive container.

2. Dissolve the saltpeter in the warm water. Pour the water over the tongue, cover the tongue with a plate that fits inside the container, and weight it down with a large, well-washed stone or water-filled jar. Cover the container, and refrigerate it for 10 to 14 days, turning the tongue every 2 to 3 days.

3. When you're ready to cook the tongue, put it into a large pot, cover it with cold water, bring the water to a boil, and drain the tongue. Repeat this process 3 times, using fresh water each time. Then cover the tongue with cold water again, and bring the water to a boil. Reduce the heat, and simmer the tongue for about 2 hours, or until it is tender.

4. Remove the tongue from the cooking water. Let it cool just a little, and then peel off the skin. Slice the tongue immediately if you want to serve it warm. If you'll be serving it cold, let the tongue cool completely before you slice it.

Makes 1 pickled beef tongue

Irish Corned Beef

THIS RECIPE COMES from an Irish family, now living in Seattle, who say it originated in County Cork. Like the English, the Irish prefer to pickle silverside, or the outer part of the upper hind leg of beef, rather than beef brisket, which Americans usually use. Many American butchers don't know what silverside is, so you may have to explain, or substitute beef brisket. Whichever cut you use, the cooked beef will have a dry texture, an intriguing spicy flavor, and, because only a little saltpeter (potassium nitrate) is used, a mildly pink color (you can double the amount of saltpeter, if you like your corned beef really red, or leave it out altogether).

By the way, the term *corned beef*, referring to the corns, or grains, of salt used in pickling, isn't used by the Irish; they call this spiced beef. Following Irish-American tradition, you might quarter and core a cabbage and simmer it in the broth during the beef's final 15 minutes of cooking.

5 to 6 pounds beef silverside

6 tablespoons brown sugar

5 tablespoons pickling salt

½ teaspoon saltpeter (available at pharmacies)

2 tablespoons black peppercorns

2 tablespoons whole allspice

¼ cup juniper berries

1. Put the meat into a nonreactive container. Whirl the sugar, salt, saltpeter, and spices in a blender until the spices are ground fine. Rub the mixture well into the meat, and cover the container with plastic wrap. Refrigerate the meat for 3 to 7 days. Turn it once every day or so.

2. Roll the meat, and tie it with kitchen string so it will fit into a large pot. Put the meat into the pot, cover it with cold water, and bring the water to a boil. Reduce the heat, and simmer the meat for 2 to 3 hours.

3. Slice and eat the beef while it's hot, or press it flat with a weight (such as a plate topped with a large rock) for 12 hours. Stored in the refrigerator, the beef will keep for weeks.

Serve the beef with chili sauce or chutney (see Chapter 9), and either potatoes fried in butter with parsley or crusty bread.

Makes about 5 pounds corned beef

Mrs. Kim's Soy-Cured Beef

WHEN MRS. KIM'S son Michael sent us a sample of this pickled beef, my husband and I ate it straight from the jar without even bothering to sit down. You might prefer to serve it with cold noodles, in a salad with Asian flavors, or as an appetizer at the start of a meal.

Mrs. Kim also makes this dish with pork, but when she does she uses a little less sugar and adds some monosodium glutamate, or MSG (which you could leave out, if you prefer). If you use pork, make sure that it is very lean.

Although Mrs. Kim's recipe doesn't mention vegetables, her sample included small green peppers. These might be added in the last 20 minutes of cooking.

2 pounds flank steak, cut into thin 1½-inch-long strips

¼ cup sugar

½ to ⅔ cup soy sauce, to taste

1. Put the steak strips into a pot, and barely cover them with cold water. Bring the water to a boil, and reduce the heat. Simmer the meat, uncovered, for 30 minutes.

Add the sugar and soy sauce to the pot. Simmer the meat for 45 minutes more.

2. Remove the pot from the heat, and let the contents cool. Refrigerate the meat and sauce in a tightly covered container. It will keep for at least 1 week.

Makes about 1 quart

Pickled Pigs' Feet, Southern Style

THIS SIMPLE RECIPE follows the general method of Betty Talmadge, the wife of Herman Talmadge, a former U.S. senator and governor of Georgia. Betty spent many years curing hams and other pig parts for a living. She says that pigs' feet pickled this way will keep for 3 weeks, but I find that, refrigerated, they keep much longer.

4 pigs' feet, cleaned and scraped (see page 347)

1 pound pickling salt

½ cup sugar

1 teaspoon saltpeter (potassium nitrate, available at pharmacies)

9 cups water

6 small dried chile peppers

1 teaspoon black peppercorns

1 teaspoon allspice berries

4 bay leaves

3 garlic cloves, sliced

About 2 quarts distilled white vinegar

1. Pack the pigs' feet into a gallon jar. Combine the salt, sugar, and saltpeter with the water, and stir until they dissolve. Pour this brine over the pigs' feet. Cap the jar tightly. Store it in the refrigerator for 15 to 21 days.

2. Remove the feet from the brine. Put them into a stockpot, cover them with water, and bring the water to a boil. Reduce the heat, and simmer the feet until they are tender, about 2 hours.

Remove the feet from the stockpot, and chill them thoroughly.

3. Wash and scald the gallon jar. Put the chilled feet back into it, and add the peppers, peppercorns, allspice, bay leaves, garlic, and enough vinegar to cover the feet. Cap the jar, and let the feet pickle for at least a few days before eating them.

Makes 4 pickled pigs' feet

· · ·

HOW TO PREPARE PIGS' FEET FOR PICKLING

Wash the feet, scrubbing them well, then scald them in water heated to 150 to 165 degrees F until the hair comes off easily. Scrape the hair off with a sharp knife, and singe off any that remains.

That's what you're supposed to do, anyhow. But after spending a whole day scalding, scraping, and singeing our homegrown hogs' eight pigs' feet, which still ended up covered with smelly burnt whiskers, I can't really recommend the method. You might be better advised to let your pigs' feet go off to the rendering plant, and buy some other pigs' feet that have been magically dehaired at the meat factory. The only challenge, then, is to find a store that sells pigs' feet. In the South, this may be easy. Elsewhere, they are often available in urban ethnic markets.

Quick-Pickled Pigs' Feet

THIS RECIPE OMITS the curing step, so you can eat your pig's feet just a few days after the pig gives them up. Enjoy these with bread, cucumber pickles, and beer.

4 pigs' feet, cleaned and scraped (see page 347)
6 cups water
2 tablespoons plus 2 teaspoons pickling salt
1 large carrot, quartered
1 large onion, halved
2 cloves
3 thyme sprigs, or 1 teaspoon dried thyme
1 bay leaf
1 parsley sprig
8 black peppercorns
6 allspice berries
1 large onion, halved and sliced
A few grindings of black pepper
About 7 cups white wine vinegar or cider vinegar

1. Put the pigs' feet into a large pot. Add the water; 2 teaspoons salt; the carrots and the onion halves stuck with the cloves; the thyme, bay, and parsley; and the peppercorns and allspice. Bring the ingredients to a boil, then immediately reduce the heat. Simmer the feet for about 2 hours, until the flesh is tender.

2. Remove the feet from the broth, and put them into a gallon jar. Add the sliced onion, remaining 2 tablespoons salt, and ground pepper. Cover the feet with vinegar, cap the jar, and refrigerate the feet for several days before eating them.

Makes 4 pickled pigs' feet

• • •

"Just give me a pig's foot and a bottle of beer."

—Bessie Smith

Souse

SOUSE IS AN OLD ENGLISH word for the cooked flesh of pigs' feet (or other pork trimmings) in aspic—that is, a tart, savory jelly. Sometimes the whole feet are covered in aspic, but in this recipe you remove the bones, thereby producing a more palatable presentation for people who tend to dwell on where those feet have been. This recipe, based on one from an old Mennonite cookbook, is especially interesting because it includes a cucumber pickle (which you can leave out, if you prefer). Souse goes well with coarse whole-grain bread and either prepared horseradish (see page 326) or a sharp, grainy mustard.

4 pigs' feet, cleaned and scraped (see page 347)

1 medium onion, quartered

2 tablespoons plus 2 teaspoons pickling salt

2 cups white wine vinegar

½ teaspoon whole cloves

1 bay leaf

1 teaspoon black peppercorns, crushed

3 thyme sprigs

1 teaspoon juniper berries, crushed

1 cup chopped pickled cucumber

1. Put the pigs' feet and the onion into a large pot, cover them with cold water, and add the 2 tablespoons salt. Bring the contents to a boil, then reduce the heat. Simmer the feet about 4 hours, until the meat begins to fall off the bones. Skim the liquid 2 or 3 times during the first half hour of simmering.

2. With a slotted spoon, remove the pigs' feet from the stock, and let them cool a bit. Strain the stock through a sieve lined with cheesecloth.

3. In a saucepan, combine 2 cups of the strained stock with the vinegar, 2 teaspoons salt, and spices. Bring the liquid to a boil, then reduce the heat. Simmer the liquid 15 minutes.

4. Tear the flesh—that is, skin, gristle, and a very little bit of meat—from the bones, and put the pieces into a flat-bottomed dish. Sprinkle the cucumber on top, then strain the hot vinegar mixture over all. Chill the souse thoroughly.

Serve the chilled souse in thick slices.

Makes about 1½ quarts

• • •

PICKLED BEAVER'S TAIL

Among the many animal tracks along the creek near our farm are shallow, foot-wide, grooved trenches. These trails are made by beavers' broad, heavy tails as the animals drag them over the sand. Beavers are making a strong comeback here in Oregon since their near-extermination in the nineteenth century. They were killed for their fur, of course, not their meat, but pioneer women didn't let anything go to waste if it could be turned into a palatable pickle. Here's a pioneer recipe for pickled beaver's tail: "Spear a beaver tail on a long stick or fork and hold over an open flame until the skin pops and peels off. Boil the tail in water until tender. Cut into bite-size pieces and put in jars. Cover with vinegar, and seal."

Pickled Pigs' Ears

NOWADAYS, MOST PIGS' EARS are sold dried as doggie toys, but if you raise your own hogs you can enjoy these chewy morsels yourself. Pickled pigs' ears make a great party food, especially when the conversation has been lagging.

This is basically a Vietnamese recipe; I've just added the ginger and pepper flakes to make it more interesting. In *The Classic Cuisine of Vietnam*, Bach Ngo and Gloria Zimmerman write that "these morsels go perfectly with drinks before dinner, and very well without drinks at any time." Drinks—the more alcoholic, the better—may be a necessity, depending on who your guests are; you might wait until they have downed one or two each before you bring out the pigs' ears. I've heard that the Burmese serve pigs' ears in salad; you might try this, too, and let your friends guess what the chewy sweet-and-sour strips are.

To make pickled pigs' ears, you must of course first get the ears. Set them aside at slaughter time, or ask the butcher to save them instead of sending them to the rendering plant. Cut off the base of each ear to leave a triangle that will lie flat. Then scald the ears in water heated to 150 to 165 degrees F until the hair comes off easily. Scrape off the hair with a sharp knife, and singe off any that remains.

4 quarts water

1 tablespoon alum

2 cups distilled white vinegar

2 cups sugar

1 teaspoon pickling salt

2 teaspoons hot pepper flakes

5 thin slices fresh ginger

2 pounds (4 to 6) pigs' ears, trimmed and scraped clean

1. Boil 2 quarts water with the alum for 5 minutes. Let the water cool.

2. Meanwhile, bring the vinegar, sugar, salt, pepper flakes, and ginger to a boil in another, nonreactive, pot, stirring until the sugar and salt dissolve. Let the liquid cool.

3. While the alum water and vinegar mixture are cooling, boil the pigs' ears in 2 quarts water for 20 minutes. Remove the ears from the water, let them cool a bit, then slice them into thin lengthwise strips. Let the strips cool completely.

4. Soak the strips in the cooled alum water for 2 hours.

5. Drain and rinse the strips, and pat them dry. Pack them into a 2-quart jar, and cover them with the cooled vinegar mixture. Cap the jar. Store it in the refrigerator for at least 3 days before the party begins.

The pigs' ears should keep in the refrigerator for several weeks, at least.

Makes 2 quarts

Pickled Salmon

THIS IS MY FAVORITE way to prepare salmon. I follow the method of Kenneth Hilderbrand, a seafood processing specialist for Oregon State University.

Vary the seasonings as you prefer; just don't use less than one part vinegar to one part water. Kenneth Hilderbrand suggests adding more sugar for a Swedish-style pickle. I like to use a red onion, which gives the pickle a pretty pink tinge.

Other oily fishes, such as shad, striped bass, and black cod, are also good pickled this way.

About 1½ cups pickling salt, for dry-salting the fish
2½ pounds filleted salmon

1 medium onion, sliced and separated into rings

1 cup plus 2 tablespoons water

1½ cups distilled white vinegar

10 tablespoons sugar

1½ tablespoons pickling salt

3 tablespoons mixed pickling spice

1 garlic clove, chopped

1. Spread a ¼-inch layer of pickling salt in a nonreactive pan large enough to hold the salmon. Lay the salmon on top, then cover it with a ¼-inch layer of additional salt. Cover the pan with plastic wrap. Leave the pan in the refrigerator or another cool place—where the temperature reaches no higher than 50 degrees F—for at least 5 days. If you refrigerate the salted salmon, it will keep as long as 1 year; otherwise, pickle it within 3 months.

2. Remove the salmon from the salt, and rinse the fish clean. Discard the salt (or save it to pickle another fish), rinse the pan, and lay the salmon in it again. Cover the salmon with cold water. To remove excess salt, let the salmon soak for 2 to 24 hours.

Drain the salmon. Skin it, if you like, and cut it into chunks or strips. Combine the fish with the onion in a 2-quart jar. Mix the remaining ingredients, and pour them over the salmon. Refrigerate the jar for at least 1 week before eating the salmon. It will keep for several weeks in the refrigerator.

Makes 2 quarts

Pickled Herring

THE BALTIC AND THE NORTH SEA once swarmed with herring, a fatty fish whose oils turned rancid so quickly that it had to be consumed or salted within a day of the catch. In Scandinavia and the Netherlands, people soaked their salt herring in water to remove excess salt, then pickled the fish in vinegar with spices and onion. Pickled herring is still very popular among Scandinavians and the Dutch, and also among their descendants here in Oregon, who rush en masse to the coast when the herring is running.

You can salt herring at home, but since the fish spoils so fast, it's hard to get fresh if you have no fishing friends. So I buy herring already salted; it's available, swimming in its brine, from some fishmongers. The herring comes scaled and beheaded. I don't bother to skin it, but you can do so, if you like, when you fillet it.

I pack my pickled herring in a jar and pull out a few pieces whenever I want them. For special occasions, though, you might want to reassemble the pieces as fillets in a dish, and garnish the dish with dill before serving. Or you might make a sour cream sauce for the herring, by stirring ¼ cup pickling liquid into 1 cup sour cream.

1 pound salt herring (about 2 small fish)

1 medium onion, halved and sliced

20 allspice berries, crushed

1 ½ cups distilled white vinegar

½ cup water

5 tablespoons sugar

10 white peppercorns, crushed

2 bay leaves

1. Soak the herring in cold water for 12 to 24 hours to remove excess salt.

2. Drain the fish well. Clip off the fins and tails with kitchen shears. Fillet the fish, and cut it into small strips. Layer the fish in a 1-quart jar with the onion and half of the crushed allspice.

3. Bring the remaining ingredients to a boil in a nonreactive saucepan. Reduce the heat, and simmer the liquid for 5 minutes. Strain the liquid into the jar.

Refrigerate the pickled herring for at least 1 day before eating it. It should keep in the refrigerator for a few weeks.

Makes 1 quart

Pickled Oysters

I'VE NEVER BEEN ABLE to eat a raw oyster, but I love oysters pickled with wine vinegar and olive oil, as in this recipe. Try these with dark rye bread.

Two 10-ounce jars raw oysters
½ medium onion, sliced
2 tablespoons water
1 tablespoon lemon juice
¼ teaspoon salt
⅓ cup olive oil
1 large garlic clove, minced
½ teaspoon hot pepper flakes
¼ teaspoon crushed black peppercorns
3 tablespoons white wine vinegar

1. In a nonreactive saucepan, combine the oysters and their juices with the onion, water, lemon juice, and salt. Bring the mixture to a simmer, and simmer it for 1 minute. Drain the oysters and onion, reserving the juices.

2. In a large skillet, heat the oil. Fry the oysters and onion over medium heat for 1 minute per side. Remove the oysters from the skillet with a slotted spoon, and set them aside. Add to the skillet the garlic, hot pepper flakes, and the peppercorns, and fry them briefly (don't let the garlic burn).

3. In a 1½-quart jar, combine the oysters, their juices, the vinegar, and the spiced oil. Cover the jar tightly, and give it a shake. Refrigerate the jar for at least 12 hours, shaking it occasionally, before eating the oysters.

The oysters should keep in the refrigerator for 2 weeks or more.

Makes about 1½ quarts

Marinated Mussels

WHEN WE LIVED near Boston, my husband and I bought mussels—3 pounds for a dollar—nearly every week in the city's North End. This Spanish recipe, which we learned from Penelope Casas (*The Foods and Wines of Spain*), was our favorite way to prepare mussels for friends. The mussels need only one day's pickling.

4 dozen mussels

2 cups water

2 lemon slices

I cup olive oil

6 tablespoons red wine vinegar

2 tablespoons minced onion

2 tablespoons roasted, peeled, and minced red bell pepper

2 teaspoons capers

2 tablespoons minced parsley

¼ teaspoon salt

A few grindings black pepper

1. Scrub the mussels well, and remove their beards. Discard any mussels that don't close tightly. Pour the water into a large nonreactive skillet, and add the mussels and lemon. Bring the water to a boil. Remove the mussels as they open, and set them aside to cool.

2. In a large bowl, whisk together the remaining ingredients. Remove the cooled mussels from their shells, reserving half of the shells. Put the mussels into the bowl with the marinade, cover the bowl with plastic wrap, and refrigerate the bowl for 12 to 24 hours. Wash the reserved shells well, put them into a plastic bag, and refrigerate the bag, too.

When you're ready to eat the mussels, put one mussel into each shell half, and spoon a little of the marinade over it. Serve the mussels at once.

Makes 4 dozen pickled mussels

Pickled Shrimp

THIS IS A FAVORITE snack in Oregon as well as on the Gulf Coast. I prefer to use black tiger prawns, whose black stripes turn pink-orange when the prawns are cooked. "They taste like little lobsters," the fishmonger told me. She was right.

1 quart water
1¾ cups distilled white vinegar
2 tablespoons plus ½ teaspoon pickling salt
1 teaspoon white peppercorns
1 bay leaf
1 teaspoon hot pepper flakes
½ teaspoon cumin seeds
A few celery leaves
1⅛ pounds large unshelled shrimp (prawns)
1 teaspoon sugar
2 small dried chile peppers
2 lemon slices
2 garlic cloves, sliced

1. In a large nonreactive saucepan, bring to a boil the water, ½ cup of the vinegar, 2 tablespoons of the salt, and the white peppercorns, bay leaf, pepper flakes, cumin seeds, and celery leaves. Reduce the heat, and simmer the liquid for 10 minutes.

Add the shrimp, and cook them for 1 to 2 minutes, until they turn pink-orange and start to curl.

2. Drain the contents of the saucepan into a strainer set over a bowl. Let the shrimp cool, and leave the bowl undisturbed so the solid matter settles to the bottom.

3. When the shrimp have cooled and the brine is clear on top, scoop 1¼ cups of the clear brine into a 1-quart jar. Add the remaining 1¼ cups vinegar and ½ teaspoon salt, and the sugar, whole peppers, lemon slices, and garlic. Cap the jar tightly, and shake it briefly so the sugar dissolves. Discard the celery leaves in the strainer. Put the shrimp and spices into the jar, and cap it tightly. Store the jar in the refrigerator for at least 3 days before eating the shrimp. Refrigerated, the shrimp should keep for several weeks.

Makes 1 quart

Escabeche

THIS IS THE SPANISH WAY of pickling fish: It's first fried in olive oil, then pickled in spiced vinegar. The result is irresistible. I use ling cod in this recipe, but any firm, white fish will do.

½ cup pickling salt

1¾ cups water

2 pounds fish fillets, cut into strips or squares

¼ cup olive oil

1 garlic clove, minced

1 bay leaf, torn in half

2 dried red chile peppers

½ large onion, sliced

½ teaspoon black peppercorns

¼ teaspoon cumin seeds

Leaves from 2 marjoram sprigs

1¼ cups white wine vinegar

1. In a bowl, dissolve the salt in the water. Soak the fish in the brine for 30 minutes.

Drain the fish well, and pat it dry. Heat the oil in a nonreactive skillet just large enough to hold all of the fish in a single layer. Add the garlic, bay leaf, and peppers, and then the fish. Fry the fish just until it is firm throughout. With a slotted spatula, remove the fish, and set it aside to cool.

2. Add the onion to the pan, and sauté it until it is tender. Add the spices and vinegar, and simmer for 10 minutes. Remove the pan from the heat, and let the mixture cool.

3. Pack the cooled fish into 2 pint jars or 1 quart jar. Cover the fish with the seasonings and liquid. Refrigerate the fish for several days before eating it.

The fish should keep for up to 2 weeks in the refrigerator.

Makes 2 pints

Pickled Tuna

IN THIS PORTUGUESE VERSION of escabeche, the olive oil is infused with the flavor of slowly cooked garlic. My recipe is adapted from Jean Anderson's (*The Food of Portugal*).

Serve the tuna as an appetizer or light entrée.

1 cup olive oil

4 large garlic cloves, slivered

2 pounds boned fresh tuna, cut into pieces about 1½ inch by 1½ inch by
    ½ inch

1 large onion, halved and sliced thin

2 small lemons, sliced very thin

2 large garlic cloves, minced

2 tablespoons minced parsley

¼ cup chopped cilantro

1 teaspoon pickling salt

1 teaspoon coarsely ground black pepper

2 large bay leaves, crumbled

½ cup white wine vinegar

1. In a large heavy skillet, warm ⅓ cup of the olive oil over very low heat. Add the garlic, and let it slowly turn golden; this should take 20 to 30 minutes. Remove the garlic with a slotted spoon.

2. Increase the heat to medium, and gently fry the fish, in 2 batches, for about 2 minutes per side.

3. In a 1½-quart jar or a 9-inch-square nonreactive dish, layer the tuna with the onion and lemon slices, garlic, parsley, cilantro, salt, pepper, and bay. Sprinkle the tuna with the vinegar, then the oil remaining in the skillet plus the ⅔ cup remaining olive oil. Cover the jar or dish, and chill the tuna for at least 24 hours. If you're using a jar, shake it occasionally during this period.

Refrigerated, the tuna should keep well for 1 week or more.

Makes about 1½ quarts

Golden Pickled Eggs

IN THIS RECIPE and the next I assume you'll use large chicken eggs; a dozen should fit in a quart jar. But you might use duck eggs, as I do, in which case you'll probably need only eleven. Or you might use bantam or even quail eggs; if so you'll fit many more eggs in the jar, and they'll pickle quickly without any piercing.

Recipes like this one appear in many old American cookbooks. The golden color comes from the turmeric.

About 12 hard-cooked eggs (to fill a quart jar), peeled
1 tablespoon pickling salt
1½ cups cider vinegar
½ cup water
1½ teaspoons sugar
One 1-inch cinnamon stick
1 teaspoon crushed white peppercorns
½ teaspoon crushed allspice
½ teaspoon ground turmeric
¼ teaspoon celery seeds
2 shallots, sliced thin

1. With a fork, pierce each egg through the white to the yolk about 6 times. Put the eggs into a 1-quart jar. In a nonreactive saucepan, combine the remaining ingredients. Bring them to a boil, reduce the heat, and cover the pan. Simmer the contents 15 minutes.

2. Let the liquid cool a bit, then pour it over the eggs. Cap the jar, and refrigerate it for at least a week to allow the eggs to absorb the flavorings. Refrigerated, the eggs will keep for several weeks.

Makes 1 quart

Hot and Spicy Pickled Eggs

THIS RECIPE IS BASED on one from India. Have these eggs on their own as a snack, or serve them as an accompaniment to a rice dish or vegetable curry.

Eggs that are several days old when they're cooked will be easier to peel than very fresh eggs.

About 12 hard-cooked eggs (to fill a quart jar), peeled

2 tablespoons pickling salt

6 fresh or pickled green chile peppers (such as serrano), slit lengthwise

1½ cups cider vinegar

½ cup water

1 tablespoon minced fresh ginger

1 tablespoon black mustard seeds

1 tablespoon crushed black pepper

2 garlic cloves, coarsely chopped

---

1. With a fork, pierce each egg through the white to the yolk about 6 times. Put the eggs into a 1-quart jar. In a nonreactive saucepan, combine the remaining ingredients. Bring them to a boil, reduce the heat, and cover the pan. Simmer the contents 15 minutes.

2. Let the liquid cool a little, then pour it over the eggs. Cap the jar, and refrigerate the jar for at least 1 week to allow the eggs to absorb the flavorings. Refrigerated, the eggs will keep for several weeks.

Makes 1 quart

Eggs Pickled in Beet Juice

IN THIS VERY SIMPLE and classic American recipe, the crimson liquid from pickled beets turns hard-cooked eggs a shocking shade of pink. I have a Mennonite recipe in which the eggs are pickled right along with the beets, but most people pickle the eggs in leftover pickling liquid after the beets are eaten. Some halve the eggs and remove the yolks before pickling the whites briefly; the yolks are then mashed with mayonnaise and lemon juice and returned to their cavities. Here's the basic recipe for whole pickled eggs; after the eggs are dyed, devil them or not, as you wish.

I cup liquid from Basic Pickled Beets (see page 107)
I cup white wine vinegar or distilled white vinegar
I teaspoon pickling salt
½ teaspoon black peppercorns, crushed
½ teaspoon whole allspice, crushed
I bay leaf, crumbled
About 12 hard-cooked eggs (to fill a quart jar), peeled

1. In a nonreactive saucepan, bring to a boil the beet-pickling liquid, vinegar, salt, and spices. Remove the pan from the heat, and let the liquid cool.

2. Put the eggs into a 1-quart jar, and pour the cooled liquid over them. Refrigerate the jar, and let the eggs pickle 6 to 24 hours. The longer you leave the eggs in the liquid the deeper the red color will penetrate into the whites. To keep the yolks from coloring, slice and serve the eggs before a day has passed.

Makes 1 quart pickled eggs

Salted Duck (or Chicken) Eggs

ALTHOUGH IN CHINA eggs for brining traditionally come from ducks, chicken eggs work as well. Salted eggs are usually *quite* salty; however, following advice from my Chinese-Singaporean mother-in-law, Mei Water-house, I use a half-strength brine.

The Chinese eat salted eggs with hot rice or congee. The Thais, having adopted the recipe, serve salted eggs with green chicken curry or simple rice soup, or slice them lengthwise and garnish them with sliced hot peppers, shallots, and lime juice. You may find salted eggs a delightful snack even with no garnish whatsoever.

1 quart water
½ cup pickling salt
12 fresh, clean duck or chicken eggs

1. Bring the water and salt to a boil, and stir until the salt dissolves. Let the brine cool.

2. Put the eggs into a jar or small crock. Cover them with the cooled brine, and then cover the jar or crock. Refrigerate it for 3 to 4 weeks.

3. Remove the eggs from the brine. Store them in the refrigerator until you're ready to use them. Then put as many eggs as you like into a small pan, cover them with cold water, and bring the water to a boil. Reduce the heat to low, and simmer the eggs 15 minutes.

Plunge the eggs into cold water. When they are completely cooled, peel them. Serve them halved or quartered.

Makes 1 dozen salted eggs

Mail Order Sources for Pickling Supplies

Alltrista Corporation
P.O. Box 2005
Muncie, Indiana 47307
800-240-3340

Ball canning supplies, plastic caps, crocks, cotton spice bags, cherry pitters, tomato strainers, and Foley food mills.

Burgess Plant and
  Seed Company
905 Four Seasons Road
Bloomington, Illinois 61701
309-663-9551

Shallot sets and vegetable seeds, including China Hybrid and Orient Express cucumbers, as well as trees and perennial plants.

Cole-Parmer Instrument Company
625 East Bunker Court
Vernon Hills, Illinois 60061
800-323-4340

pH meters, starting at $53.

Cumberland General Store
#1 Highway 68
Crossville, Tennessee 38555
800-334-4640

Squeezo and Victorio tomato strainers, food mills, kraut boards, food grinders, cherry pitters, canning tools, and other homestead supplies.

Johnny's Selected Seeds
1 Foss Hill Road
RR1, Box 2580
Albion, Maine 04910
207-437-4301

Garden seeds, including baby turnips, shallots, haricots verts, Asian cabbages, daikon, and tiny green and white Thai eggplants. Other supplies include garlic and shallot sets, Victorio tomato strainers, and kraut boards.

Lehman's Hardware and Appliances

One Lehman Circle
P.O. Box 321
Kidron, Ohio 44636

Victorio tomato strainers, Foley food mills, kraut boards, food grinders, canning tools, cherry pitters, European canning jars, and other "non-electric" tools and equipment for the home and farm.

Nichols Garden Nursery

1190 North Pacific Highway
Albany, Oregon 97321
541-928-9280

Herb and vegetable seeds, including cornichon Vert du Massy, April Cross daikon radish, Presto turnip, Baby Corn, Bambino eggplant, Cascabella peppers, and Asian cabbages.

Penzeys, Ltd

P.O. Box 933
Muskego, Wisconsin 53150
415-574-0277

Spices—whole, ground, and mixed—from all over the world.

PineTree Garden Seeds

P.O. Box 300
New Gloucester, Maine 04260
207-926-3400

Small, inexpensive seed packets include haricots verts, shallots, cornichons, daikon, and West Indian gherkins. Also in the catalog are garlic and shallot sets, tools, and a large selection of books for gardeners and cooks.

Precision Foods, Inc.

P.O. Box 2067
Tupelo, Mississippi 38803

Pickling lime, pickling salt, and citric acid.

Shepherd's Garden Seeds

30 Irene Street
Torrington, Connecticut 07790
860-482-3638

Vegetable and herb seeds, including Little Fingers eggplant, haricots verts, and garlic and shallot sets.

Territorial Seed Company

P.O. Box 157
Cottage Grove, Oregon 97424

Vegetable and herb seeds (including garden purslane, Short Tom eggplant, and Bambino eggplant) and shallot and garlic sets.

Select Bibliography

Anderson, Jean. *The Food of Portugal*. New York: William Morrow, 1986.

Andoh, Elizabeth. *At Home with Japanese Cooking*. New York: Alfred A. Knopf, 1980.

Beeton, Isabella. *Mrs. Beeton's Book of Household Management*. New York: Exeter, 1986. (First published in London, in serial form, from 1859 to 1861.)

Belleme, Jan and John. *Cooking with Japanese Foods: A Guide to the Traditional Natural Foods of Japan*. Brookline, Massachusetts: East-West Health Books, 1986.

Casas, Penelope. *The Foods and Wines of Spain*. New York: Alfred A. Knopf, 1982.

Cates, Elinor, ed. *Recollections and Recipes*. Scio, Oregon: Scio Historical Society, 1993.

Frederick, J. George. *Pennsylvania Dutch Cook Book*. New York: Dover, 1971. (First published as Part II of *The Pennsylvania Dutch and Their Cookery* by Business Bourse in 1935.)

Goldstein, Darra. *A Taste of Russia: A Cookbook of Russian Hospitality*. New York: HarperCollins Publishers, 1991. (First published as *À La Russe* by Random House in 1983.)

Holm, Don and Myrtle. *Don Holm's Book of Food Drying, Pickling and Smoke Curing*. Caldwell, Idaho: Caxton Printers, 1992.

Kuo, Irene. *The Key to Chinese Cooking*. New York: Alfred A. Knopf, 1977.

Levenstein, Harvey. *Paradox of Plenty: A Social History of Eating in Modern America*. New York: Oxford University Press, 1993.

Neil, Marion Harris. *Canning, Preserving, and Pickling*. Philadelphia: David McKay, 1914.

Ngo, Bach, and Gloria Zimmerman. *The Classic Cuisine of Vietnam*. New York: Penguin, 1986.

The Picayune Creole Cookbook. New York: Dover, 1971. (First published as *The Picayune's Creole Cookbook*.)

Ok, Cho Joong. *Homestyle Korean Cooking in Pictures*. Tokyo: Shufunotomo, 1981.

Randolph, Mary. *The Virginia Housewife, or, Methodical Cook*. Mineola, New York: Dover, 1993. (First published in Washington, D.C. in 1824.)

Roden, Claudia. *A Book of Middle Eastern Food*. New York: Alfred A. Knopf, 1980.

Schrecker, Ellen. *Mrs. Chiang's Szechwan Cookbook*. New York: Harper and Row, 1976.

Shimizu, Kay. *Tsukemono: Japanese Pickled Vegetables*. Tokyo: Shufunotomo, 1993.

Showalter, Mary Emma. *Mennonite Community Cookbook*. Scottdale, Pennsylvania: Herald Press, 1957.

Steinkraus, Keith H. *Handbook of Indigenous Fermented Foods*. New York and Basel: Marcel Dekker, 1983.

Talmadge, Betty. *How to Cook a Pig and Other Back-to-the-Farm Recipes*. New York: Simon and Schuster, 1977.

Tannahill, Reay. *Food in History*. New York: Crown, 1988.

Thorne, John. *The Dill Crock*. Boston: Jackdaw Press, 1984.

Tsuji, Shizuo. *Japanese Cooking: A Simple Art*. Tokyo: Kodansha International, 1980.

United States Department of Agriculture. *Complete Guide to Home Canning*, 1988.

VanGarde, Shirley J., and Margy Woodburn. *Food Preservation and Safety: Principles and Practice*. Ames, Iowa: Iowa State University Press, 1994.

Volokh, Anne. *The Art of Russian Cuisine*. New York: Macmillan, 1983.

Index

Page numbers of recipes are in **boldface**.

Lime-Mint Freezer Pickle, **279**
Low-temperature pasteurization. *See*
    Pasteurization, low-temperature

M

Malt vinegar, 11
in English Pub–Style Pickled Onions, 132
Mango(es)
    Freezer Pickle with, **281**
    Pickle with Shredded Ginger, Quick,
        272–73
    pickled, **162–64**, **272–73**
    for pickling, 162
Mango and Apple Chutney, **310–11**
Mango Chutney, **309**
Mango Pickle I, **162–63**
Mango Pickle II, **164**
"Mangoes" (pickled stuffed fruit or
    vegetables), 139
    Pepper, **139–40**
Marinated Artichoke Hearts, **105**
Marinated Dried Tomatoes, **149**
Marinated Mussels, **356–57**
Marinated Sweet Peppers, **135**
Mary Randolph's Sugar-Free Tomato
    Ketchup, **318–19**
Mason jar lids, 20, 21, 23
    in boiling-water processing, 25, 26, 27–29
    in open-kettle canning, 30
    plastic, 30, 31
Mason jars, 20, 21, 22–23
    in boiling-water processing, 25, 26, 27–29
    in open-kettle canning, 30
Meats, pickled
    beaver's tail, 350
    beef brisket, 342, 344
    beef silverside, **344–45**
    beef tongue, **342–43**
    pigs' ears, **351–52**
    pigs' feet, **346–50**
    souse, **349–50**
    Soy-Cured Beef, Mrs. Kim's, **345–46**
Mennonite Community Cookbook (Mary
    Showalter), 147
Mennonite pickles
    Curried Green Tomato Pickle, **148**
    Dutch Lunch Spears, **92–93**
    eggs pickled with beets, 364
    Quick Green Tomato Pickle, **270–71**
    Souse, **349–50**
Middle Eastern pickles, 32, 165, 266
    Armenian Pickled Eggplant Stuffed with
        Peppers and Parsley, **122–23**

Green Olives with Lemon and Thyme,
    264
Lebanese Pickled Eggplant Stuffed with
    Garlic, **121**
Pink Pickled Cauliflower and Cabbage,
    114
Turkish Pickled Cabbage, **178–79**
Turkish Pickled Eggplant Stuffed with
    Cabbage and Dill, **123–24**
Minty Watermelon Pickles, **225–26**
Miso, 4, 203
    Celery in Red, **204**
    Daikon Pickled in Sweet, **202–3**
    kohlrabi in, **205**
    red, 204, 205
    turnip in, **205**
    white, 202, 205
Miso-doko (miso pickling paste), 205
Miso-zuke (miso pickles), **202–205**
Mixed Fermented Pickles, **59–60**
Mixed Pickling Spice, **14**, 88
Mold, 6, 21, 31, 38, 40, 47
    Aspergillus, 200
    controlling, with sunshine, 45
    on sauerkraut, 174
Moroccan Preserved Lemons, **165**
Mrs. Beeton's Book of Household Management,
    324
Mrs. Chiang's Szechwan Cookbook, 68
Mrs. Kim's Pickled Garlic, **207–8**
Mrs. Kim's Soy-Cured Beef, **345–46**
Mushrooms
    fried-chicken, 126
    Herbed Marinated, **128–29**
    Lemony Pickled, in Olive Oil, **129–30**
    Pickled, with Ginger and Red Wine, **127**
    Polish Pickled, **126**
    shiitake, 128
Muskmelon. *See* Cantaloupe
Mussels, Marinated, **356–57**
Mustard, 15, 50
    oil, 163
Mustard Greens, Vietnamese Soured, **71**
Mustardy Dill Pickles, **50–51**

N

Nara-zuke, 211
Nasturtium Pods, Pickled, **155–56**
Neil, Marion Harris (*Canning, Preserving,
    and Pickling*), 160
Ngo, Bach (*Classic Cuisine of Vietnam*), 351
Nichols Garden Nursery, 8, 116, 118, 187,
    263, 271, 368

United States Department of Agriculture (USDA), 5, 17, 22, 25, 27, 44, 115
United States Food and Drug Administration (FDA), 163
Unprejudiced Palate, The (Angelo Pelligrini), 105
USDA (United States Department of Agriculture), 5, 17, 22, 25, 27, 44, 115

V

Vietnamese Pickled Bean Sprouts, **70**
Vietnamese Pickled Carrot and Radish, **253**
Vietnamese Soured Mustard Greens, **71**
Vinegar, 9–12
 acidity of, 9, 10, 12
 "apple cider–flavored," 10
 balsamic, 10–11
 cherry-flavored, 239
 cider, 4, 10
 distilled white, 9
 flavored, 239, **261**
 homemade, 9
 lemon-mint, **261**
 malt, 11
 "mother" of, 11
 red wine, with garlic, bay, and savory, **261**
 rice, 4, 11
 tarragon-allspice-pepper, **261**
 unpasteurized, 11
 wine, 4, 10–11
Vinegar pickles, 4, 7
Virginia Housewife, The (Mary Randolph), 91, 156, 318, 324, 326
Vitamin C, 232, 234, 235
Volokh, Anne (*The Art of Russian Cooking*), 177, 178
Volume equivalents, 23

W

Walnut(s)
 Ketchup, 324, **325–26**
 Pickled, **156–57**
 varieties, 325
Walnut Ketchup, **325–26**
Water for pickling, 12-13
 chlorine in, 12, 13
 iron in, 12-13, 46, 84
 minerals in, 12-13, 46, 84
Waterhouse, Blanche, 330
Waterhouse, Mei, 365
Waterhouse, Robert, 37, 48
Watermelon rind pickles
 dark, **227**
 gingery, **223–25**
 minty, **225–26**
Waters, Alice, 95
Weighing produce, 19
Wine Kraut, **175–76**
Witty, Helen (*Fancy Pantry*), 161
World War II, 5

Y

Yeast, 6, 21, 35, 40, 41, 47, 174
York, George, 129

Z

Ziedrich, Dolores, 274
Zimmerman, Gloria (*The Classic Cuisine of Vietnam*), 351
Zucchini
 Bread-and-Butter, **98**
 in Freezer Pickle with Carrots, 280
 Relish, **302–3**
Zucchini Relish, **302–3**
Zydeco Green Beans, **110**

LINDA ZIEDRICH is eager to hear your pickling stories, and she will consider incorporating your ideas or suggestions into the next edition of *The Joy of Pickling*. Please write her in care of the Harvard Common Press, 535 Albany Street, Boston, Massachusetts 02118.